Trevor Coult is a veteran of the Armed Forces who was awarded one of the highest gallantry awards by HM Queen Elizabeth II in 2006. He is a veteran campaigner and has raised over £250k for veterans' causes. In 2021, his petition received a Royal Assent from the Queen.

This book was only possible because of the support of my son, my parents, and my ex-wife. When suicide seemed like an option, I found help from SSAFA, PTSD Resolution.

Trevor Coult MC

EXPLOITATION

AUSTIN MACAULEY PUBLISHERS™

LONDON * CAMBRIDGE * NEW YORK * SHARJAH

A CIP catalogue record for this title is available from the British Library.

ISBN 9781398481985 (Paperback)
ISBN 9781398481992 (Hardback)
ISBN 9781398482005 (ePub e-book)

www.austinmacauley.com

First Published 2023
Austin Macauley Publishers Ltd ®
1 Canada Square
Canary Wharf
London
E14 5AA

I would like to thank the Veteran's Affairs office, the Ministry of Defence and Veterans UK. Without their ignorance and failures, I wouldn't have had the determination to keep going.

Chapter 1
Finding My Feet

I had been raised to stand on my own two feet, my father was always away with the army and life was very good for English families living in Germany. With the overseas allowance and wages, it made many families love the cheap lifestyle, my parents would spend a fortune on me and my sister and this was to the dismay of other families that didn't have that much money.

It wasn't until summer 1977 that my dad decided to leave the army and started his long process of demobilisation at St Patrick's barracks, Ballymena. And that would be the place where I would learn to soldier and start my career with the Royal Irish Regiment. My family were a little messed up with regards to the birth places of my brother and sister, I was born in Hannover Germany, my sister in Dover, England and my brother in Dundonald N. Ireland.

From an early age I was full of energy and always trying to win at everything, my parents would travel all over the Country to support whatever sport or activity I would be competing in. I was first drawn into Martial arts and the sport of Judo. I joined a local club called Murakwai which was in Ballybeen and it was perfect. With Billy Coulter and Elleen being husband and wife and both Black belts, it was a relationship that would last a long time. I would train every week and that would eventually change to two days a week with a competition every weekend.

It became something that I would turn to for a way out of many things, including school and it got too the stage where I would only be interested in Judo and everything else came second in my life. I started to show promise and after only a year or two my name was being bounced around at national level, the questions being asked were, "This guy will go far in the sport." I had been doing Judo now for a couple of years and I had won nearly every competition I had entered at my weight and grade. My living room was starting to be taken over with trophies and medals, and my parents were grinning from ear to ear with pride, and that made me happy.

However, I was having problems with my feet and every few days my skin would split, and I would have deep wounds in my feet and blood would pour from them, it had my parents and medical staff baffled. I would be going to the hospital every week for them to try a different cream of more tablets, my doctor had no idea how to fix me. My dad was beginning to get irate and one day in work he happened to mention that he was having trouble sorting out my feet and one of his colleagues mentioned that there was a professor who subjected in rare skin conditions and his name was Dr Burrows.

This was great news and my dad organised it that we would pay for private medical care, Dr Burrows organised it for me to be admitted into the Royal Victoria hospital so I could have tests carried out on my feet. We were excited about the prospect of having my feet better and we climbed into our blue and white VW caravanette. We had made it through the city centre and as we arrived at the hospital, my dad stopped short of the entrance and put his head in his hands, he then looked at my mum and said, "Joan, I know these people." It was a picket, but the men blocking the entrance were members of the IRA. At this stage, my mum and dad panicked yet tried to remain calm as I was in the back with my sister.

At this point, he just said, "Fuck it. My son needs help," and he drove into the checkpoint. He put the window down and the man approached our vehicle and looked straight at my dad and said hello Mr Coult what brings you here and smiled, my dad said, "I have an ill son in the back, and he needs help here." Then the biggest shock ever just took place. The IRA man shouted at the rest of his guys to let us in and to make sure we were looked after.

He understood completely as he had children at home, even knowing that the IRA hated anything to do with British rule or the security services they still knew what it meant to look after family. This would change in years to come when the new breed of the IRA would not give a dam about anyone or anything.

After a stay in the hospital, I was given cream to apply to my feet every night before bed and I never ever had any problems again, Dr Burrows was a genius and I made sure I always gave him praise for his great work.

I returned to Judo and it wasn't just me doing well, my sister was doing the same damage in the girls category and winning the same amount of trophies and medals, so every weekend we would be bringing home at least four new medals, with player of the day and a team event medal and individual, our names were fast taking over the sport in N. Ireland.

Then we got the chance to compete in the N. Ireland Championships in front of the media and all the top Judo competitors, the pressure had been building and expectations had been placed upon us, I was not interested in any other competitor other than a guy named Jerod. He was the only competitor in the whole Country that I was nervous fighting and that was down to his knowledge of the sport and his groundwork and holds, if we ended up on the floor, he would be far superior, so I had been working on this back at my club.

We managed to get through the preliminary rounds and we both had to fight each other for the Championship. We spent a few minutes trying to get a good grip of each other and as we were both focused, I manage to drop down and get an Ippon, yet it wasn't enough for the win. A few seconds later, I was trying my best to avoid contact and it came from nowhere another Ippon however it was him that had thrown me and now we were both on the mat and fighting for holds, he made a crucial mistake by twisting into a position that enabled me to get a lock on. I held him with the strength of 10 men. I was praying for the referee to count me out and then it came.

I was crowned for the first time as the N. Ireland Judo Champion, but the celebrations didn't end there, by the end of the day my club had won the team event and my big sister had also been crowned as the N. Ireland Judo Champion, my coach was the happiest I had ever seen him and my parents were overwhelmed with joy. My dad was thinking, *Where the hell are all these trophies going to go*? I knew he would find a way to get around this dilemma.

Most people would take time out once they had reached the top, however in Judo once you become a champion at one weight you need to keep moving up through the weights until you are the overall champion, so it never ends.

Back at the club we had my sister, Jamie, Neil, Kev, Dougie, Steven, myself and Adam who were all competing in Judo at the top level, the amount of awards and media attention we had was nothing short of amazing and the clubs name was being put in the spotlight now and gaining National interest, the club members began to grow and it became a very big club with new keen members arriving every week.

When competitions came, I would go into a trace like mindset and pre-empt what throws it would take to finish off my competitor and if it was to go to ground, how I would achieve my hold.

The coach called me and several members of the club across during training and told us that we had been selected to represent N. Ireland against the Irish Champions, it was a bit daunting and to be honest an absolute honour. We were now the N. Ireland Champions and we were going to fight the Irish Champions, the winner would be crowned as the All-Ireland Judo Champion.

What an achievement, and a pinnacle of all the hard work we had put in, all we had to do now is find out who we were fighting, there was no internet back then, so we had to just wait and see. The news of the venue came through and we all had to travel to Letterkenny. A beautiful part of Ireland and a fantastic journey with my family, all we had to do now is get on the mat.

After all, the guest speakers had done their bit and both teams were called forward onto the mat, we lined up opposite each other, it was like a scene from a martial arts movie, we were in a line running from heaviest to lightest in our weight category. I looked at my opponent up and down and could see he was nervous. I knew I was, but I wasn't letting it show, I knew he would capitalise on it so I kept as calm as I could.

The fights seemed to come and go to quickly, I was the third fight in and the adrenaline was pumping fast through my veins, my heart was about to explode and I was ready, the referee called us both up, we bowed onto the mat and moved towards the fighting area were we bowed again and the 'Hajime' shouted the referee and we were both in the zone, two national champions fighting for overall glory of the green emerald island. He was tough however kept leaving his right shoulder drop off, it was just after one minute of fighting I got that shoulder and dragged it towards me in doing so, I was able to lift him and throw for a 10-point Ippon win. And I was the All-Ireland Judo champion.

My parents were over the moon and the team were now in front on points. It was down to the last four fights. My sister won also and Jamie. We had won the team event and our club had four All Ireland Judo Champions to the delight of the coach and all his and Eileen's hard work.

I was starting off in life on a winning streak and it felt good. I had a great bunch of friends around me and positive energy. I went on to become one of the young stars of Judo in N. Ireland until it all came crashing down around me.

Because of the success of the club and how well we had been doing, word had spread through many of our families the coach had been inundated with kids wanting to join the club, and new girl called Emma had joined the club and Billy was taken back slightly as he had a daughter that lived in England who looked like Emma. The only problem was that his ex-wife would not let him see her. So, Billy took a slight shine to Emma as she reminded him of his daughter however unbeknown to him Emma had a real nasty streak and when Billy was not watching she would be nasty and stick her nails into people, I had noticed this and did not want to partner her.

The last thing I wanted to do was to upset the coach, then Billy made a decision that ended my relationship with the club. He partnered me with her. I tried to stay away from her and she was trying to hurt me with her nails and I snapped. She grabbed me by the hair and so I punched her. I was never allowed to explain what had happened and so I was kicked out of the club and my All-Ireland Judo Champion sister left with me. We continued to fight for another judo club called Ards Judo club. I was now fighting against my old club mates and they were never up too much. Billy spent time teaching them the ways to defeat me, and I now had a new coach showing me more techniques than I had ever been taught before.

It wasn't long before the passion we both had for the sport died, and after about a year we both left Judo and never returned. Billy never did try and get in touch and apologies for what he did that night and I doubt he ever will. One thing I have carried with me for over 30 years is that not many people can be trusted when loyalty takes over integrity.

I now needed something new to focus on and my parents were glad that I didn't let this keep me down for too long. I liked football and began to follow Manchester United; Norman Whiteside and Bryan Robson with Frank Stapleton were a formidable force and young Mark Hughes was becoming a legend, my parents bought me the strip with 'Sharp' written across the front and I felt like a superhero.

I got enrolled into the Norman Whiteside School of soccer at Bloomfield playing fields. My school had been asked around to see if any of the boys were interested and it was only Kenny and myself that took up the offer. It was my first time seeing up front my football heroes and I was on top of the world. I was one of the better players in my group and I was asked by the reporter from the Belfast telegraph to keep the ball up in the air as he took photographs for the next day's paper.

Now I had a new focus and new goal, and it was fantastic.

There were a few posters now being put up around Ballybeen Estate and it was promoting the Dundonald 10k road-race and 5k fun run. It sounded fun and

I thought why not enter. So, I went home and asked my mother for the £2 entry fee and then ran to the boy's high school to pay my fee. On arrival, I met a man called Lawson and he wore a Willowfield tracksuit top and explained he was the coach of the younger kids at the club. I thought great and went to warm up, as I was an energetic kid this just consisted of me staying in the heated room and then making my way to the start.

Then after only five minutes of waiting, the gun fired and we all sprinted to the front. I was being overtaken by large numbers of adults. I hadn't seen a single young kid yet, so it was good news on that front. I was chasing a friend that was known for his speed. Davy Weir was very fast, and I knew he was in the race somewhere, yet I couldn't find him. I just continued to run as fast as I could, and I began to pass lots of runners.

I could see the older runners in front, and they were preparing to do the last 5km while I was starting my run into the finish, I could see the lines of people cheering and shouting and it felt great. I crossed the finish line and was immediately congratulated by the Willowfield Harriers running coach, he asked me to join his club and said I had won the under 18s category and I won be getting a prize. It was fantastic to know that I have something I could aim for, and a new sport was born.

When I got home, I couldn't wait to tell my parents. It was something to take away the disappointment of my Judo. My father would come home from work and remain silent for a while and we all knew what was wrong yet we refrained from asking him, he would tell us in his own time.

The place where we lived was very quiet and peaceful and then it all changed within a few weeks, the housing executive had built houses out on the back field and lots of families from all over the country moved in, and they brought their problems with them, this didn't help my dad as he now was able to recognise some of the new occupants. My dad would always explain that he would be okay as he treated both sides exactly the same. As a prison officer, it did not do you any favours to pick sides in a very volatile and sensitive place to live.

It was on a Sunday afternoon that my dad received a phone call from work, and the bad news that three prison officers' names had been found in a book which had been found during a search of Provisional IRA member's prison cell search. It sent shivers through my dad that he was on a hit list. By Monday morning, Willie Burns who was a colleague of my dad's had been shot dead by the IRA on his way to work.

Meanwhile, the other prison officer who was known as 'The Vicar' had been shot and wounded also on his way to work. Late that evening around 7pm, our front door was banged, and my dad looked out the top window to see two men standing at the door. He took no time at all in grabbing his issued 9mm handgun and going out the back door and making his way to the front of the house.

Within seconds, there were screams from both the men as they were both forced to the ground while my dad stood over both with his gun to their heads. "Phone the police," he shouted into my mother. The neighbours had never seen such a fuss, both men were trying to tell my dad that they were from the United States of American and that they were in fact Mormons. Well, it was confirmed that they were Mormons after the police arrived. And that was the last time they ever called at the Coult house.

For the next few days in work, my dad was the brunt of many a joke with regards to 'No one messes with the Coults.' And it suited him just right, even the neighbours knew that they would be safe as long as this ex-soldier lived beside them, and it also did me a lot of good with regards to my young ego.

Just as I was starting to enjoy life with my new superhero dad being the talk of the estate, it all came crashing down. It was 1990 and the troubles in N. Ireland were having a new twist and instead of Loyalists against Nationalists, it was now both sides attacking the security forces and it didn't make sense. Prison officers were being attacked by Loyalists and we lived in a Loyalist housing estate.

My dad knew very well the dangers and had been issued his own personal protection weapon at the distaste of my mother. One day while at work, my dad was called for with news of yet another serious threat. It was special branch this time and they had gained intelligence that my dad and one of his colleagues had been targeted. It was an imminent threat and we needed to go ASAP, the Prison Officers association stepped into help, one night an HGV pulled up behind our house and we had everything packed and we were gone.

The place I had grown up in was now in the past along with my friends. We couldn't even tell our closest friends what had happened, and it felt strange to just pack up and leave without anyone knowing that we had been forced out of a place that we loved. Being in a new place brought new challenges and from here on in, I would run the five miles to get to my running club and then do my training and run home, so my running got better and better.

It was also coming to the end of my school years, and I had wanted to be either a carpenter or a soldier and hadn't made my mind up as to a career so I decided to try carpentry for the first year of leaving as it seemed simple enough. My sister was going out with a guy who was an extremely talented Carpenter and I thought, *copy him*, easier said than done actually.

He was great at working with wood and all types of joinery and because he made it look so simply, I thought it would be easy. I attended the Youth training program in Dundonald with many other young guys and it seemed to go well, until I actually got a job working for a joinery firm. Within a few months, I had cut my wrist, put a nail into my finger and sliced my thumb on the bandsaw, and this sealed my joinery fate. It clearly was for someone more talented than me.

This was when I made the decision to join the Military, and without letting my parents know I had come to this decision, I made my way to Palace Barracks recruiting office in Hollywood. On arrival, I was met by the soldiers who were very friendly and helped me with my decision making.

I had every intention in joining the Household Cavalry Blues & Royals until a Royal Irish colour sergeant started laughing and said, "Have you seen what the Royal Irish are doing?"

"No," I said…looking confused.

"Well, young lad, they are in Cyprus doing sports and having fun."

"Well, that's where I want to go," I explained.

And from there on in, I was a Royal Irish recruit.

I eventually found the courage to tell my parents about my new career. My mum was annoyed that I felt I couldn't confide in her while my father was pleased, I was leaving to join the army and see the world and have great memories. I felt that N. Ireland was a beautiful place yet there would always be the religious divide and constant threat over my shoulder.

After a few weeks, I was driven the Royal Irish depot at St Patricks Barracks in Ballymena, the same place where my father had been demobbed from many years before. It brought back many memories for him, and it was the start of my memories. He dropped me off and I grabbed my bags and stood in line at the guardroom waiting for the Sergeant to take us to our new accommodation.

He was very friendly to my parents and smiled as they drove away. He then turned to us and said, "Pick those fucking bags up and follow me." My heart sank into my chest, and I just followed him praying he wasn't going to thrash us on the first day.

It turned out all right actually. I was to share a room with two other guys. Michael and Davy, Davy had many years' experiences already in the Royal Navy and would be a great help when it came to weapons training and numerous other stuffs. He helped me to stay grounded and gave me that confidence push when things were not going well.

The bond all three of us shared was fantastic. Each morning, we would do each other's bed and check each other over to make sure our uniform was immaculate, this was noticed by our section commander Alan, and he was happy with our appearance for the first few weeks anyway. Then it all changed as the weeks progressed, our dress and appearance would become more tweaked and perfected to match those men at our unit.

Training was fun at times and at others, it would nearly break the spirit of the whole platoon, being told to get into working dress and a quick walk around camp, followed by, "You all have five minutes to be back here in sports kit." Well, it was sprinting around the block to get ready in time, and if we were late, it had consequences like press-ups and burpees.

Training was at times very hard with long days that seemed to just continue into weeks and months. At every corner, there were hurdles put in the way to break us completely down. To build us back up as a professional soldier, I would be showing everyone my speed and stamina when it came to the endurance running and carrying of weight. I was not the strongest by a long shot, however, what I lacked in strength I made up with guts and determination.

I had kept my fitness to a very high level when we all had to do the Basic fitness test also known as the BFT, I managed to complete 12 pull-ups, 72 press-ups and 70 sit-ups followed by a mile and a half warm and a run that I think has never been matched to this day, I ran six minutes and 54 seconds. The instructors were gobsmacked however this sort of time was being beaten day in day out back at my running club.

After only a few hours, I could see lots of guys and girls gathering at the back of cookhouse building in the smoking area and starting to mingle. Everyone was nervous and trying to make a good impression. I had already got to know the two guys in my room, so I was happy. The training started the next day with us being broken into group of eight men and these were to be called sections from here on in.

It was a very steep learning curve and the hardest physical and mental tests I had ever endured. My platoon sergeant was a character and was always making us work for our money, at the end of each week we would have to line up and march into the office, halt and salute followed by a regimental question, so there was many weeks I wouldn't get paid and this would lead to me and many others reading and learning everything we could.

The history was fascinating and learning everything from marching to foot drill and medical lessons. I enjoyed being out in the field and learning to live off the land and blend into natural surrounding the most, though when the weather changed and we got soaked followed by cold winds and frost. Well, it wasn't very much fun and many of us including me turned into complete mongs. I would just sit there and stare at a hot cup of coffee and wish to be anywhere but where I was, as the training was hard.

I never understood why at 4am, the instructors would throw smoke grenades and thunder flashes at us and shout, **"MOVE, BUG OUT...LET'S GO."** We had all been sleeping so peacefully and now we were running in different directions with our warm clothing on. Everything had been left behind, including weapon. Well, I soon learned to sleep wearing boots and keep everything that was not being used packed inside my rucksack. Many of the guys did the same however there was always a few that would reach the rendezvous without any kit or equipment to the amusement of our instructors. This type of behaviour was only tolerated once and from here on in it would have consequences.

At week six of training, we had learnt enough military drill and knowledge to be able to pass of the drill square wearing our berets. It was a fantastic achievement and all our families had been invited to watch us carry out foot drill and get inspected. From here on in, I was allowed to wear headdress and I felt proud. This would only last a few more weeks before we finished phase one training and depart for Strensall in North Yorkshire for phase 2 training, and it would be a completely new learning curve.

Well, the day came and my mother and father got to meet my instructors and were told I was doing well. All I had to do was come out my shell more and be more positive. This was a true account of what I was like, but they didn't mention I was a real character who was always messing about. This would eventually go as maturity settled in. Well, it waited a long time with me as I was still messing about at aged 37. I am just one of those guys who likes to work hard and play hard.

My instructors Michael and Alan were in fact military gurus and at times, I would think all they did each day was live and sleep tactics. When it came to Nuclear biological chemical (NBC) warfare, it went right over my head. I know it like the back of my had today, yet I still think it's a pointless subject. What is the point in living through the most destructive device on earth and spending your days rubbing power on your male friend's penis and bum as they go to the toilet, when all civilians have perished, it's pointless as we will never be able to keep the human race going.

And the instructors had us wearing our NBC suits and respirator while playing a game of football. This was to show us how difficult wearing it would be, now correct me if I am wrong here, but who in the right mind would want to play a football match wearing this gear! It was hard enough to breath just sitting still, and then we had the gas chamber to contend with, the instructors would light up CS canister tablets and get us to take off our masks while answering numerous questions, and after about 30 seconds, our eyes and face would be on fire and we would have to place the mask back on and breath properly. Many of us would be thrown from the building crying as the instructors laughed at us.

Well now you know why many soldiers hate this type of training, yet it would come in very handy in years to come, so I needed to get it right.

It was coming up to week 10 of phase 1 training and many of the recruits were now swapping phone numbers and saying their goodbyes. The home service soldiers would remain in Ballymena to continue their internal security training for N. Ireland and the general service soldiers like me and a few others would be preparing to travel to England to continue phase 2.

I had met some great guys and girls and many of these would now be lifelong friends. Soldiers have a bond that no other job or walk of life can compete with, these guys and girls would travel up and down the country just to make sure you were okay, such is the bond of Veterans.

Well, we had a week off at home before we had to be at the airport for our flights, all of us had been booked onto the same flight so we could travel together as a newly formed section, it was a great week at home and we got to relax a little yet we now were doing things in a military like fashion. Everything we were doing was now routine and our mind-sets had been changed to a positive outlook on life, things now just seemed so clear and things that used to be important were now trivial rubbish.

I spent time with my parents, and I visited my sister and brother-in-law. It was always relaxing with them, and my brother-in-law always wanted a beer and it suited me just fine. My dad had a few beers with me as he reminisced about his time in the military and the fun he used to get up to. It was great to hear such stories and the amount of travelling he did was unbelievable. This was what I wanted. I wanted to see countries and hopefully as all young recruits want. I wanted to go to war and fight alongside my new mates and do something I could be proud of, most of all do something my family would be proud of.

Chapter 2
Setting Standards

We had enjoyed our time at home with the family, and some of us had remembered to keep up our fitness levels, with doing some long distance running with sprints thrown in every few hundred metres to keep us on our toes. Then after we all met up at the airport, we just through that training out the window by heading to the bar for a few pints. Our flight was delayed and the longer we remained there, the more alcohol was consumed. It turned into a session and by the time our plane arrived, Beefy and I were a little worse for wear.

During the flight, we were very happy and continued to have the inflight hospitality, on arrival at Leeds Bradford airport this small group of Ulstermen were in fact ready for bed, and not some hairy assed drill sergeant. I am sure he would love to meet these very professional recruits of the future. I had a feeling there was trouble ahead. And so, now was the time to try a sober up.

Welshy was the oldest and the most mature of the group and in many ways he knew he could manipulate us into doing some funny things, the majority of the time he would keep everyone on the right path and stick up for every single one of us, especially when we got into trouble with some other guys during training or nights out in York. With our section, it was perfect in phase 2 training as we had an EX-Irish Ranger as an instructor known as Tommy, a big mountain of a man who looked after us quite well despite the fact he was now a Green Howard he still had a soft spot for the Royal Irish troops, and this was music to our ears.

He would thrash us within an inch of our miserable lives and push us far beyond any of our expectations, everyday would hurt and many of us had blisters not only on our feet but on our hands also. Just the sight of Tommy would make us nearly be sick with the thoughts of what was coming next. The worst lesson was bayonetting training; it would last all day and it was charging at dummies and learning to thrust the bayonet into the body while in a psychotic state of mind. This would keep our adrenalin at a high level all day, and by the end of the lessons we were all ready for bed and completely broken men.

Our platoon accommodation was right at the back of camp and it backed onto the assault course and where we would spend most days training. The great news was that we all shared the same room and could keep our morale up and help each other when times were tough, and I was the lucky one as I slept beside beefy. He was just pure morale; however, we did fallout from time to time but that's what happens when you live sleep breath the same air as someone every single day. We were both beginning to hate the sight of each other, but in many ways, we wouldn't let anyone talk about the other so tight was the bond we had for each other; it was basically like a marriage that had eight men in it.

Training was harder in Strensall than it was in Ballymena, and now we had soldiers from every other unit trying to compete for the pride of our cap badge, even knowing we hadn't even seen our unit yet. We worked hard as a section and competed for everything, when it came to the BFT and running well let's just say I had that well and truly wrapped up to the delight of the guys and our section commander Tommy.

There was the intersection competition where we had been at the front most of the way until the assault course. I was a fit guy however after getting to the wall first and helping the team over it. I had nothing left to give. My body had given up and my energy had been zapped.

I couldn't get myself over the wall and the guys had to pull me over like a sack of spuds. It was embarrassing to say the least. The guys knew I had done my best, but it didn't stop the jokes coming from every angle. I had to man up and take the slagging with a smile because if they see you getting all defensive, well it gets worse for you.

It was coming to the end of the first week of training and we had all been warned about drinking in York. None of us was allowed to be caught drunk or it would be dealt with on the Monday morning and bringing the camp and army into disrepute was not the brightest career move to have, and not great by destroying your unit's reputation before you have met anyone from it.

We got speaking to an instructor from our Battalion who had been posted to Strensall signals wing named Yax. He was a fountain of knowledge and put us all in the loop with regards to unit life. He made it sound so easy and it gave us that little spurt to try even harder.

He had explained that just because we were in training didn't mean that they didn't know about each and every one of us, and that company commanders would be asking for us to join their company. Well, I suppose no one wants a waster so I had better pull my socks up. I was working hard in training but not anymore than anyone else.

We decided that after yet another hard week, we would go into York and have a few pints while shopping, the city was fantastic and steeped in history. The women were beautiful but then again, I was new here and hadn't seen women for weeks so an average looking woman to me looked like a model and I was only a young lad with hormones running out of every orifice so that didn't help either. For now, the guys were only interested in a few beers and a game of pool.

Then day turned to night. We had managed to buy some essentials for Monday which included noodles and tuna for our up and coming field exercise, and a new torch and knife for cutting, the keener guys had bought a compass and button compass for emergencies, things I hadn't yet got my head around and would take some time in doing so as well. I had managed to purchase great socks and a hat…as a recruit, you will try anything on as long as no one knows.

I wasted lots of money in training buying all these useless gadgets like hand warmers and vitamins that keep you going in adverse weather conditions, and now I know that no matter what you put into your body, it will still break down when you are exhausted, so a good soldier sleeps when he can and not while on duty.

When we got back to camp, we were already a little tipsy from the day's alcohol intake and now we just wanted to iron our new jeans and shirts and get down to York again. Some of the guys from the other sections were in full swing in the accommodation and beers were everywhere. Chris Cowley handed us all a beer as we got ready and now, he was coming with us. The town was going to be painted green that night. We ordered a few taxis and made our way to the great Yates bar, which was always a place to see some beautiful women, if only just to look at.

Once in Yates, the pints began to flow and then the idea of some food spoilt the proceedings with everyone have a meal and the beer being soaked up, we all looked sober again. And in a soldier's eyes, the previous beer has been a complete waste of money and we must start again. And with the wages being not that great, it hurt the back pocket tremendously.

After a few hours, we decided to try other bars, and to our surprise, we could see that the instructors from camp all seemed to have another job. Yes, they were the local door men at some of the toughest bars in the city and when we approached them, they just smiled and said, "No squaddies, gents." What a bloody nerve, we would have to find another way to get around this.

After a couple of weeks at camp, we realised that the only way to get around this obstacle was to keep low in camp, so they didn't get to familiarise themselves with your face and when it came to going into the club, they worked at, well we just gave a girl a £5 note and went in with them, though I think I was the only one giving out a fiver, as the rest of the guys had no problem getting girls and this was down to having great ginger hair that was attractive.

With all this done, it seemed a great place to be, with the three giant screens and live football being played it had the making of a great sports bar. This is where all the troops seemed to bump into each other and the craic was fantastic, with three different floors and cocktail bars at each end it was an alcoholics dream and an Irish soldier's nightmare.

Once the weekend was over, it was back to business as usual and a boot run first thing in the morning followed by lessons on the training area. We would be walked through a tactical exercise and then asked numerous questions on what we had seen, then we got into our sections with someone being nominated as the section Commander while we listened to his take on the lesson. This was done to see if we are taking in any of the information and digesting it properly.

At the end of all this training, the section Commanders wanted to have the best shot, the fittest recruit and the best soldier all come from their sections. This was testament to their teaching abilities, and it added to their already growing egos.

Best drill and best endeavour were something that not many guys wanted to be bestowed upon them, as drill doesn't kill the enemy and best endeavour meant you started off shit and you finished okay, but still a bit shit. This was known by everyone apart from the guys that got best endeavour.

With only a few days left in training, the instructors began to take their foot off the gas a bit and let us begin to take charge of the small things, block jobs and cleaning would be checked over by the platoon duty student with everyone now beginning to take ownership of daily tasks, our uniforms would be checked several times before going on parade and we were now working as a team, a team that looked out for one another and when the chips were down, we would all get around the individual and give them that important lift that they needed.

The photographer arrived and we had our very own platoon photograph of the whole training team, this would be the first of many to come over the years ahead, and it was the final thing we had to do in training apart from pass off the drill square. Our bags had been packed and our rooms had been scrubbed for handover, all we did now was get ready to paint the town red.

We all had packed our kit and equipment away and as we would be travelling to Cyprus. We were told to take two sets of working dress and send the rest by freight mail and so all our kit went into wooden boxes and shipped out. This would take a few weeks to retrieve and with our leave and then travelling to Cyprus, it would pretty much be there by the time we arrived.

Our leave was over very quickly as many of us were excited about living in Cyprus, especially with the sun and sea and let's not forget the beautifully tanned women that were enjoying the sun. It was like a dream come true; well, it was until I met my new platoon sergeant. **"What's your name?"** he was screaming at me, and I had only arrived.

"Coult, sergeant," I answered.

"Coult where is your kit and equipment?" I explained that it was in freight and then he searched my bags and found bottles of alcohol that I had bought in duty free.

"What the fuck is this? I see you had time to buy fucking alcohol, I will kick you bollix in, Coult." *Well, that was a great first impression*, I thought and now for a life of misery by a mountain of a man called Billy.

I now had to try and get respect from the rest of the troops, but as they had returned from a horrific tour of Bosnia it seemed more likely that I would be the new punch bag than the new professional soldier.

It wasn't long before the Company looked upon me as Speedy. This would become my nickname for my entire career as a soldier. I would be the guy that no one would be able to beat at running, well that's what I thought until I met a guy named Derek. Derek worked in the gymnasium and was the fastest man I had come across since the days of Willowfield Harriers and the likes of Skim, Garfield, and Rowan. This guy Derek could move and I wanted nothing better than to beat him. I would train once a week now with the runners and just do company fitness.

The heat in Episkopi was something that I would need to get used to if I had any real intention of catching Derek. I had several chances and never could match his pace. In the Akrotiri 10km, I only managed to run 35 minutes and in the Happy valley hill climb I only managed to come in 3rd and even know I was happy with the position I was unhappy with the times on both races.

Then I nearly ruined the camp one night after a fantastic evening on the drink Ouzo. I woke up to a hefty bill that a rock star would be proud of. I had managed to break the three-foot fan that was attached to the ceiling in our room. The mirror on the wall, the sink was damaged and this was a few days before handing over the accommodation to another unit, and this wasn't the end of it as I had done the same damage to the room upstairs. All this would come out eventually that a guy named Andy Rainey had done the damage and as a sprog, I would take the blame.

This didn't stop the regimental police from arresting me and putting me in jail. I was there for a few days until a plan had been put in place for me to pay the damage, then both Regimental quartermasters came to pay me a visit. The Rottweiler as one was known as gave me a fantastic punch right on the chin and I knew I had deserved it. Then the other quartermaster grabbed me by the throat and nearly shook my head off until a policeman came in and asked him nicely to stop what he was doing.

I spent the rest of my time in the company now known as a lunatic with spirits, and I knew I had to avoid them at all costs, the problem is I actually liked having a laugh with the troops.

I now had learned a valuable lesson with regards to spirits however I never learn and continued to enjoy my life at battalion. It was only a few months that I had been on the island, and we were now packing up for a new posting. This time, we were going to be living in a place called Alma Barracks in Catterick, North Yorkshire and it would be a 5-year posting.

Things had moved on rather quickly and what the recruiting sergeant had said was a complete lie. *What an asshole*, I thought. Well, at least it would be easier to go home on leave and get to travel up and down the country. As all the guys were packing their bags to go on leave, we got dropped a bombshell. As we were effectively known as sprogs, we would be on rear party while the others went on leave.

The rear echelon officer gather everyone on parade that was staying behind and it looked like 30 men, however even some of these men were going on leave on the second week while others were coming back to help with duties, and so we became very aware of the new standing orders and where the emergency plans would be in the breakout of a fire or an attack on camp.

The one thing that will always stick with me was the rivalry of units and how one guy bumping into someone from another unit could kick off a riot in the middle of town that resulted in soldiers being hospitalised for weeks. It was a very intense place to go for a quiet pint if there ever is such a thing as a quiet drink in the military.

In the five years I lived and worked at Alma barracks, I was able to carry out operational tours in South Armagh and in East Tyrone as well as an emergency tour when the marching season was in full swing. I was pleased to be part of Operation Banner and get to see the Romeo towers and conduct the work I did in a place that I thought was beautiful yet ruined by the scum of terrorism.

I left 1 Royal Irish in December 1999 and transferred to the home service and a new family at 7 Royal Irish at Malone Road in Belfast, a quiet part of town with great history. I found the guys and girls to be great fun and very knowledgeable of local tactics, I needed to learn and fast. Some of the guys had been involved in shootings and pipe bombs and riots.

I wasn't a fan of this type of combat, but I wanted to learn and fast. I was good at recognition and used it to my advantage. The news was beginning to fill up with atrocities taking part in Kosovo breakaway groups and by the end of 1999, I had missed out on what seemed to be an epic tour for the soldiers involved. I got fed up of staying in camp during a peace campaign and decided only after a few months that maybe the grass was greener on the other side and transferred back to 1 Royal Irish who were preparing for an Exercise in Canada, but this was no ordinary exercise as it was going to be the first time in recent years that the whole of 16 Brigade Air Assault would bring together all their assets for a brigade exercise and this would be called Iron Eagle.

The exercise was fantastic, and I fully enjoyed my time as one of the troops in A-Company we had a great team around us, and the exercise was long at times with mile after mile of tabbing and carrying weight. My section commander was a guy named straws, he was over six foot in height and from Manchester and already a legend within the battalion. His boxing was very well known throughout the unit just as much as his fighting downtown. A guy that many others were very weary of in fragile situations.

After being in Canada a few weeks, we were all called in for a centralised brief by the Brigade Commander who at the time was Brigadier Jackson who went onto be General Jackson. He explained that during a routine patrol in Sierra Leone that a Royal Irish contingent of up to 14 men had been patrolling when they had been ambushed by a notorious rebel group called the Westside boys.

This sent a rage across the battalion that I have never seen to this day matched, the rest of C-Company wanted to know what the plan was to get them out. The whole battalion including the CO were gob-smacked with this news, we all wanted to be part of the rescue plan, Brigadier Jackson had already made his decision during a briefing at Cabinet office, and it didn't include the Royal Irish, in fact it was the complete opposite. The prime minister and his team had advised against using soldiers from the Royal Irish as they may have taken the whole thing to personal and put themselves in even more danger.

Basically, what he and his advisors were trying not to say was that we would have let the fact that our men would cloud our judgment and that we would leave nothing behind breathing in a ploy to destroy the Westside boys. This was actually a very good point and he knew how soldiers worked inside out, the plan was being put in place to let the 1st battalion the Parachute Regiment take the task on, this would be the first time a unit has worked so closely with Special Forces and would go a long way in cementing the role as the Special Forces Support Group (SFSG).

It was a great test for them, however deep down inside, every man in my unit was jealous of such a prestigious task. When we returned from Canada after a fantastic exercise, it was in every single newspaper. We had been briefed in no uncertain terms that we were not allowed to speak to the media and any such request was to be directed to the Battalion Headquarters.

Our camp was very open and the front fence was only two foot in height, so the Commanding officer put two men on the gate and at intervals he would make sure a junior non-commissioned officer was available to answer any questions that the press would ask, the front of our camp was all over Sky news channel and the boys that were being held captive were holding themselves together rather well, or at least we were being told that.

They had been held deep inside the jungle by the notorious Westside boys, these were mainly boy soldiers who were high on drugs most of the time.

It all took place on 25 August 2000 when the patrol turned off the main road and down a track towards the village of Magbeni. It was just down the track the patrol was overwhelmed by a large number of heavily armed rebels and taken prisoner. The guys were stunned at what had taken place and because of the threat of all being killed at the time by these lunatics, the Commander had made the decision not to return fire and try and negotiate a way out, they were then transported to Gberi Bana on the opposite side of Rokel Creek.

It took a while for the rest of the training team to realise the severity of the whole thing and after only a few hours word had gotten back to the PM and to Whitehall that there was a crisis unfolding. The British Army negotiated the release of six of the eleven men on the patrol, but were not able to gain the freedom of their Sierra Leone Army liaison officer and the other men before the West Side Boys' demands became increasingly unrealistic. It was shortly that day when the Westside boys decided to shoot the Liaison officer in the head while he had the other guys lined up and playing games with them.

Negotiators concluded that there was no other way to get the guys out safely and a plan needed to be in place rather than an effort to resolve the crisis, and by 9 September, the soldiers had been held for over a fortnight. Fearing that the soldiers would be killed or moved to a location from which it would be more difficult to extract them, the British government authorised an assault on the West Side Boys' base, to take place at dawn the following day, 10 September.

This was Top secret and back at camp the only man that knew of this was our commanding officer and a few men, however the time and date would be kept from the rest of the unit. We all knew what was gearing up and what the result would be, we just prayed that our friends and colleagues would return without the use of a body bag.

The ground operation was conducted by D Squadron, 22 Regiment Special Air Service who assaulted Gberi Bana in a bid to extract the Royal Irish while elements of 1st Battalion the Parachute Regiment (1 PARA), who launched a diversionary assault on Magbeni. The operation freed the five soldiers as well as twenty-one Sierra Leonean civilians who had been held prisoner by the West Side Boys.

At least twenty-five West Side Boys were killed in the assault, as was one British soldier, while eighteen West Side Boys including the gang's leader, Foday Kallay were taken prisoner and later transferred to the custody of the Sierra Leone Police. Many West Side Boys fled the area during the assault, and over 300 surrendered to UNAMSIL forces within a fortnight.

The operation known as OPERATION BARRAS restored confidence in the British forces operating in Sierra Leone, which had been undermined by the capture of the Royal Irish patrol.

After the operation, the British government increased its support of UNAMSIL and its efforts to bring the Sierra Leone Civil War to an end, both politically, through the United Nations Security Council, and through the provision of staff officers to support UNAMSIL.

Our men that had been freed would take some time to come to terms with their ordeal, I know a great soldier who spent some time in Gibraltar while he sorted himself out. Many of the other guys that had been captured decided in the end to leave the military and enjoy life to the maximum. I know it is a very hard subject to bring up with the guys that remain in the military. This is something they will never forget and always look to when times are hard this makes them realise that anything else that life throws at them is easy.

This is something that the Royal Irish now has as its history and makes the senior officers think when decision making about route selection, and it is also something that many units will never let us forget our mistake which resulted in worldwide media attention.

It was several months later that some of the guys that had been held captive returned to the unit and when they did, they got a pat on the back for enduring what most men would have fell apart during the whole process, I have never been in that situation and I will never be able to judge anyone who has. If anything, I would hope I would be able to match the calm professionalism of the guys who lived through it.

It was two years later that our Commanding officer was replaced by the most notorious Colonel that the Royal Irish would ever have in its history Col Tim Collins had been appointed our new commanding officer, word spread like wildfire and his reputation was slowly putting the fear into everyman regardless of rank. He had started off and a young Royal Irish officer and attended Special Forces Selection and passed, so he was coming back after a stint as C-Company's OC and now taking control of the unit he had been involved in rescuing.

Chapter 3
Brecon

I had just spent the past two weeks on summer leave, and I knew I was about to embark on my first real step up the ladder. This was SCBC 'Section Commanders Battle Curse.' I had heard from guys that had done it in the past and the horror stories of how hard it was. With these stories playing on your mind, most guys tend to drop out and make up excuses to get off it.

I knew I wouldn't be alone; I had the comfort of a good mate 'D'. We had served together in RECCE Platoon and both of us knew that we could pass Brecon, but a four-month course of being tested day in day out with some colour sergeant breathing down you neck was a scary feeling. We had planned to go out for drink on Saturday night and meet up with the guys in Bar-X. This was a sports bar behind the cinema in Canterbury city centre.

In turned out to be a great night, even my brother and his fiancé were there. We spent a few hours there and then went on to the nightclub bar. It wasn't a bad club in fact I liked it, it had three floors, the bottom was all pop music and dance, where all the squad do two-step guys went, the middle was more like rave where you found the pill-popping people and the top, well that's known as the Fijian floor as they play R&B and Soul. The Fijians are big men of adventure. There are great guys but I wouldn't mess with them. We stayed there for a while and decided to just hover about from floor to floor just to check out the women.

The time was now close to closing about 01.40hrs, and we were starving so we left and said cheers to spud who was the head bouncer and always looked out for me and went to the burger van. After two burgers each, we walked up to our camp, which is on a hill and when your drunk it's like a mountain. After letting 'D' go to bed, I went to my room got undressed and climbed into bed. That night, all I could think about was Brecon and the months ahead. I awoke the next day to fits of laughter and was a bit fed up. I wondered why 'D' was in fits of laughter and pointing at me. Well to my surprise while I was drunk, one of the guys had dyed my hair cosmic blue. I was gutted. In only a few hours, I was going down to Brecon. What were they going to think about my first impression?

I was failing the course from day one I was sure of it. After spending the entire day with 'D' and everyone mocking me, we had decided to make the eight or nine-hour journey in his Shogun 4x4 Jeep. The whole way, we both had butterflies and talked non-stop about what we were about what we were about to let ourselves in for. For us, this was the first time we had worked with other unit's and as we were the only two Royal Irish. We were now ambassadors for our unit. So, with that in mind, we had to be professional soldiers and show off our skills in front of the other units. We had just spent 8½ hours travelling up to Wales and my bum was indeed numb and I needed a good breakfast but at six o'clock in the morning, there wasn't many places open. So, we drove around for a while and found a pokey little shop which was getting a delivery of fresh bread and buns so we pulled over and went in.

I went straight for the hot food counter followed by 'D' and the little old man came out and in a strong Welsh voice. He said, "Can I help you?"

I looked at the counter and replied, "Two sausage rolls mate and a crusty bap," and he repeated what I had just said.

At this point, 'D' looked puzzled. Then the man said, "What's the bap for?"

Now I was looking puzzled. "It's to put the sausage rolls in."

"What?"

He said, "Sausage rolls in a bap never heard of that before." I nearly burst out laughing and paid him and ran out laughing quickly followed by 'D' now we were both in stitches and feeling relaxed we ate our food, drove to the camp front gate, and booked in for the course.

Silence feels inside the Jeep as we drove through the camp. My stomach was churning and I was beginning to feel sick. We drove to the car park and discovered loads of soldiers just sitting in their cars. Everyone was feeling nervous about the weeks ahead I could see this jock soldier throwing all his kit out of the boot and went across to see if he needed a hand plus I was trying to make a new friend. He replied, "I've lost my head-dress," so I leant him my beret. Now anyone in the army knows you can't wear another unit's beret; however, he did for the week, and he got away with it.

Well, it was now close the eight o'clock and everyone was starting to gather at the Falklands Hall. This was a massive hall were all the lectures took part and the course briefs took place. We were all seated and the DSM came in, he was the sergeant major of the Skill at arms phase (SAA) the course was then split into sections of eight to12 men and that was when I was spilt from 'D'. I could only see him now at night, trying not to look worried I headed to my classroom and meet the others I had 3 x Paratroopers one Pathfinder, an Irish and Welsh Guard and a Royal Anglian as well as a Stafford and two Gurkha soldiers and myself.

I got on well with them and the instructor loved me, he was a jock from Glasgow and supported rangers and with me from Ballybeen, a protestant who likes Rangers; we hit it off straight away. After spending most of the first day getting lectures on the does and don'ts, I was a bit tired and so went to find 'D.' I found him in a different block to mine. We went to the NAAFI for a coffee and watched a new T.V. series called Ultimate Force.

I suppose back home this show look's exciting to people, especially as it's about the Elite Special Forces, but when you're sitting beside 2 x Special Forces soldiers who are just laughing and saying what a load of bollocks, it takes the edge of it. So, I drank my brew had a smoke and went off to bed. That night, I lay in bed going over the sequence of how to take a lesson and eventually drifted off to sleep.

At 06.00 hours the next morning, the Duty Student came in our room and turned on the light. Everyone was very quiet and nervous and started to run around like headless chickens. I got up headed to the bathroom to get washed and shaved and spent the next twenty minutes queuing. Shortly after, I got ready and headed to the cinema for the mornings lecture. These went all morning. After lunch, we went our ways and headed to our section's rooms where our instructor Sgt Hendy introduced himself to us and explained the standards he expected.

It seemed achievable, yet like the others in my section I was a bit nervous, over the next eight weeks he taught us rifle lessons – GPMG lessons – L109 high explosive grenade lessons RGGs – LSW – 94MM Rocket Launcher and 5IMM Mortar lessons, he had shown us how to teach from the 'Bible'. The Bible is a book where all the lessons are in and he knew it word for word. He would sit there and say Royal Irish you've got GPMG 5 and rifle 8; rifle 8 is the hardest lesson to take and he gave it to me.

I had until the next morning to learn it. Others got two lessons each so that night, we all sat up until about 01.00am. You only got one chance so you couldn't blow it. I went to bed that night going over and over it until I was happy eventually drifting off to sleep. That night, I tossed and turned and at 05.50hrs I was first awake I got up and went to the bathroom. I couldn't believe it. I was first in, so I took advantage of it and had a good shave. I then went to my room and got ready, with a quick cup of tea.

I was ready for the day ahead. I spent the day being taught how to run a range and all the safety aspects and to a complete novice its very daunting, so I spent the whole-time taking notes. For the next eight weeks, it was Groundhog Day. Doing the same lessons in the same classroom with the same people, thank-God this phase of the course was coming to an end. It was the tactics phase we all dreaded, being out in the field Mon-Fri and only coming in to do administration i.e., shopping, washing our clothes and to do coursework. Well, quite frankly, I was a bit dubious. Well, by now, all I had left was my PAM 21 test and to a fool. It was impossible to fail, as it's actually an open book test. Thank God I had got HPS 'Highest Possible Score' and now it was time for the whole course to meet up in the Falklands Hall for the closing address.

This is where we all got our 'SAA' certificates, and those very few soldiers were given distinctions. Shortly after the presentations, we jumped into our car's and went off for a well-deserved long weekend. It was 15.00hrs on Friday and phase two started 07.00hrs Monday with an eight-mile ICFT that's a run carrying 44lbs and rifle and helmet. If you failed, you got RTU which is returned to your unit and that's embarrassing so I had to pass.

On the way back to Canterbury, we just sat there, and no one spoke for about twenty miles until I picked up a teddy bear 'D' had on the back seat. I asked him where he got it from and he said let me see it, so I gave it to him, and he threw it out my passenger window. I just looked at him amazed and he burst out laughing, Speedy my ex-girlfriend bought me it, but I want nothing to do with her. I just sat there said nothing and listened to the radio, for the next few hours we just talked about 'SCBC' and tactics which was to come our way on Monday.

We arrived back at our barracks, grabbed our kit, and went to our rooms. First thing I did was stick on a wash then jump into the bath. I gave 'D' a phone. "Right mate, ready to move at 1900hr first stop Bar-X?"

"Right, Speedy, okay, mate," he replied, so I lay there in the bath for about 20 minutes relaxing before I had a quick scrub and climbed out. I put my glad rags on and called for 'D', we had a quick pint in the local Milhouse Pub then got a taxi down to Bar-X.

The first person we bumped into was Harry, also known as Timebomb, he was also our Old Recce Commander and we all looked up to him as he should have been in the special forces. However, his hearing let him down and they wouldn't take him because of this instead he taught sniper's and without a doubt he was the best sniper instructor our Regiment had ever had, and on top of that a really good friend, as soon as he spotted us he came over and wished us both the best of luck for tactic's and bought us both a pint. We mingled with the guys and everyone was buying us drinks and laughing at my cosmic blue hair.

We stayed there until closing time at 2315 hours and then moved on to Jaspers, this is a pizza shop that sells drink, so we grabbed a few beers ate our pizzas and then made the walk to camp. Once in camp, I went straight to bed. I had loads of things to do in the morning, i.e. – sort out my belt, kit and repack my Bergan etc. We got up around 1000hrs and went into town for breakfast and to look at the local talent. Shortly after that around 1530 hours, we went back to camp grabbed our kit and set off on the journey back up to Wales. I found the trip very quick. No sooner were we in the jeep, I fell asleep and woke up at the front gate to Derling Lines in Brecon.

I felt great but 'D' looked wrecked. He'd drove the whole way and let me sleep without even stopping. "What a guy." I got my clean kit out of the back and proceeded to my room to unpack. As soon as I was done, I phoned D up and arranged to meet him in the NAAFI where we watched Top gear with a cup of tea before heading off to bed, we were both knackered.

The next morning, 0600 hours everyone was awake. I got washed and ready and went to the cookhouse to get some food down my neck because if you're running eight miles with weight on your back, food is energy.

Well after breakfast, we all went to the square and the normal roll was called, once the Directing staff were happy, we climbed into the four tonne vehicles and headed to the Brecon Beacons and onto the start point. No one spoke on the route out, we all knew that it didn't matter how fit you were, because on the day anything can happen, injuries, falling it all takes place.

After about an hour, the vehicle stopped, and we all got off the instructors weighed our kit to see if anyone was under-weight. There were a few just under the recommended weight so they were made to put bricks into their backpacks, the four platoons formed up, and the first one left with fifteen-minute intervals between each one. The course is many soldiers' nightmare, with steep gradients and when you must keep in a group and both hands on your weapon the slightest thing annoys you.

The pace was at first quite fast but after about an hour we had about sixteen drop out. I couldn't believe it. It lasted one hour fifty-five minutes which is not a bad time, but also not a very good time. I stood at the end in the group that had passed and when I looked at the failures, my confidence was boosted through the roof. I couldn't believe that all six Pathfinders had failed. We climbed onto the transport and went back to camp tactics had started with 234 soldiers and after the 'I.C.F.T'. There was now 178 and that was only day one.

It all became more apparent when it was rumoured that the Pathfinders failed so they could be sent back to unit and prepare for an operation, so it all made sense now. We spent the first two weeks in the classroom learning how to be a commander and lead men into battle. I had no idea the following year I was going to do it for real in Iraq.

We were showed how to build models and give a set of orders, map reading. Well, if you were shit, you shouldn't be here on this course because you had to know your stuff to be here, I was an ex-Recce Platoon soldier and my map reading was already at a good standard and my mate 'D' had no problems either. We got together most nights to have a chat and brew in the NAAFI and spoke about how we were both doing on the course there was times we didn't see each other for days due to work routine, patrol reports and other tasks.

It was there way of keeping pressure applied to you and watching how we coped, especially when we were being tested on grid references, bearings, distance time and speed, not to mention how the ground lays and details after detail you have to be very accurate. The third week was patrol's one and the fourth week would be patrol's two. This is learning how to take out your section of eight men covertly and gather intelligence for future operations.

The fifth and sixth week is attacking week and defence. This is learning how to defend an area from the enemy attacking and attacking the enemy positions with your men using the ground to its advantage and putting maximum firepower onto the enemy positions. Thus, keeping his head down while you attack, week seven is putting everything you've learnt over the course together to see how you've developed. Bearing in mind there's instructors breathing down your neck and taking notes on your progression to collate a final report that would be sent to your Commanding officer.

And finally, week eight of tactics and week sixteen overall known as test week no matter how well you've done up to this point this could make or break the best of us. At last, all your skills are on show and it's your time to shine. I was confident as my section was strong and most of the guys were very good soldiers, the way it works is, "You work for them and they'll work for you." However, we had one guy who's from the Alphabet Regiment known as the R.G.B.W. And to be quite honest, I'd never meet anyone like him. He was challenging at everything he did. He made tasks turn out to be epic.

Well for me, I only got two appointments on the final week, section commander and platoon sergeant. I knew I had passed and on the last day, my instructor sent for me and a guy called for Lou. Lou was with the 1st Battalion Parachute Regiment. He'd served nine years and was with his patrol's platoon. I had a lot of respect for him, he'd helped in the rescue of our guys that were captured in Sierra Leone and professionally knew his job inside out.

We were told to go and see 'Jimmy.' He was an instructor in the tactic's wing and a current serving member of 22 Special Air Service. He spoke to us both and asked us to try and do selection. He said we had done well on the course and would like us to give it a go. He gave us both handouts and wished us good luck soon. Me and Lou exchanged numbers and went on our way. I was now on a high. I couldn't believe I had impressed Jimmy but I knew I was not ready for that high profile life as a Special Forces soldier, I was on a high and D felt good. He had spoken to Jimmy. We couldn't ask for better praise.

Chapter 4
Iraq and Bust

I hadn't long past Brecon and was waiting for promotion, usually guys wait about six months to a year. Then one day I, read company details I had to report to the Company Sergeant Major (CSM) at 1000hrs the following morning for interviews, prior to interviews with the Officer Commanding (OC).

This meant good news, orders are what you worry about they usually mean you've done wrong and are getting charged so I spent that night on a high. The next day, I got up and made sure I was smartly dressed, carrying my identity card with notepad and pen in my top right pocket. After parade, I made my way to the CMS's office and stood outside for about twenty minutes. Eventually, he arrived and said, "All right, Speedy, come in, mate." So, I said morning sir, marched in and halted. He told me to relax and spoke to me about how I had done on Section Commanders Battle Course (SCBC). He seemed pleased and said I was going to pick up on posting, I didn't have a clue where I was being sent, then he told me I was going to Infantry training centre at Catterick as an instructor teaching recruits.

I couldn't believe it, only soldiers that are really good at their job or need extra coaching get these types of postings and in a way I felt privileged. I was going to teach in a training centre so I had a little bit of pressure on me but I felt confident.

It was 16 December and I was about to go on Christmas leave so I had a lot of packing to do and a paper chase. That's a document you get stamped by all departments in camp i.e., gym, clothing store and Pay office. It just covers you in case you owe money or equipment to anyone in your unit. Once it's stamped, you're free to go. Well, I had to get that completed and pack my kit into boxes and stick the address of I.T.C. on it.

It took me two days, then I was off on a well-deserved break. I had just over two and a half weeks, considering I had just worked constantly for four months it wasn't much. I spent eight days in and around camp then got a flight from Gatwick to Belfast to visit my parents. I spent most of the time in the house. With the occasional trip to my sister's in Ballybeen to visit her two daughters, Amy, and Natasha. They were little madams; everything had to be pink and Barbie. Well, I'd spent a few days home and then flew back to England to do last minute tidying up and then got the train up to Darlington.

It was a four-and-a-half-hour journey, which I spent most of the time sleeping. As soon as I got there, I ran around looking for a taxi. The cheapest one was £20, what a rip off. It took nearly twenty-five minutes. When it pulled up, all I could see was a load of guy's aged 17-24 in extended line outside the Guardroom. I lit up a cigarette and walked over to the Duty R.P. Before I even spoke, he gave me a right roasting in front of the recruits. He made me feel like an idiot, so I cracked.

"Excuse me, LCPL," I said, "next time you speak to me, get your heels together and call me Corporal. Do we understand each other?"

"Sorry, mate," he said, "I thought you were a recruit, that one was one of the many mistakes I let go."

I didn't really understand, but that was how recruits were being treated. The instructors call themselves gods and the young guys are known as scum or Joe's. I had a lot to learn. Fortunately, I was going into an all-Royal Irish Recruiting Team until I had done my induction cadre. All that consists of is a week in the lecture hall being shown how to teach recruits and how to handle them, in I.T.C. Not only are you an instructor you a father figure as well. I missed a few lectures and started helping out with the recruits.

My first job was doing range safety on the 100-metre range. It was the first time these young guys had fired weapons. So, we had to be very vigilant. The guys were okay considering they were novices. We spent a further two hours at the range and then the transport arrived. The PL SGT did a quick head count and then we went back to camp. I got cleaned up and went into the office. It was okay for the other instructors. They were all married and lived in the quarters, not me. I lived in a single bunk beside the recruits and every five minutes someone was banging on my door. Corporal how do you do this, how do you do that. At first, I didn't mind but after a week your still getting asked the same questions. It gets frustrating.

I was told to attend a lecture in the cinema behind the guardroom, the hall was packed with training staff, the Commanding Officer of the 3rd Battalion I.T.C. was giving a brief, suddenly he started calling out names. He said because of a surge in recruiting we have to many, so the MOD have opened I.T.C. Barry Budan, I couldn't believe it. It was ten miles North of Dundee and I was going up there. I knew it was bloody cold. After the brief, I met my training staff. I was happy enough. I had Larry from the Blackwatch Ally from the Highlanders and my Platoon Sergeant was Royal Irish and I we didn't get on well. He was well known for looking after number one.

Well, I had a few days left in Catterick before I had to go up North, so I went and hooked up with an old friend Pablo. He was an instructor with the 1st Battalion I.T.C and a good mate of mine. I gave him a call and arranged to meet him in the NAAFI for a quick pint. We met up and had a chat and then decided to go to Richmond for a few more drinks, Richmond is a small village outside Catterick. We went to the fleece and Weatherspoon's and then onto Harry's Bar. Harry's is a squaddie bar and a boxing ring. All the different units go there and fight it out to see who's the hardest unit.

But that night, I went it was quiet enough. There was only a handful in. So, we decided to go to Louis Bar, that was a good choice. It was packed with talent. We got a few pints and then hit the dance floor. We had a bit of a dance and headed straight for the bar, and there he was, an ex-Royal Irish Soldier who got Shafted on by our top brass and eventually decided to transfer to the Para's. After a short while with them, he went for Pathfinders and now he had done selection and was a current serving Special Forces soldier. I had nothing but respect for him.

We chatted for a while and then went our own way. Pablo by now was looking rather weathered. I tried to catch up by downing a pint but I couldn't. It was now about 0115hrs and I was knackered so I jumped in a taxi and went to camp. The next day I got up and got ready for work and went to the lecture hall to meet the new recruits. These guys were the ones that were going to Scotland with me (my recruits).

Because I was R.I.R, my new guys were all from N. Ireland and wanted to go to my Regiment. So straight away I was on guard. The last thing I wanted was some fool with no common sense going to my unit. The last thing you need is someone back in my unit saying, "Who was your instructor in training, Corporal Coult? Typical, no wonder you passed out." I wasn't going to let that happen.

There were sixteen lads from N. Ireland turned up and that made my day. I remembered my first day meeting my corporal, I thought my God a real soldier, I wonder if he's killed anyone, and they were now thinking the same about me.

So, I had to look professional. Once all the recruits were booked in, they had to sit through lectures and briefs for the first two days. After that, I took them to the QM's dept and got them all fitted up with their uniform. It seemed to go on for hours. A lot of the young recruits couldn't do the simplest of things. I showed one lad how to tie his laces; it was embarrassing for a lot of them. As soon as they had been given their uniforms and other bits and bobs, I marched them across to their accommodation and let them have 30 minutes to settle in. In that time, I went for a brew with the other instructors in the NAAFI.

The whole day was spent trying to settle the new recruits into their new surroundings. They were being treated like babies. No one was being shouted at. They were going to the NAAFI. They had mobile phones some even knew the vicar's number in case one of the instructors was mean to him. No wonder the army was producing softer soldiers. When I was in training, you were spoken to like and adult and you got a slap if you messed up and that was the end of it. And it worked because you never made the same mistake twice.

That night, we had them all in bed for 2200hrs. The next day, we got them all packed up onto eight coaches, which had been parked up on the drill square. As soon as they were all loaded up, we left two coaches at a time towards our new location Barry Budan. This was to ensure we didn't completely block the minor and major roads with long vehicles. The journey took about six hours, someone with a bit of pull in I.T.C. had arranged a coach stop at a café, so the young recruits could stretch their legs and buy some food and drinks.

I was a disgusting stinking hole, and the guys were paying £4 a packet of sandwiches the owner made over £1,000 that day and these young soldiers knew they were being ripped off. Once they were ready, we got them back onto the coaches and made the last few hours through Dundee and onto Barry Budan, the look on those guys faces. I have never seen so many depressed people in one place.

We parked up and got them off the coaches. Once they collected their things, we took them to the cookhouse for a late meal which had been booked and that's where they got their brief on the camp and found out the safety brief. It was now 2030hrs, so I took them to their accommodation and showed them how to iron their uniform and briefed them on what I was doing in the morning and before I left, I shouted. "See you dressed and washed outside the block 0630hrs don't be late."

That night, I was in the NAAFI and my life changed. My phone started to ring and my brother's name appeared on the screen, so I answered it. "Speedy," he said.

"Yes," I replied.

"Get yourself back here as soon as possible, mate, we're going to the Gulf."

At first, I thought it was a joke, but then he went on. "I get my anthrax injection tomorrow." I swore to him that I would meet him in Iraq and I meant it. The next day, I went to my boss and explained to him what I wanted to do, and was told no, so I went to my CSM and was told the same thing, no one was interested. There were loads of instructors up and down the length of Britain trying like hell to get back to their units and go to war. We were the most qualified Section Commanders in the Army that's why we were teaching. I phoned my RSM and he said, "Look, Speedy, we need Commanders badly, but we can't ask for you. You now belong to the I.T.C." I was gutted, I asked him how I could get back and he told me, "Speedy the only way you're coming with us to the Gulf is if you get R.T.U.s (return to unit)."

I knew the only thing you could get R.T.U.s for is by doing something wrong, so now I knew I was going, I had missed out on the Kosovo tour and had heard all the stories about what went on. I was working with 7 R Irish at the time, so I asked to be sent back, but got there too late. Then I was on exercise in Canada and missed Sierra Leone and C-Coy 1 R.I.R had eleven men taken hostage, after all that I was determined to go to Iraq, it was my destiny.

I spent the next four weeks teaching the recruits and carrying on as normal, now and again asking to be sent back to camp and constantly being told no, and then it hit me. I started an argument with my Platoon sergeant, and ended up throwing a cup at him, full of hot tea. His patience was running out also. Well, that didn't work. I went to bed that night trying to think something up, and eventually fell asleep. I woke up at 0600hrs and that's when it came to me, I had decided to take two recruits out of camp and do shopping in Dundee, so that night, I took two of the recruits out and we had a drink in Dundee.

I brought them back at about 0200hrs. I knew they hadn't been issued with I.D. cards yet so they couldn't get in, so when the guard asked who took them out, there reply was Cpl Speedy, and that was me sent back. The next morning, I was awoken by my Sergeant major and Platoon sergeant. "Coult, you've got fifteen minutes to get packed and out of my camp." I sat up in bed and glanced around the room.

"Can I have an hour, sir? I've loads of kit."

"Get out," he shouted.

I got up and packed away my kit, ironed my uniform and went to see the CSM. "Right, Corporal Coult, you're in front of the RSM tomorrow." I was chuffed to bits. I was going to the Gulf as a Commander. I got into the 4x4 and was driven to Catterick.

The next morning, I was in front of the RSM who gave me a right roasting and sent me into the Adjutant who gave me a right roasting and sent me to work with Parachute Company. I'd spent four days there and then they went to do their jumps, I then went and told the Adjutant that I had no work to do. He smiled and then sent me to work with the guards. I only lasted six days there, and then they went on exercise. So again, I went to see adjutant and again he posted me to the Para Depot. When I got there, the CSM told me to take off one of my stripes and that I had been bust. At this stage, I didn't really care as long as I was going to war with my fellow Rangers.

I spent the next week coming in and out of the RSM's office and phoning my RSM to be updated on the Iraq crisis. Eventually, I was sent for by the RSM. "Right, Corporal Coult, you are on Commanding Officers. Orders in five minutes." *Great, it's nearly over*, I thought. I stood outside his office waiting to be called in, then the door opened. My name got called out and I marched in and halted, he read out my name and number so I agreed, "Yes, that's correct, sir."

"Do you realise you broke standing orders and could have brought the army into disrepute?"

"Yes, sir," I replied.

"All because you want to go to Iraq with your unit."

"Yes, sir," I said.

"Well, I'm busting you to the rank of private, and do you have anything to add?"

"Yes, sir, I'd rather go to war as a private with my unit, than stay here working as an instructor."

He went mad. "Get him away." I walked out of that office with my head held high.

I was going to Iraq to fight. While he was going to sit behind a desk for the rest of his career and let on, he knew it all, well he didn't. He'd never been under that kind of pressure. The way I looked at it was why join the Army and not go to war; it's every soldier's dream and I wanted to live it.

Chapter 5
Camp Blair Mayne

After being sent back to my unit, I had to see B-company's Sergeant major. He was a good soldier and everything he did was by the book. I went to his office and waited for about ten minutes, then he arrived. "Speedy, come in here," he said. As per usual, I marched in and halted.

"Right, mate, whatever happened at the training centre I don't care. What rank are you?"

"I'm a ranger, sir."

"No, you're not. You're a section commander in 5 platoons."

"Thank you, sir. Speedy, your section is already in the gulf you'll meet them out there, now go to the CQMS and get your kit."

I was well chuffed. I was flying out to Kuwait in three days but first I had to get a medical and injections. I went immediately to meet my new company clerk and found out what kit and equipment I needed. There were loads of stuff and was this all supposed to go. The first thing I did was spray my op's vest desert colour and then I did my Bergan. I spent the first day with my Bergan and webbing making sure I had the right kit in my pouches.

The company did supply me with a packing list, but when you've been in a while any soldier who knows, packing lists just a guide and personally I thought they were just for the younger guys, all I needed was enough to survive and sustain myself, first thing I binned was that bloody sleeping bag. It's known as the bouncing bomb because it weighs a tonne and takes up the most room in your Bergan. I bought a cheap sleeping bag and it took up one third of the room, that left me enough room for five t-shirts, spare combats, socks and buffalo jacket.

Well, I had packed my Bergan and side pockets with goodies playing cards and two books and then I began on my vest by packing noodles and rations. I thought two water bottles would be enough and so a began packing baby wipes and other bits and pieces. I was basically finished, but I was also taking a grip bag so I used it for training shoes and sports kit and goodies, now I was happy. Once I was finished, I ironed my desert combats and polished my jungle boots, ready to deploy. That night, I dreamt of what it would be like in Iraq and I couldn't wait to go.

The next morning, I went on parade and got myself sorted by the medical centre. They told me I would get my anthrax injection in theatre because they had run out. I wasn't really worried. I reported to my C.S.M. and was given the rest of the day off. I just had to report to the freight senior N.C.O. as I was now baggage party, that's were all soldiers without rank carry everyone's kit and equipment and ensure it gets on the flight and loaded onto the plane, taken off and reloaded onto transport and gets to our camp in the desert, not forgetting all the weapons and x-ray machines, accounting for all the baggage and even weighing it to make sure the planes okay and can take the weight.

I went to bed early that night and was the first one over at the freight in the morning. It took two hours to load up the vehicles and then we were on the way to the airport. The motorway was at a standstill so we went through all the little villages, it added an extra hour to our journey, but it didn't matter as I would soon be in the gulf and that's all that mattered.

It had taken around five hours to get to the Royal Air Force base, at the gate I showed my identification and was let straight in, we unloaded all the boxes and bags and took them to the plane it was a civilian airline from France, how ironic was this.

While we were loading up, I could see all the troops walking across the runway and boarding the plane. Everyone was on a high. I was now getting tired and my desert shirt was starting to get wet with sweat, before I climbed aboard, I stuck on a t-shirt and dried myself down. I got the guys together and we all boarded the plane and clasped into the seat.

We sat on the runway for an extra twenty minutes, then the pilot spoke, "I'd like to welcome the Royal Irish Regiment aboard our air France flight the time in Kuwait now is 18:00 hours the flight will take approximately nine hours. I hope you enjoy your flight with us. Good luck you are all doing a good job." Just then, a massive cheer went up around the plane, and we began to move along the runway. Five minutes later, we were in the air. The air hostess came round with water and then a film came on. I have never seen five hundred angry men before. They had films on with no sound and the boys were not happy. Most of them just

46

stuck on personal radios and fell asleep. I was just about to drift off and my brother came over for a chat. He was a driver in the recce platoon and a decent soldier. We spoke for a while and then he went back to his seat. I fell asleep shortly after and only woke up for meals on the plane and they looked amazing.

We were approaching Kuwait and it looked like a scene from the Las Vegas strip. The lights and colours lit up the sky and there was the biggest oil refinery in the world, miles, and miles of twisted pipelines I'd never seen anything like it, ten minutes later we were touching down at Kuwait Airport. The plane had barely come to a halt and the humidity was unbelievable. Most of the guys were soaking with sweat. Before the troops got called forward to leave the plane, I got called forward first as I was the baggage party, so we all left the plane to unload the kit.

Four container Lorries arrived, and we loaded all the kit onto them, once finishes we climbed onto the bus and were driven to an American base. Where we got off and booked into theatre, every single soldier who was taking part in the war had to book in through this camp, I'd never seen anything like it, there were miles and miles of makeshift tents and thousands of us marines in the desert, away from any sign of civilian life. After booking in, I went across to the baggage truck and accounted for the weapons. Once we were happy, we had them all. We got back on the coach and drove through the desert to find our location.

Every couple of kilometres, there was a makeshift camp with their unit's flag flying. We were driving around for two hours and then I saw the sixteen-air assault HQ and we even drove past that. We were about 500 metres northeast of the HQ. I couldn't believe it we were the most forward British unit and the camp had a sentry at the front gate and one on the back gate and four more guards in sangers and a super sanger. Once we had been cleared by the sentry to enter the camp, the guard commander booked us in and then an escort took us to our destination.

We were taking no chances. Security was tight as hell. The only unit in front of ours were the 1,5 Regimental combat team. They were the American front assault groups, it now felt real. I was at war. We pulled up and everyone gathered around the truck to claim their bags and I just sat back until the trucks were unloaded. Once the guys were finished, I picked up my kit and was met by Dev, he worked with the C.Q., he shook my hand and laughed. "We heard what you did, Speedy, you're just right mate. I'll show you to your tent." It was right beside the cookhouse tent so that was a bonus. I got into the tent and couldn't believe how big it was, each tent was big enough for a platoon and a half. I looked around to see where three sections were and I found them at the bottom right-hand side of the tent well their kit was anyway. All the guys were away still unloading stores, I put my kit beside Stevie and Bish.

Stevie was my second in command and Bish was 2 sections commander, I then went and got my rifle from Jay, he was my C.Q.M.S, from that moment on my rifle never left my side, I went to dinner, toilet, washing, everywhere I went so did my rifle I even slept with it. About thirty minutes later, all the guys arrived back and welcomed me to the platoon, and we had a laugh. I introduced myself to the section and told them all what I expected from them. Stevie then ran off and got me my ammunition I had six full magazines, one bandolier, two phosphorus grenades and one high explosive L109 grenade. I packed them all into my assault vest and went to see the platoon commander. He said he was glad to have me and briefed me up on the current situation.

I told him I needed a few days to work with my section and show them the skills and drills I wanted them to adapt. He said, "No problem when you want to start?" I told him I needed a few hours to find my feet. He agreed and handed me thirty-two maps, and these only went to key objectives we needed to take from the Iraqi soldiers.

I got my first map which led us across the border to the oil fields and marked it up putting on all the report lines, direction of threat friendly forces and direct firing locations, I had everything on that map, in permanent pen and the maps were waterproof. Once I'd marked up the maps, I needed I went lunch, it was an American Meal ready to eat which meant just add hot water, it had peanut butter and flavour drinks like bubble gum. I suppose it was better than nothing and after all we were in the desert.

As soon as I'd had lunch, I asked Stevie to give me 100% ammo check, I wanted to stamp my authority and let the guys know who was boss. Once that was done, I carried out a complete kit check. The guys knew I wasn't a soft touch and started to work for each other and for me. Stevie then went off and took two guys with him. When he returned, he had two boxes of water and he gave out two bottles to each man. He oversaw the water and dished it out when and if someone was short. That day, most of the guys in camp were out sunning themselves, but not my section. I had them in cleaning their rifles. I didn't care if they shaved or if their boots were dirty, but what I did care about was that their individual weapons worked and were clean. I didn't really care if they had clean socks on. That night I got out my sleeping bag on the tent floor which was wooden. The tent had in fact came from Saudi Arabia and very warm, so I slept in just a pair of running shorts.

As I lay on top of my sleeping bag, I was going through what drills in my head to adapt so my section would be effective in combat, contact drills and actions on attack and counter-attack and extraction drills were my priority but before we could get that cracked I wanted them to be good at battlefield first aid and A.F.V. 'armoured fighting vehicle recognition'. This was very important because they needed to know every vehicle and how to identify them, so the next morning, I arranged a lesson with one of my mates who was in the anti-tank platoon.

I told my boss about what I had done and all of a sudden, the whole platoon wanted to do it, so I let them sit in on the lesson. It lasted about forty minutes. After that, I gave my guys an hour to chill out then I took them into the desert and began teaching first aid i.e., how to treat a gunshot wound, when to apply morphine, how to make improvised stretchers. We spoke for a while and then my boss turned up to listen in to the lesson. Somehow when you're going over a lesson and it's going well and the guys are getting all the questions right, when an officer turns up, the troops all worry and some of the stuff they come out with is comical. It makes you, the commander, look terrible.

The new guy in my section even started to bloody stutter, once I had seen him going into one, I got up and said right guys take a ten-minute leg stretch then were going to do some standard operational procedures. "Right, Stevie, come here." I briefed him up on what I expected then I broke down the section into fire teams. Me being Charlie fire team and Stevie being delta. I briefed up the boss and he just said to crack on, so I got the troops in a line and took Ricky and Con in my fire team, that left Stevie with Jay and Bo. We started with types of patrolling across the desert, and I chose diamond formation as our S.O.P with diamond it gives me maximum fire power if attacked from any angle.

We then practised coming under enemy fire, that was us firing initial bursts by the gunners and the rest of us just getting down fire, trying to keep the enemies head down. We then fanned out into extended line. Once in extended line, my fire team got up and moved forwards first while Stevie had his team put down effective fire. I had moved about 15–20 metres and then gone down.

Once I was in my position, my call sign got the fire down, that was Stevie's signal to move. We kept this going for a couple of bounds until we were close enough to the enemy position. I then dropped off my point of fire and crawled forward with my grenade man. We had to almost move lying flat on the sand because in the desert if you stand up, you're a dead man because there's no cover. With all of this going on while Stevie is still putting down fire onto the enemy position, we got to about ten metres from the position and my grenade man and I put on a fresh magazine and changed our levers to automatic and got the grenade out. He pulled the pin and threw it like a stone into the bunker. Once it went off, he was in there with a burst of automatic. He shouted at me, "Position clear." I then moved in checking for other enemies, and I couldn't see any. "REORG," I shouted that way the rest of the guys signal to move in using the path that we had already taken as that was the safe route. Once in I went around and placed them all down with interlocking ARC's facing the direction of the enemy threat, I then went through the motions of sending a sit-rep i.e., situation report and Stevie carried out an ammo, casualty equipment check known as pacessdo. I then shouted, "Stop stand up and close in." I then gave the guys a de-brief and told them where and what we needed to improve on. We practised it a further three times getting contacted from different directions until I was happy enough with the standard we were at.

We then headed back into camp. On the way to camp, I noticed right the whole way across the desert there were troops practising their drills just like what we had done everyone was excited and couldn't wait until we crossed the border into Iraq. Once we got back into our tent, I gave the guys a break and then we started weapon cleaning. I checked all the weapons to make sure they were all free of sand and carbon. As soon as I was happy, the troops then had the rest of the day off to write home and sunbathe, not me I always had briefs to go to and checks to do. Dinner came and I couldn't believe it morale hit rock bottom. We were given stew with two slices of bread. As a one off it's not bad, but that became ritual. Every dinner for the next month or so was the same. The guys started asking for good parcels from home.

Conditions improved when two containers arrived with showers in, but it took two weeks for the engineers to get them up and running. It meant no more showers standing on a crate behind a sheet with cold water. We had eighteen toilets and not one roll of toilet paper, we had to use cleanex tissue from ration boxes, every single night the troops descended on the cookhouse tent it had been fitted with massive TV set and satellite and the news channel stayed on permanently, every officer watched patiently on the progression of the war in Iraq, everyone waiting on Tony Blair to say the word. We thought it would never come then word flew around camp that General Jackson was coming the following day.

That night, all the vehicles were lined up in packets facing Iraq and left in position overnight. The next day the whole battle group got on parade outside camp and the R.S.M. briefed us up. We all stood there waiting on him and all a sudden, this lynx helicopter appeared and with it about three dozen vehicles came across the dusty desert it was the worlds press, they had come to hear the speech of the general. I remember seeing the press from the stars and stripes magazine, they were two U.S. marines. He stood on a platform towering over the battle group and announced to us, he was happy with our progress and was ready to send us into Iraq, the feeling of pride was written across everyone's face.

The speech took around fifteen minutes and every TV station and press group in the world turned up. They were hanging on every word he said and taking photos of the troops and trying to interview us, not one soldier had an interest in being interviewed we had better things to do. The satellite phones were up and running. We had been issued with phone cards each one had fifteen minutes but you had to dial 32 numbers to get through anywhere. Every phone call was being monitored as soon as you mentioned anything to do with the war the line went dead, no one was taking any chances in case the operation was put in jeopardy.

It was getting very tense in camp we all knew it wasn't long now, we had spent nearly three weeks training and preparing, then the coy 2nd in Command Came in and briefed all the platoon commanders we all knew something was up, he then got up and left the tent shortly after that the platoon Sergeant opened up a box and started placing his mail in it along with family photos and his wallet. All personal items were being taken away from us. After handing in our belongings, we all had to attend a church service in the cookhouse. That night, the O.C. came into our tent and briefed the company group on the first mission and that we were to relieve 1.5 R.C.T. at the oil fields so they could push on up to Basra.

We were all told to prepare ourselves for the worst. Some of things we were going to see would be the first time we had seen pieces of skull and bodies without limbs. Afterwards, the brief silence fell across the tent. It was now only a matter of hours before we went to War.

Chapter 6
Time Has Run Out

We all sat around the tent at our bed spaces, I was sitting on my sleeping bag checking my assault vest and adjusting my straps with green tape when the company 2nd in Command came in. "I want the whole company fell in three ranks outside tent in ten minutes, the Commanding Officer wants to brief the whole battlegroup." We all marched across to the open area. I was facing Recce Platoon and C-Company. The camera men were all there and every officer was stood to attention. Then Commanding Officer, Tim Collins arrived and the silence was deadly. You could have heard a pin drop; he then gave a speech to his soldiers that left grown men with tears running down their faces.

"It is my foremost intention to bring every single one of you out alive, but there may be people amongst us who will not see the end of this campaign. We will put them in their sleeping bags and send them back. There will be no time for sorrow. There would be no tolerance of cowardice nor a killing spree, but we will show no mercy to forces who remain loyal to Saddam Hussein. Iraqi forces who declare a truce in the face of advancing allies would be embraced by the coalition and permitted to fight for regime change in their own nation. The enemy should be in no doubt that we are his nemesis and that we are bringing about his rightful destruction, there are many Regional Commanders who have stains on their souls and they are stoking the fires of hell for Saddam. He and his forces will be destroyed by this coalition for what they have done, as they die, they will know their deeds have brought them to this place. Show them no pity. We go to liberate not to conquer. We will not fly our flags in their country. We are entering Iraq to free people and the only flag which will be flown in this ancient land is their own, show them respect. There are some who are alive at this moment who will not be alive shortly, those who do not wish to go on that journey, and we will not send them, as for the others I expect you to wreck their world. Wipe them out if that is what they chose. But if you are ferocious in battle, remember to be magnanimous in victory. It is a big step to take another human life, it is not to be done lightly. I know men who have taken life needlessly in other conflicts and i can assure you they live with the mark of Cain upon them. If someone surrenders to you then you remember they have that right in international law and ensure they go home one day to their family, the ones who wish to fight, well, we aim to please if you harm the Regiment or its history by over-enthusiasm in killing or in cowardice know it is your family who will suffer, you will be shunned unless your conduct is of the highest, for your deeds will follow you down through history. We will bring shame on neither our uniform nor our nation. We will certainly face Saddam's chemical and biological arsenal, there's no question of if. It's a question of when. If we survive the first strike, we will survive the attack, we will respect their culture and religion and not confuse it with the kind of international terrorism Saddam had cultivated within his borders. Iraq is steeped in history, it is site of the Garden of Eden, of the great flood and the birthplace of Abraham tread lightly there. You will see things that no man could play to see and you will have to go a long way to find a more decent, generous, and upright people than the Iraqi's. You will be embarrassed by their hospitality even though they have nothing, don't treat them as refugees for they are in their own country. Their children in years to come will know that the light of liberation in their lives was brought by you. If there are casualties of war then remember that when they woke up and got dressed in the morning, they did not plan to die this day. Allow them dignity in death. Bury them properly and mark their graves, as for ourselves let's bring everyone home and leave Iraq a better place for us having been there. Our business now is north."

After his speech everyone cheered and clapped the Commanding Officer. He looked a very tired and nervous. He turned and walked towards the operations tent, the rest of us disappeared into tents and packed up our remaining kit. In just a few hours, we were going.

Our O.C. gave a last-minute orders group just to clarify our missions. We were already 20 miles from the Iraqi border so it wouldn't take long to cross over, we spent the next few hours just resting and catching some last-minute sleep. We didn't know when we would be able to get some again.

No sooner was I asleep and some officer came in and shouted, "Right, guys, let's go." He stood at the tent exit and wished every single soldier good luck. He was an officer from London Irish attached to us and our press officer stood beside him.

I put my assault vest on, stuck my Bergan on my back and walked towards the vehicle, everyone was doing the exact same. Again, the silence was deadly. I put my Bergen into the trailer and called for my section. I took them off to the side and shook all their hands. "Good luck," I said. The look on their faces was that of excitement. One of my guys had come out directly from training.

"Right listen in, with a magazine of 30 rounds load, safety catch, change lever check top round is securely fitted, place magazine onto the magazine housing, right guys get onto the transport."

We sat there for about twenty minutes and then the engine started and the convoy of vehicles rolled out the gates. We drove for about an hour and then arrived at a holding area. Everything suddenly changed. Explosions could be heard for miles, we all got off the vehicle and began to dig shell scrape and then the boss started screaming gas, gas, gas.

We all dived to put on our respirators and got into cover, the Iraqi's had fired a scud missile and it hit the Royal Marine HQ. Another was fired and you could see it in the sky in the distance explosions were happening to our front, the Americans had broken into Iraq and were taking some resistance, no casualties to the allies at the break in, yet the Iraqi's had already hundreds of soldiers killed, their bodies where still burning. The Americans dug holes and just through the bodies in and filled in the holes. The second scud had come down in Kuwait City which was full of local's shopping. Innocent people had been killed, it seemed to go on for hours.

We were putting our respirators on and off every ten minutes, the vehicles would drive to the border and stop every 500mtrs and we would then get off and dig in. The vehicles stopped for about twenty minutes and when I looked over my right shoulder, I could see our Recce Platoon resting, so I got off and went to find my brother. I walked up the line of vehicles and eventually found him at the front vehicle, he was sitting in the driver's seat just starting at the burning oil wells. I walked over and stood and shook his hand and wished him all the best, we stood there and chatted for a while. We could see the burning oil wells and the trail of smoke coming from them was turning the sky black. I got out my camera and asked for a photo, so he got his mate to take one of us both, it would be something to remember, especially as it was taken on the day war broke out. I spent a further ten minutes chatting then went back to my vehicles.

The troops all looked nervous, no sooner was I in the vehicle, we got another chemical attack, I had my respirator on in three seconds flat, shouting gas, gas, gas. Five minutes later, all clear was given, another scud had been fired at Kuwait, but before it had time to impact, the U.S. Navy had launched two patriot missiles and shot it down.

We had now spent hours getting on and off the vehicles, digging in and masking up, then the message came. "Mount up, Commanders, make ready." I cocked my rifle and fixed my sights to 300 metres, that's the battle range. They usually are at 300mtrs but with all the jumping in and out of the vehicle they had moved slightly, recce platoon raced off first into Iraq followed by my company, the border was well visible.

With grey cabins either side of the road and a watch tower over on the left, the fence had been destroyed by the Americans so their M1 tanks and anthrax vehicles could enter Iraq along with our challenger and scimitars. There was light blue oil drum scattered across the road with United Nations wrote on them; it took for ever for all our vehicles to get into Iraq.

There were miles of vehicles bumper to bumper who all wanted a piece of the action. We were now one mile into Iraq and the American vehicles were scattered everywhere. The yanks had dug in and were now regrouping for their next mission. I noticed they were all wearing their chemical warfare suits and lots of Iraqi bodies scattered across the desert, T-54-55 tanks were still burning and oil wells were engulfed in thick black smoke as it covered the sky.

We drove on through and passed along route Dallas, I looked to my left and saw the R.S.M. He was handling hundreds of Prisoners of war. There were Iraqi officers sitting with their hands on their heads and the defence Platoon were guarding them. We passed them for a further kilometre and came to a stop, the American's had debussed their vehicles and were all in the prone position facing up the road.

They couldn't advance in their vehicles, an American officer had been killed and they couldn't go to attack because the pipe lines stretched across the desert and their vehicles couldn't cross them and there was no way they were leaving their vehicles and going by foot, our Platoon Sergeant jumped out the vehicle and told the Platoon to make ready. We all got out of the vehicle and spread out across the desert. "Right guys Bish, Lenny I want 2 up, Speedy your reserve section lets go, enemy to our front."

This was what I had been waiting for, I told Stevie to control the guys and I shot off with the Platoon Sgt, we had advanced only 300mtrs and the fire fight had already begun. The Americans were all behind us amazed by the way we do things, Lenny pushed left around ruins and before his section even fired a round three Iraqi's surrendered, Bish pushed right and took two gun positions and I went straight through the centre with my section and took an anti-aircraft position, the Iraqis were totally surprised buy our swift and decisive movement, not even a bullet had been fired, I was now pissed off, I wanted blood on my hands and instead I only got eight P.O.Ws, one Iraqi kept shouting and screaming he was still sitting behind the anti-aircraft gun.

I got two of my guys run over to extract him, the reason why he was still sitting there was because members of the Ba'ath Party had broken both his legs so he couldn't run, so the guys picked him up and took him to a holding area with all the other P.O.Ws. I was still pumping; my adrenaline was still going. When we returned to the vehicle, I walked off on my own for a few minutes and punched the vehicle to calm down, only then I felt okay.

We said bye to the yanks and they raced off up the road further into Iraq, we stayed firm for only an hour or so and the gun battle the Americans were having was only a few hundred yards to our front. It was an old Iraqi Army camp and they wouldn't let the Coalition have it. The gun battle went on for only half an hour, then we were given the green light to move forward. We drove slowly up the road as we had been told there were mine-fields either side of it, we got to about 30mtrs from the Americans and stopped our boss got out and spoke to their Commander, again they had taken the Iraqi camp and had P.O.W.s, one of their Humvees had driven over a land mine and another American Officer lay dead.

My boss told me to go and have a look, so I got off the vehicle and headed towards the Humvee. I had only walked about ten metres and some US Marine Sergeant came over to me and said, "You guys relieving us."

I said, "Yes, mate, brief me up and you can shoot on."

"Okay, buddy, we've got a mine field out there. That's what took out our Humvee, we also got P.O.W.s around the corner and the enemy dead, come on I'll show you."

I walked over to see the dead Iraqis and couldn't believe it, there must have been thirty holes in him, I took a glance and then said, "Cheers, mate, we'll take it from here." I went and got my section to secure the road and relieve the

Americans. We had twelve P.O.W.s and were now in Mutrash Iraqi Army Barracks.

The Americans took a few photos then pushed on with their advance, our boss got the rest of the troops off the vehicle and put them in all round defence while he gave the commanders a set of Quick Battle Orders. "Right Bish I want an Observation Post on top of that building, Len I want a gun position across that road, Speedy I want a V.C.P. on the road and a Sanger built here and this road blocked off."

I thought, *Thanks, boss, in this heat, it would take all day.* He then went into hard cover and work routine began to take place. I put two men on patrol with communication back to Platoon HQ and began the Sanger. Len had two men stopping and searching vehicles and Bish had two men on top of the building keeping watch in the direction of Basra.

We held the P.O.W.s for half an hour then from higher form we were told to let them go, we then carried out a quick search and gave them some water and sent them on their way. They came back an hour later asking for their vehicles. I thought no reason to say no. So, I let them take them. They took a bus which was in fact dug in, so once they moved it and drove off. I moved the section's kit into it as it was protected from all sides.

At this point, each section was now doing two hours on duty and two hours off with two hours patrolling it was shattering, with your two hours off you got food on, got washed, did your admin and had to catch up on sleep, this was going to last two weeks, we started doing mobile patrols around the Rumalia oil fields to stop counter-attacks and got more Iraqi P.O.W. which we escorted back down the chain to the R.S.M. and all weapons we found went there to.

Bish had established his observation point and Len had the gun up and running. My section was patrolling around the old barracks when Bish reported seeing Iraqis with weapons approximately ten metres from his location. I got four men and borrowed another four from Len and at best speed went to investigate but by the time I'd got there, Bish had it all under control.

In fact what had happened was the locals were stealing weapons from the armoury in the camp and selling them to get money in order to buy food for their families, or that was what they were saying, they had AK-47 assault rifles and rock propelled grenades, the same kind of arsenal that the I.R.A used back in Northern Ireland against the security forces. We escorted them of the camp telling them to stay away or they would be in danger. Once they disappeared, I went back to have a look and Bish was already there, and his face was pure white. I asked what was wrong and he said, "Go take a look." So, I went into the armoury and couldn't believe it. There were thousands of warheads, anti-aircraft guns AK-47 assault rifles, hundreds of rocket propelled grenades and Iraqi uniforms, I got straight on my radio and told the boss to make his way to my location, as soon as he had a look, he told his boss.

We were told to stay clear of them in case of booby traps, so we stepped up our patrols until we were virtually awake all the time, so I changed the timings to four hours on eight hours off. Hoping for some rest when the patrols team stumbled across anti-tank mines, and I don't mean one or two I mean six thousand mostly still boxed. We had to get engineers over because now our main effort was the mines and now, we had to stay here.

If the mines were to be moved or tampered with, they would surely blow up and if they did the oil refinery would be destroyed also and that would be a disaster, hundreds of thousands of gallons of oil gone in an instant and that couldn't happen.

So, we split the section in half. One half went to re-enforce Len and the other half went to Bish to boost his section strength. We had to start the roster from first light, but the boss cut it short when he came over and said he was taking Len and Bish away to guard the pumping station as Iraqis were breaking in and it needed securing, he also said to be aware of a counter-attack as the Americans had left small pockets of resistance as they punched through the main positions on their way north.

He left the platoon radio so we could get in touch with him if anything happened. I said thank you but deep down I was annoyed at how he thought six men could guard what it had taken a whole Platoon to do. The first thing we did was get everyone's Bergan packed up and in the one place, I then asked Stevie to get his team and take charge of the OP, while I got my guys to control the road and outbuildings.

It was now getting dark, so all night sights were fitted and 94mm anti-tank weapons were extended, I went over to where the boss had left the radio and it wasn't there. I flipped, if we were to come under contact, we were on our own with six men with no communications, I was going to kill him. I put the guys of my team on staggered duty with me stepping in every 30 minutes and Stevie done same at his position. The young guys were nervous also, and to be honest, I felt a little uneasy with the whole process.

We must have been there for another four hours and it was getting dark well the only light was that of the burning oil wells which lit up the whole area, all a sudden, a vehicle approached from our rear. I went across to see who it was and to my relief it was the boss and his driver young Gareth. The vehicle had no one aboard inside as the boss had decided to collect the remainder of us and take us to the pumping station. I went and told the guys to collect their Bergan's and get on the vehicle, I waited until the last of the Bergan's had been loaded to make sure no kit was left behind.

Stevie was last to collect his kit and told me all his men were through and all kit was accounted for. I was now happy, so I picked up my Bergan and walked to the vehicle. When I got there, the troops kit was sitting outside the vehicle, and they were all walking around making sure nothing had been left behind. The boss came over to see what was happening and I had to explain to him that it was not good practice to leave a Commander out here with no Communications. He agreed, however, he had been left in a sticky situation himself.

We all climbed onto the transport and moved to the pumping station, when we arrived the other Commanders had agreed to let my troops have eight hours rest and we were very grateful, the Platoon Sergeant had written a cycle of duties which went rest, VCP, guards, so everyone got equal time, the only problem was that during your rest you carried out two patrols around the station, to make sure the locals didn't break in. It wasn't that bad. It gave us loads of time to get ourselves together and anyway every few days, Milan Platoon and other elements like Recce Platoon would come in and help us with the patrolling.

The station we were situated at was five kilometres by three kilometres and on foot it took an hour and a half, every day our CSM would pop in to make sure we were doing okay and check on our morale. It was good to see he was checking up on his troops, but like all bosses, he became a right pain, but in a good way as instead of us sitting doing nothing he insisted on us keeping on top of cleaning as the guys were starting to get bored so we got them to brush roads and build more sangers.

The CSM began to lift morale, he would come now and again and bring mail and bread for the troops this went on for about a week, and then word came down. The chain that we were preparing for a Company attack, the first time and probably the last. Our company had loads of sprogs that I wouldn't trust to go to the shop and now I was expected to trust them with my life.

Chapter 7
Advance to Contact

We drove in the vehicle to the Battalion Headquarters where our boss got out and spoke to the Officer commanding the Company. He gave him a grid reference of where the company was to rendezvous. We had to drive for over an hour and eventually came to an old factory. When we arrived there, the CSM was shouting his head off for things to happen. He wanted a work party to start building a toilet area.

Our platoon supplied six guys to help with the tasks as did 4 Platoon and 6 Platoon, after an orders group with the boss, the Platoon Sergeant came out and briefed us all. We were staying here for a few days until further orders had come down the chain. All we had to do is supply a guard and a quick reaction force. This was great news as the whole Company was here and there was a lot of scope for rest.

Things started to look up when the platoon sergeant gave us fruit, eggs, and buns. The colour sergeant must have been running pulling his hair out trying to get us mail and goodies. Well things were going very well and it was the first time I'd seen the rest of the guys since crossing the border all those weeks ago. And the stories were all about what each of our Platoons had done. Four Platoon had been digging shell-scrapes due to the area they were given as it wasn't the safest place to be. Apparently once they were nearly finished, the CSM had come across and told them to move position, that happened twice so as you can imagine there were a lot of very pissed off soldiers.

Six Platoon were telling us how hard they were getting it, but we all knew they had it easy and only had one stag position to man, as soon as got settled into my bed space I gathered all the guys together and carried out a kit check. When I was happy, I got the troops to clean their weapons. Then the Platoon sergeant came in and said he wanted two guys to go and assist the CSM. I sent two guys that had already cleaned their weapons. They must have been gone for around forty minutes, so I went outside to see what they were doing and found them doing routine tasks, picking up rubbish and sweeping the road. Regardless of what your role is, you must always put hygiene at the top of the list to remain effective.

That night, we had an orders group with our boss. As a company of men, we had been picked by our commanding officer to go lead company on an advance to contact. We were to clear all enemy to our front and destroy a tank battalion. How the hell were we going to do that. One hundred and fifty tanks considering our battalion were scattered across the whole desert and we only had around 64 anti-tank missiles, it seemed like madness.

Someone somewhere knew there was either there no tanks or the enemy had run and left the tanks still in place. That night, I made sure my section got as much sleep as possible, they were going to need it. The next day, Stevie got the boys up and ready while I sat at the only table in the building and marked my map. Up, I wanted to have the route and enemy dis-positions fresh in my mind. As soon as I was happy with the plan, I explained it to Stevie, so he knew about the route and the job in hand.

When Stevie knew the score, he gave me the thumbs up and we got onto the transport. The CSM asked for six guys to do a quick area clean and all the rubbish picked up. Once he was happy, we headed off in the direction of enemy threat, we bumped into Recce and they moved to the front of the company. We seemed to drive for hours. Every time we got near villages, the locals came out and lined the roads waving and throwing flowers. I'd never seen a sight like it. It made all that we had done somehow feel worthwhile.

There was one village an old man climbed a palm tree in his bare feet just to give us a coconut, and I could see a woman bathing her child in the river and others were washing their clothes and having fun. They had nothing yet were still smiling and enjoying themselves. It makes you take a good look at yourself and get your priorities into perspective.

We had reached the end of the road and arrived at the bridge that would take us across the world-famous Euphrates River. Once we had cleared up to the river the Commanding Officer made us go back and do it again, he was determined to put us into battle. When we had arrived back at the Euphrates River, Recce went forward and secured the bridge while the rest of us stopped off and had lunch.

As soon as we were finished, we were told to get back onto the transport. We were now going to cross the Euphrates. The Recce Platoon had seen the company approaching the Bridge and had to drive across it in order to clear the surrounding area, no other British unit had been this way so Recce where on high alert, as we headed up the road either side was lined with Iraqi Tanks sitting all over the place, they had just been abandoned.

Weapons had been dropped everywhere and it was as if they had just run off, the locals came out of nowhere and began to line the roads waving branches and throwing flowers at us, the Recce vehicles were covered in flowers, we couldn't find any enemy along the road, so just kept going. Eventually, we crossed another bridge and came to a standstill. There must have been half the British Army there. The roads were bumper to bumper with tanks and Recce with the artillery and Parachute Regiment, there were American M1 Tanks sitting in lines of 5.

We began to drive on the other side of the road to meet up with our very own Recce Platoon, once with them we stopped and parked up. I wondered what was going on as I could hear loud cheering and clapping, it was the Royal Engineers, they were knocking down a building which had been used by the Ba'ath Party as their headquarters, as soon as it had been destroyed and cleaned up, it became the Battalion HQ.

Six Platoon then got sent to guard a Civil-Military Co-operation house for a few hours. That's a place where the army works from one of the town's buildings and pays the locals to clean up their own mess.

We waited for them to get replaced by C-Company so we could then head north again. We were passing through town's that looked like something off a zombie television programme. There wasn't a single person on the street. The only noise to be heard was that of a challenger two tank.

The guys on the back of our vehicle were drinking water like it was going out of fashion. The heat was making my shirt stick to my back, and I had a strong dose of cramp, now my backside was going numb, and it wasn't just me. Hoppo was giving out boiled sweets trying to keep morale high, and Len was giving out cigarettes to the troops. It had been twelve hours since the guys had a hot meal and rest, so it was time for the Commanders to start earning their money and keep the troops focused and alert.

Len got out his radio and tuned it to BBC World Service and we wished he hadn't of bothered, just as we were all on a high the newscaster announced that three scimitars had been destroyed, and as we all knew that each vehicle took a crew of three men we knew that was nine British killed. Silence fell across the troops and then it was announced that it had been a Cobra Gunship that had done it, we were all pissed off. Again, the Americans had caused friendly casualties, we were annoyed but that's the price of war at the end of the day we are all expendable.

We then heard news of a young girl who must have been six or seven years old, she had watched the British soldiers in their vehicles driving through her town, it was the first time she'd probably seen anything like it.

The soldiers had spotted her waving and smiled as they waved back and carried on driving. On the way back through the same town, the young girl was hanging by her neck from a tree, a member of the Ba'ath Party had carried out this brutal murder. It was punishment for waving at the British, now tell me what we were doing in Iraq was not worthwhile.

We moved from where the Battalion Headquarters had now been established and discovered that we had been told to move as 16 Air Assault now wanted it as their HQ and our battalion had been told to go to Al-Amarah and I couldn't wait. This town was still occupied by Iraqi soldiers, and the battle group was being spearheaded by tanks, as they roared along the road to our front along with our Recce Platoon, I spotted my brother. I went over to see how he was doing and we chatted for a while about what we had been up to and how we were both keeping. I told him we were short of food and I hadn't had a hot meal in about four days. He asked me why, but after I explained he understood. I shook his hand and said goodbye. As I was about to walk away, he handed me a pot noodle and a bunch of chocolate bars, I was over the moon.

I got in my vehicle and shared the bars out. We were now heading down the main road and it took a further two hours in which time the troops were drinking plenty of water and trying to rehydrate themselves. We were all feeling tired, and the heat wasn't helping, locals were starting to gather on either side of the road. They looked happy and pleased to see us. Then we were able to see why. Just on the outskirts of the town, the battle group had taken over one of Saddam's palaces.

It was now being used as a forward mounting base; it was the biggest thing I'd ever seen. As soon as you looked at the building, you were dazzled at the amount of gold looking back at you. It must have been as big as a football pitch and the whole roof was gold. Outside the new camp, thousands of locals gathered and watched as two vehicles with ropes attached to each one was pulling down a statue of the Dictator, it must have been twelve foot tall, and it took some pulling power for it to eventually fall. Once it had toppled over, the Iraqi people began to spit on it and hit it with their sandals. They were chanting and cheering, I couldn't believe how much they actually hated him.

He had ruled with an iron fist and bullied all his people, the statue was dragged into the palace and left to the side like rubbish. We got the Platoon together and detailed them to do different tasks as the palace had been ransacked, all the windows had been broken so the glass needed to be brushed up so the vehicles wouldn't get punchers. On top of this, the place was packed with Ammo and Warheads. There was even a cannon put outside the palace and was pointing towards the town centre. Certificates with Saddam and the Iraqi flag were blowing all over the place. Each one had a photograph of one of Saddam's loyal soldiers, so we started a fire and burnt all the things that had anything to do with the old regime.

Inside the palace was a canvas painting of him, but it had been torn in half by the locals. The rooms had been destroyed and anything worth money had in fact already been stolen. With nearly every single soldier cleaning the palace so we could occupy rooms to live in, we needed space to carry out administration. We were told that we had to guard the palace, so Recce was parked at both gates with their GPMG and 50 calibre pointing at the locals. Once all the cleaning had been conducted, four platoon supplied the guard.

There were no Sangers built as each corner of the palace had towers to our relief, these towers stood up over thirty feet and looked out over the city. As soon as we put troops in the towers, we controlled the town, and because the amount of hardware we had the locals knew it also.

We needed to now start and win the hearts and minds campaign and the only way to do that was by treating the locals with respect, our medics also had their work cut out. We started by using vehicles to patrol the town and taking notes on which parts were packed and which were empty.

We drove past the Iraqi hospital, and it been looted by the locals. I couldn't believe it. They were destroying what they would surely need later, where did they expect to be treated if injured.

Our vehicles returned to the palace and the Commander reported it to the RSM, he was annoyed by what we told him and decided to stick a platoon there to guard it and help get it up and running.

We got the Platoon together and loaded all the kit into the trailer, once aboard the vehicle we left the palace and were driven slowly towards the hospital, at the gate six men jumped off and four began searching the grounds for thieves while the other two started guarding the gate. The Platoon Sergeant got a guard list up and running while I and the other Commanders began by manning the radio in six-hour shifts.

There was an old concrete building at the front gate, so we cleaned it out and turned it into a guardroom. We then sent four soldiers onto the hospital roof and began to build a defensive position to give the gate sentry added protection. It also made the guys feel more at ease and relaxed knowing their back was being watched.

So, the front of the hospital had now eight soldiers protecting it with two guys doing patrols. The locals were now gathering at the wall and peering over, they had never seen a foreign army and we didn't mind them watching. The rest of the Platoon made their way to the back of the hospital and began cleaning out the two outbuildings so we could use them as accommodation and living quarters.

It took only an hour to clean the buildings. Then I and the other Commanders realised that the back of the hospital was far to open, and the risk was too great of being attacked while we were all sleeping. By now, the whole town knew there were British soldiers in the hospital and the crowds were building at the front gate. So, we sent two more guys around to show strength in numbers while the rest of the guys built another Sanger at the rear of the hospital.

We built a Sanger on the roof and as soon as it was built, we stuck a man in it for protection. So now we had three positions to man and two guys at any one-time patrolling, we also had eight men sitting with their kit on ready to deploy at the sign of any trouble and now we had good communications with company HQ back at the palace. All we had to do now was put up the ground Spike Antenna on the hospital roof and get a radio check to zero.

The locals were now coming in and starting to clean the hospital. We would only let a handful in at a time and only the ones who used to work there. They brought brushes shovels and bags and began cleaning each room. The women were very friendly and wore garments to cover most of their faces. The men we did not trust so we searched them coming in and going out for the first few days and then once trust had been built, we let them come and go as they pleased.

Once six o' clock came, everyone was out and we stepped up the guard to two men on each post, that was mainly to keep each other awake and secondly you feel more reassured when your with another person, because we were in Iraq not to conquer but to liberate we got an Iraqi flag and flew it from the pole above the hospital. It was another ploy to win the hearts and minds campaign and it seemed to work. We had lots of people coming up to the gate and giving us, ammunition and I don't mean a few rounds. I mean boxes of ant-aircraft rounds and 7.62mm and 5.56mm. We just said thank you and piled it all up, a young kid came over and started chanting at the guys on the gate and pointing across the road at a ditch. We informed the boss who then sent a team of four guys across to see what was wrong.

They then came running back over telling the locals to stay away from the ditch, there were hundreds of rocket propelled grenades with no safety pins, that meant they were live and ready to explode, we got on the radio and the engineers arrived and disposed of them.

Every few days, the CSM would appear to see if we needed anything and to make sure the troops morale was okay, he would bring mail and newspapers. The only downside to him coming was when he arrived, we would all run off and let on to do work so he wouldn't think we were slacking.

We started to build up a strong rapport with the locals and they were allowed in to clean up and burn rubbish, we began to sorry for them in their ripped clothes and bare feet, they used to come round the back of the hospital and watch us eat, It got to the stage were we would give them some of our food and water. They would beg us for water, we must have given away boxes. They would even bring bottles of coke and Fanta to the gate so we could buy them, twelve bottles for five dollars were a bargain. A young lad even offered us bottles of whiskey for ten dollars. He brought it to the gate and we couldn't understand that from a town with nothing he was able to get us a bottle of Jack Daniels.

As soon as word got out that locals were offering us all kinds of stuff, soldiers from all over started to descend on our camp seeing what they could buy. The hospital was coming on quite well as the locals were working hard in trying to restore it. They also felt at ease because they knew that we were protecting them.

Then I heard an argument that had started at the front to the hospital. I ran over to see what was wrong and discovered a woman was about to give birth so the boss got on to HQ and asked for the medical officer to assist in the birth, she refused to come and help and insisted that she didn't do births. This really upset the troops as they now wanted to know how they could win the hearts and minds of these people. We showed them how to assist the woman and then sent them on their way. The next morning, we were all talking about it to the boss and telling him that we all felt disgusted by the actions of our medical officer, and he even turned round and told us he felt disgusted also.

That night, we could see bright lights had started to appear in the town, along with gunfire and tracer fire, the whole town was lit up. Shortly after that, a truck came racing towards the hospital with four Iraqis in the back and two in the front, they were going screaming at us for help. We ran out to see what all the fuss was and found this body in the back of the truck covered in blood. I got the guys to get the boss up out of bed.

I handed my rifle to one of my guys to hold and jumped into the back of the truck. I managed to turn the man around and he looked very pale. the truck looked like someone had spilt red paint everywhere as his blood-stained body lay still. I checked his pulse; it was shallow and he was not breathing. I started to give mouth to mouth to revive him and then the boss arrived and started shouting at the locals to calm down, the guy was a member of Saddam's Ba'ath party who the locals had been scared of for years, but now we were in the town they had all got together and trailed him from the house where he was hiding, once they had got him outside they had repeatedly shot him until he stopped moving.

There must have been a dozen holes in this guy. I managed to get him breathing and got two of the guys escort him to the medical officer were he later died. Now the locals knew we were in fact here to help them; it turned out that the guy had lost too much blood before he had got to us; the locals had carried out this brutal murder because he was a Ba'ath party member, they had shot him and then let him bleed for a while before bringing him in. So that it looked as if they were helping. Instead, they really killed him that was the vocal talking point for the next few days.

After that, we got the go ahead to start doing patrols around town on foot. However, only had six men kitted up and ready to deploy if we got into trouble. The first few patrols went into the town without a hitch. One night, I took my section and patrolled up the town. I was smiling and saying hello and being friendly to the locals and they seemed to be very happy and glad to see us. I could see my guys were a bit hot so I stopped the patrol outside a shop and got the guys to close up and grab a seat on a bench. I waited until they had all had a drink of water, while they were sorting themselves out, Stevie and I discussed what route to take next. We decided to go right into the town centre, so we headed off in that direction, the locals were cheering us and saying thank you British so I decided to chance my arm. I could see that the local barbers were still open so I went for a chat. He was very friendly and even offered me a free haircut which I refused.

I told him I would come back when I was off duty, but that was just not to offend him. We carried on up this street and a guy was selling burgers and soft drinks, he too offered us food and drink, but there was no way I was eating that, especially with the diseases these places had, but I did accept a coke and gave one to each of the guys. We took a seat while we drank the coke and had a chat with the locals.

I didn't have the guys all sitting around me because of the threat so each time I stopped I made sure the guys doubled up and watched their arc's. We must have been on patrol one for an hour and the boss was getting worried. He was on the radio and sending out vehicles to find us. It upset me slightly. I told him I was on route and would be figures 15 and his reply was, "Best, Speedy, hurry, hurry." I thought that was ignorant. I don't know what they do in Sandhurst but it must be part of the course they do that turns them all into nervous wrecks.

Our boss was a good guy though; he did give us some slack and let us off with giving him a bit of banter, but that's what being in command is all about you have to take the rough with the smooth.

When we got back in, I wondered what was up. It turned out he was just worried of our whereabouts. And after explaining to him we were all big boys with guns, he sorts of calmed down. I remember that night, the Platoon Sergeant had been given bacon by the CSM and the morale had gone sky high. It was the first time we had seen meat in months let alone taste it. He called us over individually for a piece. When all my guys were finished, I went over and I must admit he had cooked it well. He also gave us fruit and bottles of cola; I don't mean ordinary cola. I mean the army cheap imitation cola made by a firm in England which now had a contract to supply us and which meant we had to drink it.

We all preferred the Iraqi's bottles of Fanta. Anyway, the next day, explosions were going off in the town centre, some of the locals came and told us it was coming from the bank. The boss gave us the thumbs up to investigate, so my section went to see while the boss had a further nine men on standby. We arrived at the bank within a few minutes. I left two guys on the front door of the bank to guard it and sent two up onto the roof to watch for anything suspicious.

Other Platoons were taking sniper fire at their given locations so we were a little lucky. The boss and I began to search the bank we caught people inside and just asked them to leave through the nearest exit, the guys on the roof caught one guy climbing out the roof, and, he got extracted also.

As soon we had cleared the building of people, we had to get on the radio and call for engineers to assist us. The bank had been getting used to hide mines and grenades. There were even stinger missiles on the floor. The locals didn't have a clue what kind of damage these would cause if they were to explode and considering children had been in the bank playing, it was really lucky no one had been killed already.

When the engineers arrived, the crowds started to build up outside the bank so I had to call the guys down from the roof down to help hold back the crowd, but we were outnumbered at least 50 to 1. The crowd was now over a thousand strong and the engineers were about to blow up all the ammunition. I told the guys if they thought their life was in danger to cock their rifles to scare the crowd.

We managed to push them back a few metres; it gave us a chance to spread out slightly and just as we thought we had the upper hand, one of the men collapsed in front of me. I ran over and hit this Iraqi with the butt of my rifle because he was kicking one of my men. I trailed him into the bank to see what was wrong. He then explained that it was the heat, and he was thirsty so it told him to get out his water bottle but he couldn't, he had run out of water.

I gave him one of my water bottles and told him to watch his name on the stag list once we got back in. The crowd was now too strong for six men to control so we told the engineers to help us with the crowd. They helped us push them back at least 100 metres. We then told them a bomb was going to explode in the bank in ten minutes. The crowd seemed to calm down but that was just the calm before the storm. When the bomb exploded, the crowd rushed at the bank. They thought we had blown the safe and wanted money.

It ended up with all six of us fighting hand to hand combat, some of the locals were trying to take our rifles of us. I had enough and told the guys, "Right, make ready if anyone grabs your rifle fire a warning shot." Thank God they didn't fire. I ran across to the boss and told him, do we have QRF on the way and his reply was no. I told him to get on the radio or we would end up being killed.

He then got his radio and insisted we had an angry crowd and needed assistance at our location and within minutes a vehicle turned up and along with a further twelve men. At this point, my guys were soaking with sweat and needed time to sort themselves out. I handed over to the QRF and got my guys together and headed back to the hospital for a well-deserved rest. When we arrived back at the hospital, I told the guys to go and wait around the corner while I spoke to the boss. I took him to one side and gave him a right roasting for putting my men in danger and not requesting the QRF sooner. We exchanged words. We both had been under intense pressure, and we needed to let off steam. I think we both made a few bad calls that day.

I went and got the troops. At this point, Stevie had already unloaded the guys so we went back to our accommodation and got our wet clothes off. I debriefed the troops and shouted at Con for not having enough water before deploying on patrol and as a punishment I made him fill the whole Platoon's bottles, and also made him dig a toilet as the one we used to be full.

All it was, was a plastic chair with the seat broken and a deep hole in the ground, so you could sit and urinate it had a curtain wrapped around six-foot pickets so you had some privacy. It seemed to take him forever to get it up and running so I sent another guy over to give him a hand. Once he was finished, I made him burn all the rubbish and dispose of it. After that, he never messed up again in fact he always had the right kit.

That night, the boss was ordered to go to Company Headquarters for a brief, he was gone for about three hours. When he returned, he took me and the other two Commanders away to brief us up on what had been said.

The 1st Battalion the Parachute Regiment were arriving in the morning to take over and we were pushing further north, the only people who were up there were the Pathfinders, CIA and the S.A.S apparently it was a red area, meaning gun battles were still taking place. I took down grids and started to mark up yet another map. I called Stevie over and briefed him up on what I had been told.

We agreed not to tell the troops on the gun battles but did however tell them everything else because the last thing you need is a bunch of guys going into a situation worried, because then they spend their time sitting on the back of the vehicle day dreaming instead of having their mind on the job and observing their ARC's.

It was a further two hours up north. The whole way there we could see more tanks left abandon and for the first time I spotted a BRDM. This is a troop-carrying vehicle used to get Iraqis from A to B and a very capable vehicle. At last, we were moving.

Chapter 8
Olympic Stadium

We had travelled most of the morning and by now it was 1100 hours and getting very hot, most of the guys had cramp in one way or another, and the boxes of water on the vehicle were slowly dwindling away. I was trying to stretch my right leg, but it was too stuck amongst the daysacks and with people sitting all over the vehicle there wasn't much room to move about.

This was not an ordinary company move; it was more of a massive show of strength. The whole battle group was now advancing to this stadium, this would soon to be our last move and soon we would have a well-deserved rest.

I couldn't wait to see the other guys; it would be a bit weird to see so many faces in the one place, but I was looking forward to it anyway. It didn't take that long to get to the stadium. It was the first proper road we had driven on since we had left the UK and it even had lights on the centre barriers; it looked like a dual carriageway from back in England. We even went past a garage and bus stops, the road seemed to go on for miles, then there it was sitting out over on the left, it was massive, the Olympic stadium.

I could already see soldiers on patrol around the stadium and the entrance had a challenger two tank protecting it from attack. On closer inspection, I could see camouflage nets hanging from the top of the stadium and nearly touching the floor, these were being used to conceal the soldiers from peering eyes. The locals would gather at the wall and watch us doing our administration and cleaning and to be honest the last thing you want after spending day in and day out with them in that heat, is them staring at you.

As we approached the gates to the stadium, the crowd split and let us through, we were the third vehicle in the B-company packet and another six vehicles followed us, as we got to the gates a pissed off looking challenger two commander reversed his vehicle to let us in, I suppose sitting there all day isn't the most exciting of jobs, but at least they had spent their time in vehicles as we and the Paras had to do all our advances by foot. We drove in and could see that A-Company had already parked up with their vehicles facing out so they could deploy quickly to any incidents.

We were directed past them and parked up to their right, the RSM had allocated our company with sixty metres of space and our company HQ had the same amount of space for at least twelve people three vehicles and all our stores, so it was going to be a tight fit. For the first time, they could relax and catch up on some well-deserved sleep. I told the troops that before they all dispersed to speak to friends, I wanted their weapons cleaned and feet sorted out.

We also unloaded the crates of waters and piled them up beside the Platoon sergeants bed space, it didn't take long to sort out our area, once the Platoon sergeant was happy, we sent four guys into the stadium to help out with tasks. I positioned myself against the stadium wall and my section slept around me. I then went for a walk to see who was where I walked by A-Company and they were all having food. Then I met the RSM, I said, "Hello, sir," and he just smiled. I think he was glad to have us all back in one piece and now he could start to enforce discipline back into the troops; it had been nearly three months since I'd seen some of my mates and even my brother. I walked by the Pathfinders and straight into our Recce vehicles that were parked up in one extended line.

I asked where my brother was, and he pointed to the top of the stadium, the cheeky bastard had only moved into Saddam's private suite. It was where he would sit to watch the athletics when he visited the stadium.

I headed up the stairs and caught a glimpse of our Commanding Officer Colonel Tim Collins. He was standing there just staring out into the local town smoking a cigar and wearing a pair of shades. He had this look of total satisfaction written across his face, guarding him was a member of the Special Forces Pathfinder platoon. I couldn't understand why he had a minder. He had a whole Battalion here to look after him.

I carried on up the stairs until I reached the top. I couldn't believe how easy Recce had it, and half the Platoon were sunbathing and my brother and the rest were having a card school. I joined in for one game then went and sat on my brother's bed. I couldn't believe he had an American cot bed. I had been sleeping on the dessert sand and concrete for over three months and would have killed for a bed. He had salad cream, tomato ketchup and HP sauce not to mention other bits of food, we made a promise if he could get me a pair of United States Marine trousers, the I would get him an Iraqi Bayonet. I told him where I was sleeping in case, he needed to see me and then I headed off. Just as I was about to walk off, he shouted, "Trevor, Mum wants a word."

I thought, "Yes, good one." And when I turned around, he was standing there with a satellite phone. I grabbed it off him and it was my mum. We spoke for a while and then I gave the phone back and headed back to my company area.

When I got there, the guys were all having food and changing their clothes 4 Platoon were getting ready to go on QRF. Four of the guys were away getting more rations and the CSM had managed to get a satellite phone and the guys were all queuing to use it. I told Stevie that my brother had a phone and to go and see him if he wanted it, but not to tell the troops or my brother would crack up.

So, the two off us just kept that to ourselves. By now, 4 Platoon were on QRF and we were getting ready to go on so we packed up all our kit and placed the Bergan's into section lines. Every time the CO wanted to go out, Recce Platoon and Milan escorted him, so as we were relieving them. We were all chilling out and the CO came out jumped into a vehicle and shot off out of the stadium with just a driver. We all started laughing, then someone shouted, "Are you supposed to be escorting the CO?" Well, there he is on the main road.

Well, I've never seen three vehicles move as fast up that road. It was almost comical, we got onto the balcony and started to get comfortable when the RSM came in and seen us all relaxing he decided that we were causing a scene and made us all go outside and sit beside the vehicle. We were all a bit annoyed and people walking past us could see that we were upset. Sarah Oliver came across to us and started handing out sweets and lollies to cheer us up.

I went for a walk to the back of the stadium and saw an Iraqi long flatbed vehicle which they had sprayed red in colour to make it look like a civilian truck. On the back of it was a scud missile. They were hiding their rockets so if we were to blow them up then civilians would have been injured or even killed. These were the sort of tricks they were playing at so back home in our country, the news would have said British soldiers attack civilians and so many were killed. It was just one of Saddam's ploys to turn the public against us and what we were doing.

The next day, I went in search for my friend 'D.' He had just arrived back in and was glad to see me. We chatted for a while and exchanged stories. He even made me a coffee, and then he had to do some admin with the troops so I went over to Nicky and joined in on a game of scrabble. I didn't last long. So, I told 'D' I'd see him later. That night, I was sitting reading a book by Chris Ryan *the One That Got Away* and I was able to place a lot of things he and done i.e., the road to Basra and Iraqi Arsenal and dispositions and it all made sense now. I read about two of the chapters and drifted off to sleep with my jacket on. I woke up about 0215hrs and I was going down it was freezing all I could hear was people moving around trying to get warm and one guy even got out his gas burner and started to get a hot drink on.

I got up and went over and joined him. "It's bloody freezing, Speedy," he muttered. I gave him a cigarette and we chatted about the locals and how they had been treated over the years. He then asked me if I was looking forward to tomorrows tasking, to be honest I didn't even know what was happening in the morning so I let on I did so he would tell me. Apparently, the Commanding Officer was going to a meeting on neutral ground to meet the bosses of the local Militia and rebel groups and word in camp was that the CIA and SAS were going to be there undercover in case violence broke out. We were going as a Platoon to control access.

I took a drink of his coffee and went back to sleep. At 0800hrs, I got woken up by Stevie for an orders group with the boss. He told me exactly what the guy had told me earlier on that morning and that we were leaving at 1000hrs, so I wrote down all the relevant information and went to brief the troops up. We were going to the local hospital.

We got onto the transport and were escorted by two Recce vehicles, one in front and once behind we headed along the carriageway to the end of the road and turned left past all the stalls where they were selling fruit and bread. We carried on up the road for another couple of hundred metres and arrived at the hospital front gates. We reversed the vehicle up against the wall and immediately stuck two guys on the gate and sent four off to patrol around the outside of the hospital, this was just to show the locals that we were in control. We even put an extra two guys on the gate.

Inside the hospital gates, we had a line of Recce vehicles with their guns pointing in alternative directions, crowds were building up all over the area, so we needed to show them we had a lot of manpower. Anti-tank Platoon turned up in their vehicles and began to park up in the dead spot area to give us extra support. We must have had at least one hundred men on the hospital guard and a lot more on standby if called upon.

I got off the vehicle and took control of the gate. I began stopping everyone and asking them for some sort of identification. Most Iraqis don't have any so were turned away. I couldn't let them in as my boss was inside and I wasn't taking any chances. We must have been there for an hour or so then the rebels started to turn up. At first, I wanted to shoot them because they turned up with grenade and belts of ammo hanging off them and brandishing Russian AK-47 assault rifles due to this place being neutral ground I was not allowed to intervene.

They were being cocky towards us and knew we couldn't touch them. We got our own back by escorting them around the hospital. We knew who the CIA were; it wasn't hard to spot them. They stood out like a sore thumb with short sleeve shirts, trousers and hiking boots. They even had long beards and slight tan and then with belt and 9mm pistol strapped to their legs and an MP5 mini machine guns, it wasn't hard to spot.

However, the British SAS, now they couldn't be found which was just as well it would be a pointless exercise to be special forces if we could spot them. Well, we must have been at the hospital for around two hours and then the CIA began to leave shortly followed by rebel grouping and then three of our Recce vehicles followed by a Humvee. Then the CO and three more Recce vehicles moved out. Once they were out, it was our key to load up and follow on.

I went back to my bed space and got a brew on, I hadn't sat down five minutes and all hell broke out, gun fire lit up the sky with red tracer rounds which were all coming our way and whizzing over the stadium, there was a gun battle taking place in the town. Straight away, we got our kit together and onto the vehicles, as we entered the town it fell silent, you couldn't hear a single thing, so we turned around and headed back. We were now making arrests and weapons were being found, the Americans had produced a pack of playing cards with Iraqi's most wanted printed on them, so it was getting easier to spot them.

The only problem was there wasn't a single packet in our battlegroup. It was only the front-line soldiers who had them and that didn't involve us because we were now holding ground and not sieging it. We had now reached our line of exploitation.

By now, the Pathfinder Platoon had moved off on their next task, but we knew our Recce Platoon were up to any task that the Pathfinders got tasked. I remembered back to an exercise we done 'Eagles Flight' were A-Company captured the whole Pathfinder Platoon in a barn. Due to a lot of patrols going out we had to go and patrol the old part of town; we had heard the locals in that part of town were anti-British and that break away groups from the Iraqi Army where there in hiding.

So, we got all troops together and checked for torches and made sure night sights were fitted to most of the weapons. The troops were all briefed to stay close together, and we got onto the transport and were escorted by Recce Platoon to the old town. It wasn't that bad, all the streetlights were on, but hundreds of people were still out on the streets. They were gathering around our patrol, we decided to put one team in the centre of the road and the other two on each side of the road, so we had one up and two back. We had four men in each team, so twelve men armed to the teeth wasn't bad. I had my night sight glued to my eye, everywhere I looked so did my rifle, I trusted no one.

I even started to hard target past dark roads always scanning to make sure my troops were okay and not getting nervous, then I heard chanting from ahead of the patrol and even more people filled the streets. I remember thinking if we get attacked the quick reaction force wouldn't get here on time to help us, for the first time in weeks I actually felt uneasy as we continued on up the street for a further hundred metres. I remember thinking that this looked like a scene from Black Hawk Down.

Then the towns lights went out and everyone started cheering. I couldn't see a thing. I started to panic and put my CWS to my eye. My radio was going berserk and gun fire started. I got on my radio and told everyone to make their way to the centre of the road and close up, I knew now the guys were probably shitting themselves because I was, but as a Commander, I couldn't let them see I was scared. So, I got everyone within five metres of each other and carried on up the road where I was able to see the rest of the guys who had gone to ground. As soon as the Platoon sergeant spotted me in his sights, he came over to see if we were okay. Just then, Iraqis came out of building and began firing into the air.

We made ready and put the weapons into alert position. I put the sight to my eye and put the safety catch to fire, took aim, I could see this Iraqi looking straight at me and then he froze. It was the rebels; they had come out and were scaring all the locals away.

We began to crack on with the patrol and crossed over a bridge and came to a crossroads, everything seemed to be happening in this one patrol. I could see Iraqi's running and the Platoon Sergeant ran off and ordered the guys to go in hot pursuit. "Army stops, or I'll fire and gun shots." I ran and took my guys with me. I could see men sitting on their knees with their hands on their heads. At first, I thought it was serious, but in fact it was a bloody joke. The Military police had spotted locals stealing fuel from a garage and wanted us to assist in their arrest.

We were exhausted that night and all in need of a good sleep. The next day the stories and rumours were going round camp on how the rebels had to help us and so on, I refused to bite. The next morning, we were told of the Para's where on route to relive us, our war was over we were going back to Kuwait. I couldn't wait. Apparently, we were holding up the whole army because every few years. Units move around and the Southern Highlanders were going to Canterbury. We were going to Inverness and the Highland Fusiliers where in Inverness and they couldn't move so we had to be sent back.

Our observation Platoon had to deploy to Northern Ireland and other units had to be moved around. We spent a further three days there packing up and getting ready to move. Then the Parachute Regiment arrived and took over our positions.

They knew what they were doing, and I knew they wouldn't take any shit. We moved off and headed south towards Iraqi and the Kuwait border. We stopped short on an airfield and regrouped, for the first time the guys let their hair down. It was roasting so the desert shorts were deployed, and radios were turned onto BFBS, and guys were cooking and playing football on the runway. Others were repacking their kit and cleaning their clothes.

I went for a cigarette and noticed that all around the airfield were Iraqi tanks and bunkers. There were even minefields over to our right-hand side; we had been given two days to relax before we loaded up and headed to Kuwait. I remember hearing that Richard Branson was coming to take us home so as you can imagine we were all excited. We got into the vehicles and proceeded to head further south. We were all amazed by the sight of vehicles, we were leaving Iraq and there were hundreds upon hundreds of vehicles lining the roads bumper to bumper still waiting to enter the war zone and it stretched from about four miles into Iraqi all the way back into Kuwait. We thought it would never end. This show of awesome fire power let everyone know that America was not a country to be messed with.

Chapter 9
Held in Kuwait

We had been driving for a few hours now and the end of the American convoy was just in front of. Some of the Americans were stopping and exchanging dollars with the locals for Iraqi money as it had Saddam's head on it and would make a great for souvenir. The Americans wanted bits and pieces to take home to their families. We got onto a main road and could now see the military police controlling the traffic.

The guys were waving and cheering. We continued up the road and past the satellites dishes which had been blown up during the first Gulf war. They hadn't been repaired due to the amount of people that had been killed, and it was now classed as a graveyard. We passed the brigade kitchen and turned left. We carried on a couple of hundred metres and arrived at camp Blair Mayne. There was a sign hammered into the ground saying 1st battalion The Royal Irish Regiment.

We were all very proud of what we had done and were now looking forward to flying back to the UK. We knew there was still work to do and all the administration and packing up was about to start. The CQ was going to ask for a work party and every Tom dick and Harry would surely want a hand to pack up their stores. We parked up all the vehicles in company lines and began to unload. We took all our kit across to the tent and then we had about an hour to relax before we began to graft.

I went across to the toilets and couldn't believe it. I knew once the guys had found the toilet roll it would be stolen so I grabbed a roll first. Well, they do say first come first served. I went back over to our tent and the jobs were being detailed off to the troops, it took only a few hours to sort out, If anything was missing it would have fallen on the shoulders of the CSM of the company, so it was counted then recounted so we were sure, once this was done it was all taken over to the RQMS, and now he wanted it all recounted. He had a hard job of keeping the account accurate.

By now, Iraq had been taken and the regime had truly fallen, there were only die-hard loyalists that remained and were still fighting in pockets of small groups, the RSM had decided that the news was now going off and videos were now getting shown in order to get the war out of our heads which was a great idea, the C.O was now doing things with the battalion to keep us all busy, so we wouldn't think about Iraq. Which was a great idea as it was still eating away at some of the guys.

It wasn't until we were all back in Kuwait that we started to feel relaxed again, we had no equipment as it had all been packed away and now all the sunbed kings were starting to come out and lay outside their tents to get a bit of colour to go home with. Others were doing weight training using a brush and two jerry cans filled with water which was actually very hard to pick up. Instead, I decided to go for runs and used to run out towards the fallen satellite dishes; this was also a great opportunity to top up on the tan.

When I returned from my run the atmosphere in camp was electric, the rumour we had heard about the virgin flight and Richard Branson was in fact true, we were now waiting about a week to fly home but the British government couldn't get us a flight and Richard Branson had gotten wind of it and used this for his own propaganda. He had arranged for his airline to fly to the gulf and drop off supplies. He also let the world know that he intended on bringing home the troops. He was going to pay for it out of his own pocket, but British Airways got wind of it and a whole argument had erupted. They didn't want Virgin Atlantic getting all the publicity and so that ended our flight hopes once again.

Instead, Richard Branson was on the news for taking back our freight and not our soldiers. We couldn't understand British Airways. Why didn't they come out and collect us? The British Government that had once ordered its soldiers into war to fight for peace had now finished with us; we had done our job and now we were being left in the desert.

We spent the next two weeks waiting on a flight. The flight manifest had already been made out and contained all the married personnel first and then senior non-commissioned officers and mainly officers.

Most of the guys I knew to be married were between seventeen and twenty-one, which I thought was too young for me. Anyway, we were by now getting fed up waiting on a flight that would never come. We decided to organise an inter-company sports competition. This consisted of football, rugby, rounder's, netball, and a tug of war contest. It lasted for three days, which was great as it seemed to be the new vocal point, and everyone wanted to win it. It got so serious there were boxing matches during the football matches. If someone had been a pain to you in Iraq you got on the football pitch and ran at them, then all you had to say was you were going for the ball, but then again when you punch someone square on the chin there's no excuse really is there.

I got picked by my boss to captain the rounder's team in my platoon which wasn't bad but I had never played rounder's so it was a bit of a challenge. I picked twelve guys for the team and went for a practise with them. We were rubbish there wasn't one person on the team with talent and that included me. I couldn't even hit the ball and the guys that could hit the ball didn't know how to run. And to top it all off, the ones that could hit and run, ran the wrong way so really, we had no chance.

So, I got a rumour started that five platoon were practising like hell and were in fact very good at rounders, so when it came to our first game against nine platoon c-company they were all nervous. We chose to field first and caught out seven of their players and when it came to us, they only caught out five of ours and we won. I couldn't believe we had won because we were rubbish.

I went back to the tent and told the boss who just laughed and said c-company must be really shit. Our volleyball team had won also, that was due to it being completely Fijian. Back in Fiji, they all play the sport on the beach, and then news came in that we had even won the rugby match so all in all, our company was doing well. The next day was a completely a different story. My rounder's team got destroyed by A-company which wasn't really much of a surprise. We were glad to have even got to the second round, and on top of that, our rugby team got destroyed by the A-company Fijian team. It was an eye opener and now the whole unit knew that all B-company were rubbish at sports.

Now we were out of all the sports finals. We did what we were best at and went back to sunbathing and reading books. I started to go for walks in the desert with Stevie's Walkman a towel and a pair of shades just to get away from all the noise. When I was on my own, I would just lay there and think about what I was going to do as soon as I got back to the UK. I found myself starting to take two or three showers a day mainly to pass the time as it was so boring.

Then an American had come to camp with a handful of the Iraqi playing cards; these were being sold for six dollars a packet which was a bargain. I went in search for a packet to keep as a souvenir but to no avail. They had all been sold in about five minutes and there was no chance of getting a packet. I walked around camp on a mission to get a packet. I ended up giving some guy twenty dollars and a Kosovo t-shirt in exchange for a packet, which was a bargain as I hadn't been to Kosovo.

The Commanding Officer knew the guys were becoming restless and fights were now starting to break out between the companies so they had to act before things really got out of hand. They organised a trip for each company to go to an American airbase to do some shopping and relax for the day so it would calm the guys down before the flight. It also gave us a chance to buy bits and pieces the only problem was hardly any of us had money and we couldn't get any, until someone said that there was a cash machine there.

On the way there, we drove past Kuwait City and it looked fantastic the houses were all the size of our hotels back home and the cars were massive and brand new. Every street was lined with palm trees you could tell they wanted for nothing. It was a different world from Iraq or even England. They lived like kings here and had everything even the poorest of people had swimming pools in their gardens.

After heading past Kuwait City, we came to place called Doha it was the biggest military base I've ever seen. We parked up the vehicles and arranged a time for everyone to be back at the transport. We got into small groups and then headed off in different directions. The place was massive, inside the complex there was a McDonalds, Wimpy, KFC, Subway and Pizza Hut. We couldn't believe how the Americans had been living, but there was one problem and that was the queue it meant queuing up for at least two hours. I placed myself in the subway queue, I stood there just looking around and noticed all the different uniforms there where Czechs, Norwegians, Germans and the Americans very own delta force who were easy to point out. They walked around with ray-ban shades on and thought they owned the complex.

That night, we had operation plunder, which meant that the RAF turned up to check our bags to make sure we weren't taking any illegal items back to the UK, the guys had Iraqi money, knifes, assault rifles, military uniforms and other bits they had gathered up during the war and now we were getting it all confiscated. Again, I got picked to do baggage party by my CSM and now I wasn't in the best of moods. This time, I stood back and let the guys load up their own kit onto the transport.

When we arrived at RAF Brize Norton and there were elements of the regimental band playing us off the plane, a few of the men began crying as it was a relief to be back on British soil and the emotion for some was too much to handle, the journey seemed to last forever and when we pulled up at the barracks, I could see all the young kids crying and running to hug their dads and help them with their kit.

There were guys giving out more beer so I grabbed a can and went to my room. I didn't bother unpacking my kit yet. I got my music system up and running and played some tunes. For the first time in a long time, I had peace and quiet and was able to lay down on a proper bed with pillows it felt brilliant. I just lay there with a can of beer and began to think about my career and where I was going with it. I had passed Brecon, been in Milan and RECCE, done operations all over the world. Now I really needed a challenge.

I ended up working in our training wing. We had been back now for four days and I knew I was due promotion. I had been bust back in February and had kept my nose clean. I only got bust because I wanted to go with my battalion to war and the whole unit knew it. I thought loyalty was a good thing I had even been given local rank in Iraq and was hoping to keep it, but as soon as I arrived back in camp, the incoming Commanding Officer took my rank away again, I couldn't believe it especially after what we had just endured.

I had commanded men in battle and done my job well, but now I was over, and I didn't matter anymore, this was not loyalty. Everyone was in utter shock that I was being demoted especially after everything I'd been through it was an insult.

I was at my lowest point in nine years. I didn't regret giving away rank and position as I knew I could get it all back but I could never go to Iraq again. I was proud I went to serve my Country and being able to serve under Colonel Tim Collins and I would be sad to see him go as we would never get a commanding officer like him again.

Chapter 10
New Challenges

I was now enjoying my new job in the training wing at 1 Royal Irish and working under the command of Major Benson. He was the most respected member of the unit having started off his career as a young ranger and risen through the ranks to be the Senior Officer. Not many men ever reach such a position and I had huge respect for him.

My old CSM was going to take over as the training Warrant Officer, and what he didn't know was not worth knowing. For now, I was working for Jimmy Mac, and each day brought fresh ideas and a new challenge. I was having to raise my game in this new role.

It was an area that others thought I would flourish due to my background and previous rank. Officers knew that having been bust from a Corporal to a Ranger and then placed into a section that would be commanded by a Lance corporal would have me undermining his authority, especially if he was to make mistakes. So, the best place for me to would be assisting in courses and helping with administration while working in the training wing. I thought it was being run well and I enjoyed the workload.

I had refused to accept the punishment from my new Commanding Officer. Having returned from the Gulf War and being told that the new CO wanted to speak with me, I was in good spirits. Even the RSM was smiling at me as he thought I was getting promoted. My name was called out and I marched in with my head held high, then the biggest bombshell ever.

"Ranger Coult, I understand why you got sent back from ITC. It was stupid, yet I know why you carried out such actions. You may have done a great job in Iraq however you have brought the name of the Regiment into disrepute and for doing that I award you 28 days jail."

I looked at the RSM and he was in as much shock as me. I looked back at the CO and said, "Sir, I do not accept your reward and I wish to take it to court Martial." At this stage, the CO began screaming at me and the RSM told me to get into his office. I walked out stunned and stood next door, the RSM came in and began to explain that I would be better off just accepting it and carrying on with my career. I couldn't do it, especially as I had been bust from Corporal to Ranger, sent back to unit and still carried on as a Commander while at War, and now I had my rank taken away again and now he wanted me to go to jail. What type of a person does this to someone.

I had been given 14 days to make my decision. I had already decided that I was letting my solicitor take the case on. However, I was doubtful how this would work out in the long run. I decided to go downtown for a few beers and shower my head with all this mess. I happened to bump into Tim Collins who had been shafted by the MOD on his return from leading us in War. I explained what I was going through and asked for his advice, but he was reluctant to give it as I was going against a Colonel. However, in the end, he owed them nothing. He explained that what was happening to me was known as double jeopardy and I couldn't be tried twice for the same mistake.

It was music to my ears, and I proceeded to the RSMs office the next day. I explained I was taking the Colonel to court, and he looked surprised. I knew my career would hang in the balance however I knew I was right.

I watched as the weeks went by and as the case arrived, I was told to pack all my kit and equipment away and prepare for time in jail.

I travelled to the Catterick court martial centre in civilian clothing with my best uniform ironed immaculately, my boots were like glass, and I was well prepared for the case. My barrister was wearing his formal attire and he came and shook my hand. I was getting nervous until he said, "Mr Coult, just sit and listen. Please do not smile, grin, or smirk at your senior officers and let me do my job." I was a little taken back by his remark, but I understood.

I went into the court room dressed well and I waited for the judge to arrive, my Commanding Officer was there along with my Adjutant and several other Senior Officers from the Army legal team. The judge looked at me and then looked at the Commanding Officer. He stated that he had read all the case notes and asked the prosecution what their intention was. They replied that I had brought my Regiment into disrepute and I had been in-subordinate to my Commanding Officer.

Every time that army legal stated 'The Army Act of 1955' my barrister counter-acted it with the Human rights act. We trumped every old legal hoop that they through at us. In the end, the Judge told the Military legal team to be quiet and asked me to stand up. I thought the worst was about to happen, and then he said, "Mr Coult, I can see from the way the notes on this case and your operational insert from Iraq that you have worked under a cloud for some time. I can also see from the way your Commanding Officer has handled this is not that of an Officer. I can only apologise that we had to have you here today and for wasting taxpayer's money."

Colonel, having read the notes from you and your Adjutant I can only say this, "How do you expect to look after a battalion if you cannot look after one soldier, you cannot punish someone twice for the same charge, Ranger Coult is to be promoted back to L/Cpl, case dismissed."

Now I know what my barrister had told me, however I couldn't help clenching my fist and saying, "YESsss." At the point, my Commanding Officer looked at me with disgust. I knew I would have to tread lightly for some time.

I got changed, grabbed my kit and equipment. I couldn't get the smile off my face all the way back to camp, I had now embarrassed the Colonel and I knew he wouldn't ever let me forget it.

It had been a few weeks since the court case now and I was beginning to wonder if he would ever promote me, the judge had insisted I was to be promoted yet he didn't give a damn. I asked my boss and I always got the same answer back, "Wait until he sends for you, I gave up asking in the end and continued to work in the training wing."

I had carried on working with very little expectations for promotion until our Commanding Officer was to be posted. Then I got wind of a jungle exercise in Brunei. I asked to be sent to C-Company as a soldier in a rifle section and to my astonishment I was allowed to go. I mingled back into the rifle company very well, and the troops in C-Company are a very tough bunch of men. My section commander was a guy from Liverpool and a good bloke, he was newly promoted and very keen indeed, we got on okay, however I was there as just a guy and not a Commander.

The exercise was fantastic and moving through the jungle was very hard work, it took all day to move through in a tactical formation and I would finish each day soaking with sweat, it was now week 4 of the exercise and we were all told the Commanding Officer was coming for a visit, so as per-usual we cleaned everything and prepared for his team to come rolling in.

We spent that night in camp and made sure we had a good meal inside all of us. The final phase would be in a few days' time, and we had to prepare defensive positions for the final attack, we were going to defend an area and try to stop the Special Forces from attacking it. These guys had put themselves forward for SAS selection and now we had to be aggressive towards them. I am sure they would not be a walkover.

We were told to get outside and form a half circle around the OC, who then braced us all up and handed us over the Commanding Officer who then explained how well we had all done in the jungle. He was trying to tell us about the arms plot move and where we fitted in. He then said now I must do a job that pains me. This just goes to show that even if you are a complete mess. You can still get promoted, he called me out in front of my company and threw a L/Cpl tape at me. I saluted, turned and fell back into the ranks, the RSM began to scream at me, **"L/Cpl Coult get out and pick that up."** I refused point blank. I didn't want the tape to be given to me like that; it was a disgrace.

After the brief, the RSM called me away and was still screaming at me. I explained to my OC and CSM that I didn't want it and that they could keep it. This was seen as an insult to many of the Officers. Yet I was very determined to stick with my gut feeling. If I could have gotten away with it, I would have punched him.

This was beginning to eat away at me, my OC was also upset with the actions of the Commanding Officer. However, his hands were tied, and I would prefer he didn't put himself in a compromising position on my behalf.

As soon as we arrived back in the UK, I was on interviews with my boss. I turned up wearing no rank slide. The CSM spoke to me and told me to listen into the OC as he was on my side. I got called in a saluted. He asked me to take a seat and explained that what the CO had done in Brunei was a disgrace and that he didn't want me to have such pride I would ruin my own promotional prospects. After 15 minutes, he persuaded me to wear it, all I had to do now was keep my head down and get some courses under my belt.

I returned to C Company where I knew the majority of the older guys and I fitted in quite well with the kind of regime they had. They were the Company of men who were known as the guys who could drink until 0700 hours and then do an eight-mile run carrying weight. They were left alone to explode at weekends and then they always produced the goods on a Monday morning, and great company to be around.

We had been warned off with another operational tour of Iraq; it would be known as OP TELIC 7. It went down well with the troops. Many of the guys who had served during the liberation of Iraq had moved on and there were only a handful remaining within each Company group.

We had a training cycle being put together by the Training Officer and his team, and all the in-camp training was starting to unfold, previous experience was being put to good use and vehicle commanders were being put through their paces by our Motor transport platoon. We were picking names to send on team medic courses and language training courses, basically we were now moving into a period of transition and preparing for yet another operation.

After only a week of training, the OC asked for all the NCOs to stay behind after dinner and he wanted to speak to us in the cookhouse. As always, we were slightly worried as to why he wanted to speak to the Commanders. We would be working from here on in multiples of 12 men. Each platoon would be split into two equal teams and that would give us six multiples when we arrived in Iraq, this Ops Cycle would consist of, Escorts, Patrols, Prison guard, Rest, Rear Idler, and QRF.

This sounded like a nightmare operation, especially as there were numerous units based in this location, the camp was called Shiaba log base or better known as SLB, it had a fantastic built hospital, and it was relatively safe compared to other outposts like Basra Palace.

We knew the threat was real and how the insurgency had improved considerably since we had left Iraq back in 2003, the trouble had increased. Since the capture and execution of Saddam Hussain the country had fell into chaos and extremist groups and rebels owned different parts of the country. There were now soldiers being killed daily and mainly from sniper fire at checkpoints or roadside bombs.

We would spend day after day learning about our Counter-measure equipment, this would help to keep us and our vehicles safe from radio-controlled devices. It was classed as secret. We were allowed to let other Nations carry it when they worked with us on certain operations, however we were bound by the Official Secrets Act not to let them know how it worked.

After a few days of the Command group tweaking the Orbat, we were finally broken into the multiples that we would work with on operations; this would now make the training easier and give everyone a chance to get to really know each other and learn from one another. It made a world of difference and helped us to get our tactical drills the way we wanted them.

My Multiple Commander would be big Strawman, a legend within our unit and known for getting the job done. I first stumbled across this 6ft 4 giant when I was in Limassol on a night out. He had been punched from behind by another soldier from our Unit called Andy Rainey. The one thing that always stuck in my mind was not only did Strawman have a leg in plaster at the time. A car had been speeding up the main road and had hit Strawman. He had been flipped over and jumped back up and stood in a boxing stance ready for the fight, many guys including me looked on in amazement as he ignored what had just happened and was looking for Andy.

From that day onwards, I thought, *this guy is either crazy or hard as nails and I never wanted to be on the end of his temper.* This was 10 years later and now he was my Platoon sergeant and my multiple commanders. One thing was for sure and that no one would mess with our band of brothers, and we all knew it.

The training was intense and had been designed to see how far we could be pushed; it was working as many of us were drained and feeling fatigued. Our drivers were now working through the night and getting very little rest, the Commanders had been given 'Wavers' which covered them in the unlikely event of an accident, so we hung on in and continued with the tasks.

We had now been working together for some time and we knew each other's strengths and weaknesses, it was a great bunch of guys and when morale had begun to drop slightly we knew who to turn too, it would be Ashley, he would always lift the troops by just cracking a joke and it helped us many times over.

We continued getting briefed with the latest developments in Iraq so we knew the policies and local intelligence, as well as any cultural issues that could occur. Iraq had fallen apart since the war, and it was more dangerous now than it ever was before.

The insurgency had taken a new twist and it seemed that the rebel groups had made improvised explosives that were far superior to anything we had ever encountered before, and that is saying something, considering we had spent over 25 years trying to defeat the IRA.

It was now September 2005, and we were about to deploy on Operation TELIC 7. The guys were now fully prepared for what would be a testing six months. My team were always having a laugh and it was great to be part of it.

Well, it was soon becoming routine and another very hot and humid day, the troops were starting to call it Groundhog Day.

As soon as we had settled into a routine, we made a location board and got all the guys to write where they would be what time they left and what time they expected to return. This was used in case we were ever to be crashed out in an emergency.

We couldn't spend all day relaxing as we had timings to stick to and daily briefings to attend. This would be from the battle group battle space. We needed to know what we were doing and what areas we would be working in and what the intelligence pictures were. We also needed to find out weather reports for the next seven days and who was going on R & R and most importantly who had been injured or Killed in Action (KIA).

So far, we had been lucky. There had been numerous rocket attacks into camps all over Iraq, especially up in Basra. SLB was a very quiet place. Our most likely attack of any kind was going to come from a Locally Employed Contractor as there were over 1000 of them working all over the camp, many of whom were wearing our combat boots and uniform.

The Platoon Sergeant was a friend. We had gone through the ranks together; he had been promoted before me. He was a tough Irishman and when he shouted everyone heard him and was not one to be messed with. He made sure that he carried out a nominal roll call just before the boss got there to make sure we were all seated.

The brief was rather in depth and we found out what every other Company had been up to. The Battalion had been quiet overall. There had been a major incident with B-Company as one of their Platoon Sergeants had lost his mobile phone while out on patrol, but instead of reporting it to the Chain-of-Command, he took a young Ranger back out into a dangerous part of Iraq, with no other call signs to support them and no Counter measures in place for roadside bombs. He had placed his life and the young Rangers lives in grave danger.

He was sacked on return to camp and sent back to the United Kingdom. His career now surely it tatters. He had been a good soldier but as any soldier will tell you, you are only remembered for your last contact or course, not for the years you had done superbly before.

This was to be the topic of conversation for the next few days, as the rest of the troops would go to the small village. I would start to go over to the Hospital, not because I was injured but because they had a great NAAFI and let's not be naïve; that's where all the hot nurses and doctors would hang out, so it was very pleasing on the eye to sit there and just chill out.

The following day, it was my turn to stand up in the coach and brief all the occupants of the actions on contact. I had all ranks on my coach. When all the seats were taken, I walked up and down the coach counting every single man.

I gave the headcount to the Packet Commander and then began my brief... "Sir, ma'am, troops! As you can already see, the curtains are closed on each coach. You are not allowed to open them at all while the coach is moving, no lights are to go on whatsoever. This will show the position of the coaches while they are moving."

The road we are about to travel down to the airport is very dangerous indeed. As you can see from the vehicles that were parked outside, we will have flank protection and the rest of my Company will escort us there. If we come under attack from gunfire, you are to remain in your seat with your body armour and helmet on, the ground troops and I will deal with the attack. If we hit an Improvised Explosive Device, we have enough team medics and trauma trained personnel to deal with the incident. I will ask you all to sit back, relax, but do not sleep during this journey, I hope you all have a fantastic leave.

As soon as I had finished giving the mandatory brief, I got off the coach to give my boss the thumbs up 'Boss, we are ready to move.' He turned, acknowledged me, and waited for the rest of the team to do the same, within a few minutes we were off to the airport.

These types of patrols were very tiring for the drivers and commanders, not to mention the top-covers who would spend all day scanning the ground to the left and right looking for anything that was unusual or stand out. By the time we had finished for the day, our eyes were tired, and we felt drained, especially with the hot conditions.

We had been doing this task now for a few weeks and I was starting to become complacent. I couldn't afford to slip up, then news began to circulate that we would be moving to Baghdad as part of security for the General and his team, it was the lift we all had needed.

Then the boss came into my tent and said, "Speedy, you're going with the OC on a reconnaissance of Baghdad support unit, you will be leaving tomorrow morning at 0500hrs so start packing your kit tonight, breakfast is at 0430hrs." I spent most of the night sorting out my kit and helmet along with night vision goggles.

My kit was packed then unpacked and packed again, I had a good sleep that night and when one of the guys on duty came to wake me, it felt like I had been sleeping for about 24hrs, my body was refreshed, and I was raring to go. I went over to breakfast with my bags and rifle and waited to be called to the transport.

The OC was already at breakfast with the Regimental Sergeant Major, he just winked over at me and with his southern Irish accent he said, "Yul right Speedy son?"

I just replied, "Aye, sir."

"Enjoy yer recce, kid." On that note, he stood up put his paper plate in the bin and walked off.

I finished my breakfast, loaded my kit into the back of the vehicle and waited patiently for the OC to arrive. His kit was already in the vehicle, we waited for about five minutes then he climbed in: 'right Speedy boy, let's get to Baghdad.'

The journey lasted a few hours before we finally landed in Baghdad, from here we were then moved onto a Merlin helicopter and flew just above the roof tops all the way into the green zone, we passed through a series of checkpoints before reaching an Iraqi checkpoint and into Maude house, this was where the 3-star General stayed.

He was the second highest ranking soldier in Iraq who worked alongside the US 4 star General, who was based inside Camp Victory and the only way to get there was to drive down route Irish, known as the most dangerous road in the world. You had to drive out of the green zone, onto the highway and into insurgent territory. This I was not looking forward to as I was very nervous and apprehensive about.

The boss went straight into the Ops room and begun to receive briefs. I started to take notes and pictures and began to put together a slideshow for a briefing for when I returned to my company. I then went to the American PX, this was a massive shop in the green zone used by all fighting troops, whether you were close protection, green berets, special forces or just a contractor. They all used this area, so as you can imagine the security was very tight.

The OC returned after two hours and began to brief me up on life at Baghdad, it seemed very relaxed in camp, yet outside was a different story. The guys from Support Company had been very busy with patrols and duties, yet on a stand down day they were allowed to just chill out and relax. This I thought was fantastic.

He explained that in the morning we were going on a vehicle patrol out of the green zone and up to Camp Victory, and American base where we were escorting a drops vehicle back to the Maude House. This seemed very straight forward and it would give both of us a chance to see how these guys conducted themselves and we could learn from it.

We all loaded our personal weapons and got into our vehicles and patrol formation, the vehicle I was in was given the dreaded task as tail end Charlie, basically keeping all civilian transport away from the back of the convoy. Actions on attack were starting to run through my mind and I was happy with the drills expected of me, after only a few minutes we headed out through a series of checkpoints, most of them being American.

On the horizon, I could see an M1A1 American tank, its barrel pointing towards a block of flats on route Irish. There were several US soldiers all facing out towards enemy threat with their sights scanning every possible attacking position.

Our convoy was now out heading at a reasonable pace along the road, radio checks and situation reports were happening every time we crossed below a bridge or passed a certain report line on the map. It was running smoothly, and everyman knew his job inside out, rehearsals had paid off.

We were now only a few hundred feet away from the US Camp. I could see the build-up of traffic towards the entrance. It was when we were going to be vulnerable. We had to slow down approaching the American checkpoint, there were warning signs everywhere.

Lethal Force will be used, *"STAY BACK."* The warnings were real, and they meant business. We entered the base and straight away we all unloaded our weapon systems, making sure that we caught the ejected rounds that flew out of our rifles.

We had a quick brief. The boss stated he was going for a brief and a drops vehicle would be here in a few minutes. Our task was to escort it to Maude house and that was our cue to go and grab a coffee. We had a few minutes to recharge and chat about the journey down.

The drops vehicle arrived and got into position within the convoy itself, we were just waited on the bosses' vehicle to return and then we would be on our way back to the green zone, it was just a few more minutes and we were all information; the radio checks got carried out by each vehicle.

We gave a radio to the drops vehicle so they could have run commentary on the patrol and keep in communications if any situation that occurred.

I got myself into position back-to-back with Tam. The other guy doing top cover with me, and we headed back out of camp onto Route Irish. Again, the atmosphere was strange, we drove down the road for approximately one kilometre, the convoy stopped. I could hear shouting from the front. I had a quick glance; my arcs did not afford me to get drawn into the situation. I did manage to see a white vehicle parked at the side of the road; it looked static.

The convoy then began to move again, just at the same time the white car began to reverse towards the convoy. My personal role radio was going berserk, people shouting orders across the radio.

I then heard air horns followed by warning shots, these went straight into the engine block. The car was gaining speed. I turned and noticed what it could only be classed as insurgents running with a heavy weapon and they began to assemble it. I aimed my weapon and began firing it, informing the others that we were in contact. I gave a quick steer to the others. I was 200mtrs away from the enemy and it took me three bullets to get on target.

I gave a steer for the driver to move his vehicle alongside the other call signs, they were taking incoming fire. I thought if I could get our vehicle alongside theirs, it would cover their extraction – it worked. I could see the strike marks as the rounds bounced off the road to the front of me. Tam the other top cover sentry had been controlling the other side of the vehicle at the time, not being drawn into the situation and remaining focussed throughout.

It seemed like forever; we had a vehicle stall on the central reservation, and it needed to be bumped from behind to get it over, another snatch vehicle helped with that. After a few more minutes, we were extracting back to the same US Camp that we had just left.

We needed to regroup and discuss what had just happened, as we were the last vehicle in the convoy, it was left to me and Tam to give covering fire for the rest of the convoy; it had been a scary few minute. I was scanning the unclear flats to our front, there was gunfire coming from the top floor, but I was looking for the flash from the muzzle 'not seen'. As soon as I could identify it, I fired a burst of 2–3 rounds of ammunition until the flashes stopped.

All in all, it had been well controlled by everyone involved. We parked up the vehicles near the PX, I noticed a few of the guys did not speak, the commanders were all at the OC's vehicle getting a debrief. Everyone else was smoking cigarettes and writing down notes about the contact, we all knew that statements would have to be written as soon as we got back to BSU.

And this was just meant to be my recce of Baghdad! It turned out to live up to its reputation, I was going to have to give a very in-depth brief on my return. We had time to reflect on the situation, everyone in the patrol had now re-bombed their magazines and we were all ready to go.

The boss gave quick battle orders and we started to leave the US Camp again, this time we were slightly more observant than usual. Everyone, including me, was on edge as we drove onto Route Irish. I was amazed that the white car that had driven at the convoy, which had quite a few magazines of ammunition fired into it, had now disappeared. This is normal routine with insurgents. They never want Coalition forces to recover their dead, and in a lot of respects their casualty evacuation was fantastic and almost as good as our own.

We arrived back at BSU; the journey seemed very quick this time as we had a lot to do as part of the after-action review. The boss called every member of the patrol in and questioned us on our actions during the contact. I was very happy with what I had done.

My OC was happy the way I had handed myself and after a few days, we were flying back to SLB, I was now the talk of the Company, and the guys were really looking forward to a tour of Baghdad.

On return to camp, I was sent for by my OC and CSM. They wanted to hear everything about my contact on Route Irish. I carried on as if it was an everyday occurrence and it was soon forgot about, and the troops were now being selected by the OC. He was making sure that he had the right calibre of men for the job, especially considering the previous contact.

I had made the cut. I was going to Baghdad and the troops that had been selected were guys I would trust with my life; everything was running smoothly once again.

Chapter 11
Making of A Soldier

News started to circulate that the Battalion were putting together a platoon of the best soldiers within the unit. It was going to be hand-picked by the Commanding Officer, and if anyone wanted their name put forward for selection then now was the time to do it. Then information slowly got drip fed across the Battalion. The platoon would be of full strength and attached to the 3rd Battalion the Parachute Regiment based in Colchester. It sounded great so I made sure my name was on the list that was put forward.

Then the truth started to come out, the boss briefed a few of us and said, "Guys, this will be very hard, but you will be trained up to fight in Afghanistan. It will be the first-time troops have entered a place called 'HELMAND.' It is ruthless and one of the Taliban strongholds within the Middle East this is where the poppy fields are and where they get their opium from, so they will fight very hard. Without the opium, they cannot buy weapons so prepare for a battle."

We had heard all this rubbish a thousand times before. We just nodded and smiled. "Yes, sir." That was all officers wanted to hear, and one of my default settings. We still had three weeks until the end of this tour. It was on everyone's lips for the entire time. We all wanted to know who the Commanding officer and his team had selected. It was not long before the OC had an orders group and explained who was going to take part.

He explained that the chosen platoon would leave theatre a week early and proceed for three weeks' leave. On their return to Fort George, Inverness they would begin training on conventional warfare. Sergeant Spence would be dealing with the training side of things and would be the platoon sergeant, straight away the platoon had been given the best sergeant in the battalion, the section Commanders were going to be Robbie, Strainer, and myself. I was ecstatic at the prospect of going into battle with these guys.

The platoon commander was going to be Sean and he already knew all of us, the Command element of the platoon was looking very strong indeed and the fact that most of us that had been picked were already in Baghdad was amazing stuff. It was hard not to smile for the remaining time in Baghdad, not only was our time here coming to an end, but we also now had something else to look forward to.

I got to know Spence a little while out in Baghdad and had started to ask him what he thought it would be like in Helmand, he said, "Not sure, but I can tell you this for nothing, we will be prepared for every eventuality." It wasn't long before the new brigade started to arrive.

Baghdad had now come to an end for the selected few, we were flying home for a few weeks of well-earned holiday, then back to work for preparation of another operational tour, I got myself a flight back to Northern Ireland and arrived at Belfast City airport where I was met by my parents, as per usual they were pleased to see me, then I began to be chastised by my mother on why I looked so thin, but this is what mothers do, they tend to insult your weight, so that you let them fatten you back up. I enjoyed it as my mother's cooking was fantastic so the first thing, I asked for was an ulster fry; she was great at them.

My dad just smiled; he knew that if I was getting one then so was, he. The journey home only took ten minutes and that was long due to the amount of traffic at the bottom of the Sydenham bypass, it was good to see the place again.

When I had settled back into my surroundings, I explained that I was going on another operation in a few weeks' time, my parents looked confused. They had not heard of guys doing back-to-back tours before, it was not the correct procedure, however it was what us keen soldiers lived for.

I made sure I spent quality time with my family on this visit and after what seemed like a few days. My holiday had come to an end. I had bought some kit and equipment to help my next tour run smoothly and I made my way to the airport, I was sad leaving my family, yet I knew I had a family back at camp also, and we all go on like brothers.

Back at camp Spence left us alone for the remainder of the day, we all thought he was going to be relaxed at training. Then the next morning, **BANG**, he turned into a monster. He started off by taking us on endurance runs to build up our stamina, then running with weight began to make an appearance. Soon we were running with full combat equipment fighting order (CEFO) the platoon was starting to take shape. Along with the patrolling across ground, and the contact reaction, it was all good. The one thing that I hated was casualty extraction. We were running with casualties for about three miles, then being told the Helicopter landing site (HLS) had been moved.

He was teaching us break contact drills, lifesaving drills. We were all starting to perfect the drills the way he wanted us to. Spence was starting to get the platoon to work the way he wanted, and it was with blood, sweat and tears.

We spent nearly two weeks going over all kinds of scenarios, and when he was ready and was given the thumbs up by the boss, we were ready to get on the coach and travel to Colchester. We were now *Ranger Platoon* and part of C-Company 3 Para, and this is where we would remain until the operation was over.

After many hours sitting on the coach, we arrived at our new barracks; it was early hours in the morning and the rest of camp were still asleep. We remained on a strict training cycle for the next two weeks and prepared for an overseas exercise in Oman. This was where we put the whole battlegroup and attachments to test, we conducted a live firing operation in a safe environment as we put the last things together before doing it for real in a foreign country with a real live enemy.

The Commanding Officer asked for our platoon to meet him in the cookhouse; it was 17 March 2006 and St Patricks Day. He gave us a great welcome and handed over a bottle of whiskey to the boss. He wished us well and thanked us for being part of this operation.

The exercise brought out the competitive side in everyman. The Paratroopers were excellent and worked for every inch on the battlefield. They kept us on our toes and made us fight for everything, nothing was handed over easily and the sheer determination and drive from each soldier kept us at the top of our game, and we were loving this.

After a few weeks of tweaking our drills and fine tuning our skills the exercise had come to an end, the feeling through the unit was that we were ready. We now just wanted to get on with this tour and get to do what we did best 'Soldiering.'

Back in Colchester we had two false starts before finally getting on the coaches and making the long journey to RAF Brize Norton. The feeling of nervous excitement was etched across everyone's face.

We were now on our way to Helmand and to the Camp that was being built for our arrival known as *Camp Bastion.* This would be the hardest, most dangerous operation I would face up until now. After what it seemed like a week on a flight, we were suddenly ordered to place our helmets and body armour on for the descent into Camp Bastion. Then all the lights went out as to not attract attention, then with a sudden dive we were heading straight down at 70 degrees to the landing strip, and we had arrived safe and sound.

The boss spent the next two days on briefings at the joint operations cell (JOC) and it wasn't long before maps needed to be waterproofed and marked up. I was given over twenty maps to sort out, as we did not know what areas we were in fact going to, we had to spend time on every map; it was all getting serious and very quickly.

Spence was straight off on task and made sure we had everything we needed the amount of ammunition he brought back was colossal. There was enough to start a small war, and we would be self-sufficient if caught out by enemy forces.

The next few days in bastion were fast and furious, with mine awareness training, zeroing and Arabic lessons. Along with our own patrolling skills and basic field-craft, we were very busy over the next few days.

When we got a spare minute, it was trying to workout were to find the medical tent, or the armourer. Well certain things you keep to yourself, but a spare gas plug and cylinder for my rifle was top of my list. Along with any spare first field dressings (FFD), these would turn out to be life savers in the right situation.

Then came the lessons on rules of engagements (ROE) and the flying lawyer, then wanted to get drilled into us that they were in fact on our side. If we needed them after an incident, then they would make their way to our location, or if needs were, we would make our way to them.

It was now 10 May and orders had been descended from the boss that we were moving as soon as possible, myself, Robbie and Davy started to get amongst the guys. Pressure was starting to build on the platoon it was natural, especially when you did not know where you were being sent to.

It wasn't long before we were flown by Chinook to Forward operating base (FOB) Price. This was a small camp on the outskirts of Gereshk. Our task was to take over the running of the of the base from A-Company 3 Para. They themselves had been tasked to move somewhere. The camp was very small with a super sanger that overlooked the area for kilometres, a joint British – American forces base, with a lot of history.

We worked out which section was going on notice to move first, we had to track down the motor transport representative (MT rep) and find out which vehicles were ours, in case we got stood to.

We got the drivers within the platoon to sort that out. Alan took a few guys to help him with the communication side of things, while the boss went to sort out some more Arabic lessons, it isn't long before we have section tents. This makes it a lot easier to admin the section. I have two good non-commissioned officers (NCO) within my section.

I have really landed on my feet here with two great NCOs within the section, Alan and Luke are taking quite a lot of pressure off me and maintaining the discipline and morale while I spend most days trying to keep on top of the constant briefings and changes to the mission.

The boss and Spence had come up with a cunning plan. The platoon would be split while in camp. It would be broken into two multiples. This would give maximum rest to the guys and make sure the work was evenly spread amongst the guys. It was eight hours on guard, followed by eight hours on quick reaction force (QRF) then the eagerly awaited eight hours rest.

With most units trying to set precedence and show how important they are, we were told to stay away from the pathfinder's compound as they tend to get rather upset, the US Rangers were living across from them and ate in our cookhouse and were very approachable with exception to delta force and other departments and agencies (ODA). They ate in their own cookhouse.

The first patrol for Ranger Platoon had arrived and was very testing, it got rid of the cobwebs, we knew our fitness was of a good standard, but the heat made it worse than we had expected. There were signs of dehydration in some of the guys, but overall, it was a learning curve.

The maps we had spent time marking up made it very easy to navigate, the locals seemed curious why we were patrolling around their neighbourhood, tomorrow will be a lot better and we will learn from today.

After only a few days orders came down that we were to fly out to reinforce an Afghan Army check point, it was going to take place over the next 24 hours and we were to make our way to that location and to conduct an offensive operation. We were to drive there by snatch vehicle, not the most robust of vehicles but it least it got us from A to B, it was only a short drive from FOB Robinson, so we waited until it was getting dark and made our way there.

After a few hours driving, we pulled up at the side of the road. There were old Russian tanks scattered around old defensive positions up rusting away. The compound that we were going to enter had old gates on it. They were 10 foot in height and wide enough to drive a lorry through. Each wagon had dismounted their troops, so we could react if fired upon.

The night seemed to pass without any enemy activity, though the Icom scanner kept picking up information of Taliban moving around our location.

The following day, we were told again to move locations. This was becoming the normal thing to do it felt like we were chasing the enemy around the battlefield. We were told to move to the District Chiefs house, which was in Sangin, one of the most dangerous places in Afghanistan and a hotbed of Taliban activity.

This time, the intelligence had been that 400 Taliban fighters were making their way to Sangin D.C. This was going to be the battle that we had wanted. Spence for the first time was wondering what the hell was going on, were we being used as bait by task force Helmand as it felt like we were just being thrown at everything that moved.

It felt weird moving through Sangin. There were no people about the buildings looked unoccupied and the roads were in a terrible state; it gave me a bad feeling. I pointed out to some of the others a building near the bridge it had a plaque saying 'Taliban headquarters' above the door, then it had writing in Pashtun beside it.

We drove over a narrow bridge. This time, we had more dismounted guys than normal. The place was deserted, and the building looked like it was still being built. We parked up the snatches in reverse order as it forded us some sort of protection but not much.

We all dismounted for the vehicles while the boss gave a set of quick battle orders to the platoon, as we entered the house Davey took his section straight up onto the roof and placed his men out into position then gave them arcs of fire, they had a sniper rifle along with the 51mm mortar.

I was feeling nervous, my section had been tasked to stay in the middle floor and help where it was needed so I split the section up to enable that we could cover three separate positions.

Getty was told to keep his men on the bottom floor where he would remain throughout the battle, his orders were to deal with the casualties if we took any. He conducted ammo resupplies to both sections and most importantly to protect the vehicles. Thank God I didn't get his task as it was a lot to deal with. No sooner had we spread out the messages coming across the radio were that the Taliban had eyes on our building. "Well at least one of us could see the other."

We started to place our night vision sights on. The guys on the roof could now see a snake of vehicle lights in the distance and they were approximately only one kilometre away from us. The boss got onto the radio and asked if we could change our rules of engagement to card 429 (war fighting) and was ordered to remain on card alpha until fired upon. This was not what we had wanted to hear, what was wrong with pre-empting the strike, we were in Sangin valley, Helmand province, and sometimes you must love your idiotic government as they make life or death decisions from their nice offices in London.

The night seemed to pass without incident and just as well, because we now knew that we had to stay on card Alpha. It was already starting to become an operation like no other. We had so far been moved all over the battlefield trying to interdict Taliban movement, we had been close to getting overrun on two separate occasions and the only thing that had stopped us was luck, but that would surely come to an end!

OPERATION MINIMISE has now been called again and we knew it was going to be bad. News had come in that A-Company have been in contact most of the day in Sangin and two of their soldiers had been killed in action (KIA) and they had also five casualties, that was a massive blow to morale and very hard to stay positive when this type of news keeps coming.

The morale of the troops in Sangin had dropped to an all-time low, they were running on fumes and their rations were close to running out also, not to mention the ammunition which was dwindling away and more importantly their 81mm Mortar ammo was starting to run out.

This was a shock to the battle group who had not prepared for such a setback, back in the UK the Defence secretary had informed everyone that we would probably finish without a single shot being fired. How the hell could someone with his stature in parliament be so wrong. He became infamous within the military circle for such a bizarre comment.

The Commanding Officer has spent a few days at Brigade Headquarters getting briefed on an operation which will involve the whole Battalion. We will fly at low altitude into Sangin using three chinook helicopters and carry out an air assault while Apache gunships fire into depth and likely enemy positions.

We carried out rehearsals and it took three attempts to get it right. The OC and CSM stood off to a flank watching us until he was happy. The last one was the best, **GO GO GO**, the quad bike drove off at speed into the distance, but not too far away so it didn't get protection, we then ran off the Aircraft keeping good spacing between each other before moving to the left. The guys all lay down on their belt buckles and began to interlock the arcs of fire automatically. No one had to prompt them. Everyone was now happy and above all the OC was comfortable with the rehearsals.

That night, orders were given for the operation. It would be called **OPERATION ATAL**. It already sounded great. The battle plan was to have American troops on our right-hand flank providing protection. While the Canadian soldiers would be on our left flank doing the same job. It would be done in one clean lift. Five Chinook helicopters would lift the entire fighting force and drop them off right into known enemy territory. It would be unexpected by the Taliban and the sheer size of our force would have them on the back foot from the start.

We all boarded our specific Chinook helicopter destination was Sangin. It was going to be outstanding. I was apprehensive about the outcome and the only thing that was always certain was if it went bad, I would be home first.

After what seemed like 10 minutes of pure radio checks, we lifted off as a complete fighting force. We were completely packed. It reminded me of sardines in a tin. I could see out of the window and the other Chinook helicopters we were flying sin a fighting formation very low. They were weaving left and right then suddenly we lifted to about 1500 feet and the warning came down the Chinook by word of mouth. Ten-minute warning followed by five minutes. I could hear gunfire already. The door gunners on each Chinook were engaging targets and I could see green tracer rounds flying into the air, the sky was ablaze with tracer fire it looked frightening.

We began to grit our teeth, then before any Heli had landed reports or casualties came across the net. The green tracer rounds had in fact came through the bottom of one of the Chinook helicopters and they had a casualty, nothing to serious just a gunshot wound to the shoulder. Our Chinook landed facing towards the Sangin dried river. The door gunner was suppressing a position as we all got up from our seats and started to get off the Chinook. We began to take incoming fire and needed to get off quickly. We knew that we had to do exactly what we had practised back in Bastion. This time when the Quad drove off the back of the aircraft, it got bogged in. We had to climb over dean and all his ammunition. The drama was that the quad was carrying far too much weight and was now ineffective.

This was typical. They say that no plan survives contact and it sure as hell had not. We eventually got ourselves into a formation and began to space out. The boss called in the commanders and wanted to push on with the battle. We each identified our targets and began to push forward. The exchange in gunfire was unbelievable. The enemy fire was accurate and stopping us from getting a foothold.

Robbie started us off by suppressing positions that were pinning us down which gave Davey the chance to move into a good position and get eyes on depth positions. This also gave my section the time to breath properly and think of how to move across the open ground. Spence had pre-empted the strike by putting down smoke to mask our movement across the ground while the boss was manipulating us the way he wanted to good effect.

Assault, Suppress, Reserve, that's the way we moved through the green zone, it was working well, we stacked up at the side of the first compound. *"Ready,"* I said to O. Driscoll, he nodded at me, then with Luke giving suppressive fire he threw the L109 grenade into the compound. *"GRENADE…then BOOM."* After only a few seconds we each entered the compound. He went left as I went right, scanning everything that moved with the weapon aimed into likely threat locations. There was nothing there. I called for the remaining members of my section to enter the compound, they came straight in. *"Right, Speedy, where is not clear,"* was the first thing Luke asked. I pointed to some of the outbuildings, he got the guys to pair up and each pair to clear the remaining positions.

We continued to do this for the next couple of hours. The other two sections had their chance. We started to rotate through the lead section. It also gave the reserve section some time to re-bomb their magazines and distribute the ammunition equally amongst the section.

The look on the face of Spence was priceless. He could now finally get rid of a lot of weight. He had been carrying *10%* of the ammunition and as much as his body could physically carry so when we asked for a re-supply, he couldn't get it off quick enough and who could blame him.

He had been keeping us under control and tactically aware of who was where and what the remainder of the coy were doing, it was going well, yet the enemy fire was still fierce, other platoons were still engaged in a firefight. But then again, they were closer into the town and had the stronghold to deal with.

After we had taken our positions, we waited for the rest of the company to reach their own objectives as we had now reached ours. All we had to do now was interlock arcs and get sentries posted. The fire fight that 8 platoon were involved in seemed to last forever and the OC was starting to get annoyed with the whole situation. He got the forward air controller (FAC) to call in fast jets which took no time at all as they were already in the air stacked up. Then suddenly, there was a *whooooosh* shortly followed by a massive cloud of smoke in the shape of a mushroom, then a colossal explosion that shook the ground.

There were a further three more J-DAM bombs into key positions before radio messages began coming in. All three platoons gave their code word across the radio this meant that we had reached our objectives. We then took it in turn to extract into Sangin D.C. There were still other call signs in contact right across Sangin. Apache gunships were engaging with Hellfire missiles, and it sounded like and looked like a scene from a movie and the most surreal thing I have ever seen.

For the next few days, we continued to try and engage with whatever locals we came across, but every time we thought we were getting somewhere, we would have our base attacked and this was not some burst of gunfire from a hidden location it was from four or maybe five positions at the same time, and at times it was overwhelming.

The intelligence would be drip fed to our platoon every single morning and evening and the casualties had been mounting up, we had 17 now and four guys killed in Sangin. I knew that Spence and the boss felt it would be the place where we were the most vulnerable and if we were to lose a man that would be the place and it was etched across their faces. I did not have the heart to tell them that I knew what they were thinking. It's not exactly something that you bring up in a conversation.

Spence decided for maximum rest to break the sections down into fire-teams, this would enable us to cover all the Sanger positions and with two hours on and six off during the day. It would be chilled out. We would be able to get lots of rest while at night it would be three hours on and again three hours off, everyone seemed happy with the rotation.

For the next couple of days, we received continuous attacks onto our camp, it was relentless and at one stage I thought someone's got to run out of ammunition soon, whether it was the Taliban or us, but I knew we couldn't keep this up. It became routine as they would hit us with Mortar fire which would land just outside the front of the camp in the wadi. At the same time, the front gate would be attacked with automatic fire and rockets, followed by Sanger 4 being fired upon, this was a terrible Sanger to have as it was vulnerable and easy to hit from the building that sat only 100 metres away.

It was 6 September 2006 a day of tranquillity, a day to sort out administration and most of all I had planned to go for a dip in the river, my boots needed a clean and I had planned to wash the t-shirts that I had in the top of my Bergan.

After breakfast in my bunker, I made my way to the surface of the ground and started to chat with the other guys, the craic was great, the guys were taking the piss out of each other, and this became the normal routine, to get you through the day.

Lunch seemed to pass with only a few engagements with the enemy, back at Bastion reports were coming in of other outposts being in contact with the enemy, but that was just second nature now I am sure every patrol base was either loving this experience or hating every minute of it, we just wanted it to end.

I was sitting beside the biggest tree in the orchard when Spence looked across and said, "Davey get the commanders together for a brief." Some of the rangers got up and moved to the different Sanger locations to let the commanders know of what Spence had said it was now 1645hrs. I was already there so just remained where I was.

Spence waited for a few minutes until all the guys had sat down in a line, the threat from attack, was always there after all it was Sangin, but from previous intelligence briefs and from experience of our time in Sangin, we had never been attacked. At this time, it was always after the call of prayer and on cue.

It wasn't long before the guys had all sat down. Luke came and sat down to my right. I looked at him and shook my head he just smiled back at me and carried on eating a vegetarian meal. On my left was Stella. He was just sitting there taking in every one's conversation. He was a very intellectual person who kept himself to himself.

The brief was about the amount of activity there had been in and around the battle groups' locations and it didn't look good. Statistically, we had killed hundreds of enemy forces, but it meant nothing. To be honest, I personally did not feel that we had gained anything especially when most of the time we couldn't find any bodies and could only see blood trails.

We had come to the end of the brief, Davey was finishing his service support and wanted the weapons cleaned and the orchard area looking respectable, basically he wanted us to smarten up a bit and he had a valid point, with everything that goes on in a place like Sangin you tend to let somethings slip.

Davey had just finished off his brief by saying something that will never leave me, I still to this day remember every single thing that took place that day, he said, "*Right, fellas, it's near time to get your helmet and Body armour on, so get to it,*" that was repeated by Spence, who added, "*STAND TO.*"

We never got that far, just as I looked up I could see Davey and Spence walking over to their kit, and then, *whoooooooooooooosh… BOOM…*it was followed by a deadly silence or it felt like it, everything around me was quiet the orchard was filled with dust and what I can only describe as a white flash.

My ears felt like nothing was going in. I couldn't hear a thing. The explosion was the loudest thing that I had ever heard. It had been a Taliban mortar. They had been firing during the day and having had one mortar land out the back of camp. They had been judging distance and had worked out exactly what they needed to get it right in the middle of our camp.

It had landed right in the orchard and only 20 metres from where every single commander was sitting. It was a direct hit and the red-hot burning metal had flown straight at every single one of us. The tree I had been sitting against had taken a lot of the metal that had been directed at me. It wasn't the end of the attack as it seemed to go on forever.

Once the dust had started to settle slightly, I was in battle shock. I looked at my combats and I was covered in blood. My legs and arms were red, and I was numb. I didn't know how I felt at that exact moment and my ears were not working properly. I didn't even know that Robbie was screaming for me to get into cover. I looked at the floor beside the tree. Luke was still there. He was lying on his side; his spoon was still in his mouth.

I looked at the other side of the tree and Stella was still sitting there. I was being screamed at from the other guys. I started to get a grip of myself and tried to help Stella. I could see that he had shrapnel in his back and stomach. It looked bad, I helped him do his body armour and he limped into the trench. Robbie began shouting at Luke to get up but he never responded.

Then I was grabbed by Robbie. He came running from cover and shouted to grab Luke's legs. I began to come around. While Robbie had his arms along with Craig, we dragged Luke into what was a trench, but big enough for about a complete section to take cover in. We were screaming for a medic; the enemy mortars were still landing in the camp.

It sounded like we were being overrun by the Taliban as every single Sanger was engaging the enemy and the amount of ammunition that was being fire was colossal. After what seemed like a lifetime, I saw a shadow appear from the dust, it was the company medic Billy. He was a big guy, so to see him run through the orchard while bombs were still dropping around the D.C was amazing and showed that he was a very brave and courageous guy.

Just as Billy was about to enter the trench where we had moved Luke into, an explosion threw Billy straight into the trench and on top of Luke. He didn't even flinch. He began to carry out lifesaving drills. He even carried out a tracheostomy. He didn't even know that the explosion had blown his sight completely off his weapon. His combats were burnt a bit and there was a piece of burning metal on his daysack.

He worked on Luke for a few minutes and then told us to get him to the medical room. I cannot remember what I was thinking. I just knew Luke was in a terrible way. The attack was still in full motion. My ears were still not 100% but at least I was okay. I could hear Spence shouting for a head count. He wanted to know how many of the platoon had become casualties, but at this early stage and amongst the chaos, no one knew.

The only thing that was certain was that Luke had lost a lot of blood. My combats were covered in it. I remember the look on his face. His eyes were wide open, and the dust had begun to settle on his pupils. The medic had to sweep the food from his mouth where he had been eating the vegetarian meal earlier during the brief. The look on everyone's face was that of worry and confusion.

It seemed very fast, but we quickly got him on a stretcher and began to run through the impact area and into the medical room. We were still under heavy fire from the Taliban. It wasn't until I had reached the medical room that the severity of the attack was noticed.

There had been four other soldiers injured during the attack. Stella had back and stomach wounds. His face was pure white. He looked in serious pain. Another young paratrooper who had only recently joined the company and now he had a hole in his right hand, were the shrapnel had passed straight through it.

Spence had been wounded also as shrapnel had hit him in the legs, arms and buttocks and he was bleeding badly.

It seemed a long time before help arrived to extract the casualties, the OC had to order Spence to get on the chopper and get medical help as he wanted to just patch himself up and stay with his men, but the OC was not negotiating. Just before the Chinook took off Spence shouted out at me, *"Speedy, I will be back in a few days, tell Davey he is in charge and get amongst them."* I was seeing red mist from the attack and needed to gather my thoughts.

The Chinook arrived with the Medivac team flanked by two Apaches who had already began to engage positions. The fire support tower was still engaged in a fire fight also. It went on for what seemed like forever. I ran back to the ops room to tell them that Davey was now platoon commander and that had come from Spence.

The CSM was still pissed off. He had taken this badly especially as we were under his command. Everyone was in shock with the amount of damage the Taliban had inflicted on us in one strike.

I managed to take myself away for a few minutes as I had wanted to cry for quite some time, but I would never let the troops see me. I took about 10 minutes to clean myself up before going from Sanger to Sanger, to see how the guys were dealing with things. Davey and Robbie were already sorting out the troops, and morale had taken a massive blow. The three of us spent that night walking from Sanger to Sanger talking to the troops. We wanted to make sure that everyone was okay. Robbie had a word in my ear. He told me to get my bloody combats off, I agreed.

This was the worst day that I had ever witnessed. The troops were mentally not in the right frame of mind. It took a few days to lift everyone's spirits. Our boss was in England on R&R and would be upset that he had not been here for us, and now our platoon sergeant was injured and he too was angry that he had to go, and along with Stella and Luke. Morale couldn't get any worse.

From this day forward, every member of the platoon became closer than they had ever been before. Every single time I think about the attack I get it in 3D, it plays over and over in my head, and it never goes away it keeps happening every single day.

The following day, we were left alone to carry out personal administration and come to terms with such a loss, just before lunch time the OC sent a runner to bring me to the operation's room. I arrived a bit dishevelled to a man with a smile from ear to ear, to put his hand out and shook my hand followed by, *"Congratulations, Cpl Coult, the Brigadier wants a quick chat."* I was still none the wiser than the brigadier came on the radio. ***"Cpl Coult, I just wanted to congratulate you for your work in Baghdad during what seems to be a most complex ambush, your actions have been rewarded with the Military Cross."*** I was stunned and had no emotion, I was still in shock after losing one of our guys, I couldn't tell anyone as we were mourning as a platoon.

We spent the remainder of the tour fending off attacks from the ever so bold Taliban. By the time the Royal Marines arrived to replace us, I had a new respect for the sheer determination of the Taliban. I didn't agree with their methods just their spirit.

On return from a horrendous tour, I had developed a newfound love for operations and tactical awareness. It began to take over my life. I had my kit packed for deployment and I began to stay away from trusted friends. I became a recluse.

I trained and prepared for what would be the icing on the cake. I went to Brecon in Wales and attended the Platoon Sergeants Battle Course (PSBC) this would have me return to Helmand as a Platoon Sergeant (if I passed).

The first thing I needed to do was collect my Military Cross from Buckingham Palace. My family were ecstatic at the prospect of seeing the Queen and watching me getting awarded it. It would be a day I would never forget, a day of reflection and a day of mourning all wrapped up in one. I would eventually share these experiences but it would take some time to come to terms with such traumatic events.

After a few days in camp under medical surveillance to see how we were all coping with stress, I was able to get a flight to Belfast. My parents had organised a party which was fantastic. My unit had plans already in place that would take up most of my leave. The Regimental Colonel wanted me to meet me in Ballymena for Lunch. Then there was Councillor Jim Rogers OBE, who wanted to arrange for me to be received in the City Hall. Then there was Alderman Michael Copeland MLA, who wanted me to join them in their members room at Parliament buildings Stormont for lunch. All this was because I had been awarded the Military Cross. On top of this, the people of East Belfast wanted to host me in the Welders club.

When I arrived home, I was moving from venue to venue to meet and greet. It seemed to never end and became exhausting. Apart from this, I would spend most of my leave at home with my parents as it was relaxing and quiet and I needed it this way. I was on edge most of the time and found it very hard to settle, my parents showed tremendous patience with me, and we spoke about what had happened. Every time it got difficult; they would change the subject. I explained that I was not finished in Afghanistan and that I wanted to return as a Platoon Sergeant, it was met which strange looks.

After a few more days, I was back on the plane heading back to camp, this is where I would begin my new journey and prepare for a new operational tour and this time I would be in charge. I just prayed it would run smoothly but as all soldiers know. Nothing survives contact with the enemy even the greatest of plans get ripped apart when the bullets begin to rain down on you.

It wasn't long before the Platoon Sergeants Battle Course had crept up on me and was now a thing of the past. I had managed to get an instructor's recommendation, but fell way short of the illusive distinction that the chosen few get, but overall, I was very pleased with giving a good performance and not embarrassing myself. It can break the toughest of men!

When I made my way back to camp, I knew my unit had already deployed to Afghanistan and I was excited yet nervous about joining them. They should now have been well settled into their new surroundings and carried out numerous patrols which would have made them more at ease. I would arrive to a platoon who were now gelling well together.

The day had arrived and I and a few others were making our way to Helmand, the drive to RAF Brize Norton was always a long one filled with boredom and anticipation of what lay ahead, the flight lasted forever we needed a refuel and headed to Cyprus, we landed and spent a further 15 minutes taxiing the runway before coming to a stop. Then an announcement came across the speaker that we would be here for two hours as the plane refuelled for the last leg into Afghanistan. We quickly made our way off the plane and across the runway to the terminal.

Once inside, I knew the layout so I went and signed for a mobile phone and phoned Luba and my parents. I must have spent an hour on the phone just talking rubbish. I was always guaranteed an update on the situation in Helmand when I spoke with my dad as he was glued to the television for the entire time I was deployed.

It must have been the quickest two hours ever. As we were soon ushered back towards the plane for that final leg, I grabbed the same seat that I had been sitting on and put my earphones in, only to be woke up once and that was for a bite to eat. I quickly devoured it and fell back asleep thinking of all the jobs I needed to do to quickly bring myself up to speed with the rest of the guys.

When I had settled into my new role and unpacked my kit, there was something that I needed to do, so I made my way across the man-made bridge and into the Orchard area. I needed to see for myself what was left of the place that caused me so many nightmares in the past, it was where I had been sitting listening to Spence just before the Mortar landed killing Luke. I sat there for a while enjoying the peace and quiet. Then Robbie came over with some of the remaining guys from HERRICK 4 and requested a photograph of us all. I said yes before we walked back over towards the operation's room for a cup of coffee.

I would report to the boss every day in Sangin. We worked off each other and it was great that not only was he listening to me but also teaching me at the same time. Now that my predecessor had left. He took it upon himself to teach me how he had been taught by the outgoing Platoon sergeant known as mentoring and I was very keen and willing to accept as much knowledge as I could get my hands on.

I would learn before leaving on any patrol I would first make my way to the CSM and we would discuss over a brew the casualty evacuation plan for our patrol. I explain that when the platoon gets to certain checkpoints and RV points on the ground then I will secure each point just in case of contacts with the enemy and if needs be will get my search section to secure crossing points to enable him to get a quad to that area, either to extract a casualty or to resupply us with ammunition. We would examine every possible outcome and go through scenarios until we were both 100% happy with the plan. I could then go back and brief the platoon of the casualty extraction plan in the event of such an incident.

This would become routine until we were both happy of our plans for all areas within the AOR and then it would be a quick pop into the Ops room and a chat of which plan we would go with. As soon as he gave me the thumbs up, I would depart for the task in hand.

The OC explained the brigade are about to mount an operation deep into enemy territory and he has insisted that 7 platoon are going to conduct the operation. My boss is over the moon that we are going to fly into their own backyard and fight them. It is a little bit daunting but great for the troop's morale.

The town of *Sar Puzeh* gets mentioned at the Orders group, it means nothing to us right now, but it will be etched on every one's lip for a long time after this operation. The intelligence that is being filtered down to the troops suggests that there are over 250 Taliban fighters with an array of weapons from a Dushka which is a Soviet heavy machine gun firing the 12.7×108mm cartridge and ZPU .50 anti-aircraft guns to AK-47 /AK-74, and 107mm rockets and RPG through to SPG-9s not to mention areas that conceal possible IEDs where we could be channelled into, it will be a hell of a battle.

As the platoon sergeant, I start my preparation by checking weapons and night vision optics. I want to be 100% accurate when the boss asks if we have all kit and equipment. The batteries need to be fully charged and the ECM completely faultless. There is a lot to get done.

The boss goes away for a brief and after a few hours he returns to the platoon. He looks excited yet slightly worried, he eventually calls me over for a chat about the operation. *"Speedy, this will make or break the platoon, it will not be easy, and to top it all off. We are about to drop into a hornet's nest with hornets everywhere."* I just stare at the boss with my mouth open. So, we are to stay on the high ground with the Paratroopers below us! This could be a major problem; we will just have to wait and see. I can tell that everyone is now watching our platoon. Depending on how well we perform will shape how the company get used in the future. It will also show the wider army how good the Regiment is under enemy fire.

That night as we prepare for the Air Assault. Everyone is going through their job in their head. I am making sure we have enough ammunition for the job in hand. I decide to carry a Bergan in order to pack it with spare ammunition and bombs for the 60mm mortar. I also have a stretcher and spare batteries. I went for a walk and noticed the boss is awake already. He has not slept due to rehearsing everything in his head, he has a lot of pressure on his shoulders, but is trying not to show it.

We are now all standing on the HLS in Sangin waiting for the Chinook to arrive. The OC and CSM standing off to a flank talking. They are gleaming with pride. Both wishing it was them going into do the assault. They are excited for us. The noise of the Chinook approaching makes everyone stop talking. It lands and a gust of sand and dirt goes across everyone. We bend over and struggle to our feet with the amount of weight that we carry. I break into a gentle jog and board the aircraft. We sit down in reverse order. So, when we land, we can run straight out into what fate awaits us.

The Chinook wastes no time to move off the HLS and into the night sky. It is early hours in the morning and we are hoping to surprise the enemy with a dawn attack. I start to get déjà vu. This feels like a repeat show. I look around the Chinook in my night vision goggles. Everyone is quiet. No one dare talk. We go through the plan in our heads and prepare for whatever is waiting for us. The news comes down that it is a HOT LZ. *Shit*, I think, *the HLS is awash with red and green tracer flying all over the place.* This Chinook landing cannot come any sooner.

The door gunner tells us it is going to be HOT. The boss shakes his head. He is ready for it but could do without it. This will be called as he sees it. Everything now rests on the Quick Battle Orders that he will give in contact.

The Chinook lands and the door gunner is now engaging enemy fighters in the distance. We all run off behind the quad bike and the worst news possible happens. The Bowman radios across the ISAF troops have all dropped their fill, no one has communications to the CO. Even worse, we cannot speak to one another across the battlefield. It seems that the ECM red once switched on ruined the signal on the radios, so we now must fight this with just Personal role radios (PRR).

Already we are spread out across the open ground. The Chinooks have gotten offside weaving in and out and keeping only 30 foot above the ground as they leave us in what can only be described as hell on earth.

The boss makes his way forward to a group of men. I sit there not knowing what the hell is happening. At least we have 360 arcs of protection. He returns to tell us disaster with the Comms, before pointing in the direction that he wanted us to travel in, and we then move off towards the high ground. Automatic fire and battles are taking place to our rear right. We begin the climb onto a feature. I have the FSG with me at the back, the boss has the FSG CSM with him at the front.

We have moved only 100mtrs before we are forced to go firm in the dirt. Bullets are whizzing past our heads and to the front of the platoon. The boss is now within the enemies' arcs, and they respond in kind as I can hear bullets hitting around where he is at.

He has now sent one of our sections to protect the Commanding Officers tactical group. This just gets better and better. Our firepower within the platoon has dropped. However, we do have the FSG, so it balances itself out.

The boss is now relaying everything back to me at the back. It seems like only five minutes into the battle when I hear the APACHE opening into enemy positions. A 107mm rocket flies over my head. It was very close to the boss, then

I hear the boss screaming, *"MAN DOWN, MAN DOWN, SPEEDY GET THE MEDIC UP HERE."* My CMT tries to run forward to assist but I grab her. She is keen to get the casualty treated. I refuse to let her move forward, we are taking too much enemy fire and I cannot afford her to become a casualty, I need the troops to suppress and win the firefight before we can move forward, they boss is shouting for heavy fire. The section Commanders are pinned down at this moment. A few seconds later, I hear FCO's being screamed and a heavy rate of fire going down.

We are winning the firefight. I move forward with Caylie; she begins to conduct basic life support onto the casualty. We move him slightly into a bit more cover. Some of the FSG group sit there with their hearts in their mouths. I think they already know the outcome.

After a few minutes, Caylie looks at me and shakes her head. Without hesitation, I begin to distribute his ammunition and serialised equipment. I take his Garmin GPS and leave my broken one in his backpack. The boss's radio is broken so I take his Bowman and give it to the boss he needs it. I cannot leave his backpack there so I decide to strap it onto my already heavy equipment. At times like his, you seem to get extra strength from somewhere.

I get Joe and a few others to help me extract the casualty back into cover. I let the boss know that he is KIA. He looks pissed off. I use my new radio to find out where the RSM is located. The enemy fire is still coming in and now me and my band of men are carrying a soldier killed in action all over the battlefield to the doctor. My back is about to break with the extra kit and now my platoon has no platoon sergeant until I return from handing over the FSG CSM.

I get back to find the platoon have moved forward slightly. The boss is now furious that we keep taking enemy fire from our right flank, and we cannot engage back due the paratroopers in the low ground. It feels like we are being used by the CO to draw in enemy fire so they can identify the enemy and then kill them. We ask can we come off the high ground and are refused point blank by the CO. He wants us to stay there.

This is a nightmare!! Matt has taken his section forward and is now controlling the fire fight, we have a slight reprise for a few minutes. The incoming enemy fire towards our location is relentless. This is something out of a war movie. I have never felt so helpless, now being able to return fire.

I meet up with Tony. He is mentoring the Afghan Army and has his team of merry men from the Royal Irish with him, and they are spread thinly across groups on Afghan soldiers. Tony is trying to keep a cool head while everyone around him is going mental. He tries to beckon me to go to his location, but there are bullets and RPG's flying towards us. We stand and argue over who is going to go to who. We end up laughing. This is bloody crazy.

I manage to crawl into a broken compound wall where I find a dozen or so soldiers sitting in cover. I drop me Bergan down and join them for a drink, the bullets are hitting the wall near my Bergan. I can see the guys are laughing at the fact that my US Marines Bergan could be destroyed. I look at my Bergan and look at them, Caylie shouts, "Speedy, it is not worth it." I get up run towards my Bergan and bend over to pick it up. Just then, a bullet hits the wall in front of me, I roll down into cover and now I have my Bergan. Everyone just stares at me and thinks, you are completely mental. I know but I have my Bergan intact.

We continue to move across the hillside for a few more hours, every step is vital, an RPG flies straight towards Bubbles. He is stunned for a few minutes but continues to dodge bullets across the open. This is becoming surreal. An APACHE directly above us fire the 40mm rounds and the empty casings are landing on top of us. It seems like the whole world is exploding around us. The boss is keeping the troops motivated at the front. We dare not take our eye off the ball for a moment.

We continue to move forward in short bounds. Matt has now been tasked to secure a possible HLS for the T4 to be extracted from the ground. His section is taking heavy fire from all directions. He manages to control and secure the area with his section. After all, he is a very experienced veteran from the Iraq war.

After being in contact for nearly 14 hours, the enemy fire whittles away. The Commanding Officer decides to call an end to the operation once there are no enemy left to engage. He moves the whole entire fighting force onto the 611 MSR and patrols us to a pre-designated HLS. I can see the frustration etched on every one's face for what the hell was the point in this, what did we achieve?

We were greeted by the Boss and CSM on our return. They were full of praise for what we had to endure, however the news that the Taliban had now fixed our company with the laying of dozens of devices was not great. The Taliban had us exactly where they wanted us. No one would admit how vulnerable we had become. Our patrolling formations had to be tweaked to perfection. Dave and Treo had now got twice as much pressure on their shoulders.

We had taken them for granted for far too long and Treo was now the companies answer to every IED. The poor dog was working around the clock.

I think we expected far more from Treo than anyone else had ever done before, Dave had bags below his eyes and looked completely shattered, he and Treo would never let anyone down. It was as if they were robots. I would make a point of popping across and chatting to him. Hopefully, gaining not just a work asset but a great friend into the bargain.

We get orders from the boss that we are to move out at last light and carry out a patrol. We would then find somewhere to lye up and return to camp in the morning at first light. It wasn't long after leaving camp that the guys and Treo came across a device in the ground. We marked it as per orders and moved around it.

We continue with the patrol and find a second device. The guys are not happy and again we mark it and box around it. we come to a compound and we secure it by sending in Ronnie and his search team. Davy looks pretty pissed off with the whole situation as he knows he is dicing with death at the front along with the rest of his team. There is nothing I can do about it as orders are orders.

We put sentries on and spend the night getting some valuable rest. I decide to cook some hot food and check up on the guys, the new boss Mr Ward has started to find his feet and very fast, I take a picture of him sleeping to be used as ransom in the near future. He just laughs. I begin to take the piss out of Chips, we call him that because he eats junk food and it also annoys him.

He is enjoying this time and relaxing with the rest of the guys. Cupples has still not put any food on. He walks from radio-to-radio checking to make sure not only we have enough batteries left but also making sure the ECM has been switched off and that we are only using one set while we are static.

The next morning, the sentries have woken everyone and the guys do not make breakfast as we are about to return to the DC. We all pack away our kit and get ready to leave this compound. The boss surprises me by packing up first and is waiting for the rest of us.

He gives the section commanders a quick set of QBO's and we leave the compound. Again, I sit near the exit counting everyone out, checking dress and equipment. I send a radio message to the DC. Our interpreter is full energy. I have asked him to carry a video camera to film the patrol and the route we take back to the DC. This I will use to help brief the Marines on how we conduct patrols.

I have changed the patrol matrix about. For some reason, I have decided to put the CMT 3 with the boss at the front. That way if we take casualties then it gives me a better option and we can react a lot sooner than having to run from the back. It is something I have learnt from Sapwan Quala.

T and Davy are at the front with Dave and Treo and they are searching for every grain of dirt. A lot of rests on them doing their job to the highest of qualities, the platoon snakes out and follows in the footsteps of all three men and Treo the dog. I see the platoon begin to disappear right down an entry. The walls are over 15ft in height and are now channelling us into alleyways. There is nowhere else to go. It is right on the edge of the Green Zone.

The new boss is happy to be going back into the District Centre. Only a few hundred metres from the pipe range. Then out of nowhere I first see a mushroom black cloud to my front then I hear the most deafening explosive to date. I look with pure panic etched across my face. I know it is right in the middle of the platoon. I start to run forward shouting at Caylie. She already knows what has happened. I can hear the boss sending a message to the Ops room screaming, ***"HADES 4 1 ALPHA CONTACT IED, WAIT OUT."***

I can hear screaming from the platoon. We get to the guys and I can see the Interpreter lying a few feet away from the rest of the platoon the high corn field around him has been cut away by the large explosion. I can see his face is badly marked. His nose has been blown completely from it. His fingers have all been blown off his hand leaving just his index finger and thumb. He is covered in blood and screaming for help.

I know this sounds terrible, but I left him and prioritised who needed help first, and it wasn't him, it was my radio Operator Justin Cupples. The CMT was already working on him. Caylie got down and assisted in treating him. It was a token gesture she was a great medic but not a miracle worker. Justin had stood on what the IED report claims to be 3 x 105mm tank shells that had all been placed together, to cause one massive explosion.

It had been intended for the boss, with the fact that Justin has a large antenna and so does the boss they initiated it at the wrong person, and he just happened to take the blast. I will never forget looking at him and seeing so many people trying to save his life. Tourniquet applied to his left leg and his left arm. Both been blown off from the blast. The corn field half been torn from the ground and claret everywhere.

We managed to get Justin and Rock onto stretchers. The CSM always true to his word had grabbed anyone that was available and ran to our position to assist in the extraction of the casualties, one of them now being a T4, which meant injuries so severe he was not going to survive, in fact he had died right there as the impact had taken place. The only thing that was a saving grace was that he would not have felt a thing.

Dave and Treo have been at the front of the patrol trying to detect signs of an IED. Treo has found everything up to date. The poor dog has worked wonders. However, we must remember Treo is not a robot. If the Taliban decide to dig in an IED deep in the ground, then not only will he find it hard to detect, but the equipment we use cannot detect it either. In fact, a whole section of men has walked across it, before it went off!!

The CSM was fuming. I think having given him the chance, he would have killed someone at that moment when he spoke with me. We were both ready to kill, as both parties were extracted. I could not push the troops out to exploit the area due to possible secondary IEDs I had to keep everyone where they were, which meant they all had seen what was going on.

I do not know why I decided to do this, but as out of pure respect, I ask some of the guys to check around where Cupples had been lying to maybe find his wedding ring. I am not thinking about his wife and what we are going to do when we see her.

I do not have to ask the guys to clear up. They start to cover up all the blood with sand and dirt. We do not want to leave any sign that we had been dealt a massive blow. This will take a long time for the guys to get over. I have been conducting myself to what everyone expects from a platoon sergeant. There is no time for crying, you remain strong, not only for your men, but because that is what is expected from you. You cannot ever let your men see you are weak.

The CSM and OC. Speak to me when we have returned from the patrol. They know I am at a breaking point and encourage me to continue being the strong person that I am. I now get asked to keep an eye on the new boss. He was nearly killed and he knows it. I know they are telling him the same story and to keep an eye on me. It is what you do.

This is where the CSM starts to add bullshit into the company. The guys are all now complaining about tasks being given out and shit jobs from the CSM. Y This is where only the veterans understand why. The CSM is keeping everyone busy with tasks. It is because if they are busy and bitching at him. It stops them from thinking about Ranger Justin Cupples. No one has time to reflect and the job continues to be done without fear. I respect the CSM for his pure drive and how this whole situation was conducted. I do not think anyone else could have done it better.

The OC waits a few days and then visits our platoon to find out how the guys are coping after such a blow within the ranks. He tells the platoon that when Ranger Cupples in being repatriated from Bastion onto the flight home. He will be sending eight men from our platoon to help carry the coffin. There is an instant smile across the guys' faces. I need to sit down with the boss now and discuss whom we can let go. We must remain focused and have firepower to remain operational yet I need to be flexible and understand.

After a shuffle of troops and dropping to only two sections, we manage to get guys away for what is a very important day in Ranger Company. The last chance that the guys have to say goodbye to a brave soldier and very good friend.

This hit me hard. It had been the anniversary only two days ago when I lost young Luke here in Sangin and now Justin had been taken by the hands of evil. I knew that if I made it out of this place, I would never again carry out frontline operations. I had finally reached my limit and I wanted out.

I matured as a person and as a soldier while working with some of the bravest men, women and dogs. I got to see young men like Ralf turn into a man and save the lives of myself and numerous other good men, I watched as the world's bravest dog and his handler Dave Heyhoe found bomb after bomb and kept us alive day in and day out. I looked on as my radio operator was killed and taken from us in one of the most brutal attacks I have ever witnessed. Men are being ripped apart by flying metal fragments and bone.

This place has left me and thousands of others scarred for life. I will never look upon the Taliban as peaceful people and I will always put them in the same league as the IRA. When I see what they are capable of, it reminds me of the two soldiers that were savagely ripped apart in Belfast by these animals who called themselves Nationalists.

Chapter 12
The Dreaded Transfer

After returning from another horrendous tour of Helmand, I had decided that enough was enough. I was being ear marked for an E1 posting away from operations with the battalion. This would be a well-needed break that I had wanted for some time, not to mention a promotion to colour sergeant. I was excited about the new prospect and what the future would entail. All I had to do was keep these demons out of my head.

There were nights that I wouldn't sleep. These constant memories of explosions and friends being killed would forever haunt me. My deep love for frontline soldiering would never go away, but the more I got into the learning aspect of having everything in lines and fully prepared, the more I knew I had a serious problem.

I asked to speak with the company sergeant major (CSM) and explained that I wanted to transfer out of the unit. He was a little shocked to say the least. "Right, Speedy, walk out of my office and come back in again, I'm not sure I heard you correctly."

"Spence, I am serious. I want to settle down with the missus and start a family, mate."

"Right don't do anything stupid. I will have you in with the Commanding Officer and we will see if we can find you a posting to where you want to settle down."

"Thanks, Spence, it's about time I grew up and stopped all this messing about that's all."

After two visits to the Commanding Officer of 1 Royal Irish, I had made my mind up. I had come up with two ideas and put them both to the CO and he threw them back at me with the comments of "That's not where we see you headed,

Sgt Coult. We have plans for you. So, you are not willing to let me go and set roots and start a family? No Sgt Coult we want you to go to OPTAG."

I said I would sleep on it, but after a few phone calls to guys at OPTAG, I quickly was informed that they were about to expand on the teams and that the team I was going into was being deployed to, you guessed it HELMAND!!

The next day, I returned to the Commanding Officers office and said, "Thanks but no thanks, sir. I have put in my transfer papers and I am starting the cadre next week." The CO and the RSM were both stunned at my decision, but they didn't have to go through each day with my thoughts and emotions going around and around in my head. I was struggling to come to terms with some of the horrific sights that I had seen and been involved in. This seemed the only option to put it all to bed.

I spent some time on the phone to my partner and to Pete. He was the training Warrant Officer at my new destination. He would become a very reliable and likeable guy who would always have my back. It wasn't long before I packed up my four boxes in Ternhill Barracks. I didn't really want to explain my reasoning for a quick departure. All I know is that I would miss the guys that I had served alongside in many campaigns and the Craic that we all had in the Sgts mess, but I wasn't naïve I knew someone would take my place as soon as I drove out the gates.

After beginning to pack up my room in the mess, I started to look through some old pictures from nights out with the boys and previous overseas exercises. Things I knew I would miss. But to get over all these nightmares, it was a sacrifice I was willing to make.

That night, I had a few beers with Spencey in the mess and yet again we played pool for a Guinness. I won the odd game or two but it was another cheap night on the beer for him again. I had an early night with dreams of expectations and how I would start a clean slate at a new place of work. All I had to do was keep pro-active and things will return to normal. Well as normal as I could expect anyway.

I drove the long drive from Shrewsbury to where our new flat was situated, it was a quiet little village called Little Dunmow, only a stone throw from Stansted Airport and 30mins drive to Colchester. We were still building up on furniture and for the next few weeks we would spend our evenings sitting on a blow-up blue sofa watching the 50" television that we had always wanted.

I spent a few days reading over the course criteria and thought it was going to be the easiest course ever put together. Basically, it was going to be a doddle, and most of the staff that worked at the facility were past their sell by date and hanging on for dear life to get the all-important pension. *Not much competition,* I thought.

As soon as we all meet up for the day 1 briefing, I thought it was being ran by Pete the only Warrant Officer with a sense of humour and knew his job at the place. We had a clerk who stood up and stated that he had no qualifications and this was a last resort... *Well, what a real belter,* I thought, and a real insight to what I was about to undertake!

The course was the easiest course I had ever completed. We spent eight weeks being taught the I and D rules only to be told on the last week that the rules had now be changed and to forget everything we had been taught up to now. I was fuming at this.

Out of eight of us that had started the course only three finished it, which says a lot for them, one of the Staff Sergeants who had come from the RMP failed the basic fitness test but was given another chance at the end of the course. I could have put in very little effort and still have passed.

I just kept thinking, *be true to yourself have integrity and dignity and everything else would fall into place.* I kept my end of the bargain right until I stopped working there.

I continued to move around the workplace from job to job, until I reached the training wing. It had a great team of guys. All of whom where Ex-Infantry with the odd Royal Marine to give it that cherry on the cake. Our job was to teach all the military annual training tests as well as the operational build up training, easy to us when we worked together.

I started work as member of staff on 6 December 2009, and was soon the talk of camp as the guy who had the Military Cross and who was very pro-active. Jobs would be sent in my direction, and I would try and complete them ASAP and report back that the job was done.

I undertook many a task and at one point I was on the Mess Committee, the PRI secretary, the unit TRiM Coordinator, Right-Turn instructor and a member of the training wing teaching staff and detainees. I was just enjoying the new routine.

I had worked at the place now for a few years and was being warned off for an operational tour in Afghanistan. I knew my days on frontline fights were well and truly over and I needn't worry that way. However, this would be a completely new challenge, rather than kill or capture the terrorist. My new job would be to work alongside them and make sure they were in fact healthy and ready for the Afghan authorities.

Having been warned off for operations. I now was having trouble in getting some pre-tour leave. It seems that the Military Provost Staff only want duties filled and you basically must go sick to get time off. I would have spoken to the welfare officer about this, but there was no welfare officer up until 2013. We were told to just 'get on with it.'

I managed to get some of the leave that I couldn't take transferred across to the following year. I was about to spend the next few months on courses and learning how to process the detainees from point of capture to transfer. It looked difficult but it would all fall into place the minute I began doing it for real.

Over the next few weeks, I would find myself being sent to the Intelligence Corps to learn how to use the Biometrics data capture system and learn how to enrol a civilian onto the database using iris scans and fingerprints, not to mention DNA swabs from the mouth.

This would be known as the HIDE system. We are looking to try and find the insurgents/Taliban/Al-Qaeda suspects and the devices we are using are called the HIDE and SEEK systems, ironic wouldn't you say.

We began to carry out in house drills and practice scenarios that could very well occur in theatre, moving the detainee from A to B would be something we all had to master and using and learning the prohibited five techniques that would land any ISAF soldier in a world of hurt needed to be known as if our lives depended on it.

We had a few Pashtu lessons organised so we would at least be able to communicate with the Taliban prisoners and have a basic understanding of what they were trying to tell us. I already had a basic knowledge of the language however all I really knew was commands, like put your hands up, turn around, place the weapon on the ground.

Now I needed to know, do you need a tashnab (toilet) and I am about to conduct a talashi (search) my priorities had changed, but my professionalism for doing what was right was never in question.

During our pre-deployment training, we got to see who we would be working with, the guys were a great bunch, and then the theatre Captain came in. He was an LE officer and always full of ideas. However, the Warrant Officer would prove to be testing, it was only a matter of time. Both individuals lacked operational experience, mainly from being on the ground as most of their previous tours had been from an office in camp so far back, they had to send forward for their mail.

I had made sure I had taken out all 15 units of PAX insurance just in case I got injured, pretty naïve of me to think I would be covered for all types of injuries. What they never tell you that in the small print there are clauses and while you are all in Afghanistan. They can change the contract without your written consent. So, what you signed for before you deployed and are covered for can be changed without you knowing and you then receive no compensation on your return.

I had spoken with my wife on several occasions and we both knew that it was not going to be a very difficult tour. Being at the back this time had its privileges and they were clean clothes, showers every day, fresh food, pizza, Internet, television, phones, coffee houses, the gymnasium, basically it was a holiday in an operational environment. However, every few days someone with rank would try and justify why it was dangerous, and this would come from someone who had never left camp Bastion!

Our training went well and our medical training was great. Most of the guys I was deploying with were in fact first aid instructors and many of them had deployed frontline in the past so we didn't lack experience on that front. Jonno was a great instructor and was always keeping up morale. So, we were at least guaranteed a bit of a laugh and usually at one of our expenses.

Jonno took most of the pre-deployment medical training and was able to mark us all off the nominal roll. It was a paperwork exercise to give us all the tick in the book we needed prior to leaving Colchester for a long journey back to Helmand.

It was 3 November 2011 and I had said my goodbyes to my wife and son, it was never nice going away from the ones you loved, but it was my duty and my way of life that I was now used to.

My wife had everything that she needed, all the contact numbers for house repairs, and the bills paid and everything else would be covered by warranty. I would arrange to phone her once I had landed in Afghanistan and leave a message, she had even managed to buy me a new laptop for the deployment, but as all guys who deploy from a marriage know…she will get her own back by spending a fortune on stuff we will never know about.

It was getting late, and we loaded the car with the usual deployment kit, a Bergan packed to the point of almost exploding, my grip bag and daysack. I helped put my son into the car seat, but no sooner had I fixed him in. The wife came over to check I had done it correctly, that the normal way we conducted every task whether it be big or small.

I went back into the house to do the normal routine before getting in the car. I checked upstairs to make sure all windows had been closed and then the back door to see if it was secure. Once I was happy, I carried out a quick check for passport, F/Med and dog-tags not to mention wallet with a few quid spending money for the first few weeks of buying fatty foods and sweets in the NAAFI at Bastion.

It was only a short distance to the main gate of MCTC and it looked like it was the meeting point for everyone before we loaded onto the minibus. The atmosphere was electric. Everyone was excited to be deploying, some would save a small fortune for deposits for a house, while others would finally be debt free on their return having been given a £5k operational bonus at the end of the six-month tour.

It was shocking to see how many were in fact naïve about the situation and how we could be deployed to collect these detainees straight from a contact. Some of the team struggled to pass their weapon handling test, never mind the knowing the rules of detention. The word amongst the team was, "We are only qualified to stay in detention facilities." This was something that annoyed me, because we are in fact soldiers first detention subject matter experts last.

My wife and son had given me a kiss goodbye and I was a little teary eyed at the prospect of missing them, especially as my son was only a few months old, I had already spent a lot of time arranging my R&R to take place so I could be home for my son's 1st birthday.

I gave it a few days each way so the middle of my leave would be his birthday, and a fantastic way to spend it would be having his mum and dad home.

It was now 21:33hrs and the excitement on every one's face was plain to see. Jim turned up driving the white mini-bus and Andy drove the van with all our baggage on board, I decided that I would go with Andy and try and keep him awake during the drive to RAF Brize Norton.

This was the Royal Air Force Base that all deployments across the world would deploy from. It housed all our troop carrier planes and it would be our home for the next 10 hours or so, because when you fly with the RAF, they expect you to be there nine hours before the pilots get out of bed.

It took quite some time to make the long journey to Oxfordshire and all I wanted to do was get some sleep. We arrived at the RAF camp at around 0200hrs in the morning. We pulled up outside the terminal and began to unload the vehicles of our kit and equipment.

We had a few weapon bundles that needed to be monitored right up until they had been loaded into the checkout desk and they were in the hands of the RAF staff. Again, I was already starting off this tour pissed off with the RAF. Now we were being told that we could not carry hand luggage onto the plane. Only helmet and body armour were permitted to be brought on board.

The carrying of helmets and body armour is now routine when flying in and out of theatre due to the threat from ground to air missile strike from insurgent activity and small arms attack when taking off and landing. And I was becoming a seasoned veteran having completed several tours in this operational environment.

We hung around the departure lounge for nine hours while the planes were being checked over and the baggage was loaded. There were clicks of soldiers beginning to unfold in the lounge, because the army had been cut back to such a small force it seemed that everyone knows knew each other. With only a few brigades of fighting troops and constant overseas operations, we were starting to know a lot of the guys from each unit.

It seemed like forever to get on the plane. once we were called forward to board, we tried to stay with the person that would be the least pain in the ass to sit beside for the long journey. There is nothing worse than someone who talks complete rubbish placing himself on the seat next to you. That's why many of the senior ranks that board these planes seem to always have the bag. The bag that we had to hand in. Yes, they seem to have sneaked it on, and it now sits on the seat next to them. And we walk past and sit on the next empty seat.

We knew that the flight would take place in stages, the first stage was flying to Cyprus were we would have to refuel if we were to make it all the way to Kabul.

But just as we were called forward to board, there was an announcement that the flight would be delayed now until 0800hrs. This was because an emergency medical team and all their equipment had been sent for and we had to wait for them to arrive. This would not upset anyone at all. In fact, we all knew how vitally important these teams were in theatre.

At 0807hrs, we were finally called for boarding, this would be done in the usual way, Officers followed by Warrant Officers and Senior Non-Commissioned Officers' then NCOs and other ranks. The whole process took about two hours to get us all on board.

We were very lucky that our party of nine were all senior ranks. And that we didn't have to wait that long and we would be all sitting as a group on the plane. However, right from the word go the Warrant Officer who would effectively be our boss for the next six months wouldn't sit near us. He made all of us feel uncomfortable, and this was not even day 1 of the tour, what a great atmosphere this was going to be.

Once on board, the plane I managed to get a window seat beside Steve. Well at least I would have a good journey, as Steve had the same sick/funny sense of humour as I had. The teams where we would find ourselves in had still not been finalised by the CSM. He kept everything to himself. I had already begun to have doubts that this tour would be easy.

I was dreading this tour. I had completed nine previous operational tours and this was the only one where we were being called Sgt Coult and Sgt Steve in a chilled-out area before we deployed. This only meant that on tour it would not be an enjoyable one.

We all sat down and got out our music players and books to keep us company throughout the journey. Then over the speaker, we heard the captain telling us to listen into the safety brief. Then a few of the RAF stewards took their position up and down the aircraft and showed us how to use the seatbelts. Use the lifejackets and get to the drop-down oxygen masks, something we had seen a thousand times before.

I then reached into my pocket and grabbed my iPod shuffle, I was never one for up-to-date technology, and beside the point that my wife had already downloaded 54 songs. Many of which made me relax and just fall asleep anyway.

After only 20 minutes I had fallen asleep, no sooner had a closed my eyes I was nudged by Steve, "Hey up fella, its scoff time." Well, I was hungry, and I would have been upset with myself if I had of missed a meal. So, I was happy to be woken up for breakfast. In fact, it was well received and a great surprise. The RAF hot breakfasts were always nice, well I thought so anyway.

I had been hungry for about three hours now, so an egg, sausage, bacon, beans hash brown was going down rather well. After breakfast, we only had an hour left before we began to descend into RAF Akrotiri for that final refuel and it was also a place where mobile phones were available to all theatre troops to phone home for free.

As we approached the runway in Cyprus, I could see how beautiful the sea looked, and the temperature was beginning to rise in the cabin.

I could feel myself sweating and it was a little uncomfortable. I couldn't wait to get off and relax with a cold drink from the little shop at the arrival's lounge.

However, as we landed, we were all quickly ushered off the plane and into the smallest room available at the airport. It resembled a cattle pen, but after some high-ranking officer complained about the lack of free space we were allowed to move into a bigger room.

It was a great weight off my shoulders to be able to phone home and just have a few minutes with my wife Luba and son Sebastian, especially as it kept them happy to know I had made it this far and was okay. They both seemed to be in good spirits which was refreshing to hear, and she spoke about her chores and daily routine that had taken up most of her day. It wasn't long before we were all being told to prepare to board the plane for the final journey into Helmand.

I tried to have some sleep during the final leg of the journey, but it was impossible, especially as my mind was running overtime with thoughts from previous tours I had completed in Helmand. The motionless faces of a few friends who had died beside me and the look on their face as they passed away was something I would never be able to forget. I was reliving every contact over and over again when I went to sleep. It was this reason I had walked from my old unit and tried to start over again.

It would never go away. When I just thought about that day, I could hear the explosions and see the devastation as if it was happening again. Running forward to find Justin's body, or the 17-hour contact in Sapwan Quala where my platoon was used as bait to take direct fire from the Taliban for the 2 Para snipers to engage the enemy mussel flash. Then carrying the FSG CSM after he had been killed by a single bullet which had hit him in the side of the body armour.

Getting the CSM to the Regimental sergeant major was horrendous. I was in contact and running around like a lunatic to locate his party, and those thoughts would remain etched on my mind until the day I died.

We were about to descend into Camp Bastion when the captain announced that all lights in the cabin were about to be switched off, and that personal protection equipment did not need to be fitted. This really pissed me off. Especially as we didn't need to wear it and they had removed our hand luggage. It never made sense with the RAF.

We landed in bastion with the sound of clapping coming from many an idiot. It was usually when we returned to the UK that people would be found clapping.

I looked outside the window and it was like a small city of lights and tents, something that had changed significantly since my last visit a few years earlier, it had been described as a city the size of Reading. But looking at it from above it was now bigger than Reading.

It was an amazing sight; each Nation had the own part of Bastion camp and their countries' flag flew from their HQ situated in each of the locations. There were thousands of civilian contractors working on various projects within the camp. Large painted pictures and road signs explaining how to get to various emergency locations, as well as the threat state which was dotted around the camp.

We taxied for about 10 minutes on the runway before we came to a complete stop. The captain said, "On behalf of myself and the crew, I would like to welcome you all to Bastion and hope you have a safe and enjoyable tour." It left a lump in my throat, as I knew what could unfold and quickly things can change in Helmand.

As we all got up and headed for the steps, I could feel how hot and humid it was, there were four coaches sitting on the runway waiting to take us to our temporary accommodation in Bastion 3.

Once we had driven at the 10kph speed limit to our sleeping area, we then had to wait on a safety brief from the arrivals team. It was followed with us being given our phone cards and then the baggage trucks turned up, and not before time as we were completely worn out.

That night, I didn't even have a dream. As soon as my head hit the pillow, I was asleep.

The next morning, we went to breakfast as a group and it was fresh rations and cooked very well. It would have put most breakfast houses in the UK to shame. Our CSM was at our location waiting to drive us in the minibus to visit our facility, this is where I would spend the next six months. And hopefully, there was at least somewhere to relax after being with the Taliban all day.

I thought we were all going to be driven to Bastion 1 United Kingdom Temporary Holding Facility (UKTHF) but half the guys on the bus got dropped off at the facility at Bastion 3 currently being called TORCHLIGHT by every other person apart from my senior corps members, it was meet with eyebrows being raised and extra duties heaven be hold you called it TORCHLIGHT.

It was known by all members of the Special Forces based in theatre as TORCHLIGHT, because it was where the Exploitation took part, and torchlight was the old way of carrying out interrogation. But because of human rights and smart-arse lawyers we now exploited instead of interrogated, again another play of words.

Once we had arrived at our facility, it was very distinctive indeed, with *NO WEAPONS BEYOND THIS POINT and NO PHOTOGRAPHY* and guards everywhere you looked ranging from Pte's to Captain's. We rang the bell and waited for the gate to be opened, there was a sign stating that no one was allowed to enter without permission from the Theatre Provost Marshal, now that was how important this place was deemed to be.

When we got let in, I felt a little uneasy for a while, the reality of the place was overwhelming to me as I had only ever been on the frontline trying to kill these guys and now I found myself coming face to face with the very same guys who have killed my fellow soldiers and who would kill me the first chance they were given.

The guys seemed really pleased to see the new fresh faces of us as we entered their place of work, and I was not surprised as I was always happy to see me replacement when I was working in Sangin DC. I grabbed a cup of coffee and waited for the guys to come to me and explain what the place was like and how it managed from day to day. But surprisingly, everyone wanted to know what was happening back at MCTC in Colchester.

That was a place that the Sergeants were in fact running while others basked in their own self-importance rather than looking after the troops, this was well renowned throughout the mess and many great guys stopped attending the functions and socialising because of this.

And the fact that they preferred working in Afghanistan with insurgents than back home at MCTC told a very alarming question about the place.

Chapter 13
Adjusting to Theatre

I was shown what my new living accommodation would be and it was by far the best bedspace I had ever had on operations, it gave me a warm and fuzzy feeling knowing I had space to relax and enjoy my down time when not on duty.

I was moved into an iso container that had been specially adapted to sleep in, it had air condition and an antenna for a television. One bunk bed and one single bed, one for each of us. It was going to be a guy from the Navy called Spud, me and Reders and they had given me the single bed, what a great start to the tour.

With three guys and all their kit and equipment to be stored as well as somewhere to relax, it looked more like a storeroom than a place to sleep. It was 8ft wide and 20ft long and to be honest it was still better than anything I had ever slept in before, especially as it was so far back from the frontline, I could walk to the gym. Well, if I ever felt the need to choose the gym over a burger, then I could.

It wasn't long before I headed back to the transit accommodation and collected my belongings and took it to my new surroundings. There is nothing that would upset me now, especially as I knew where I was going to be for the next six months, so the onus was on me to make it home from home.

And looking back at the previous tours I had here, this was like a 4 star hotel compared to living on the frontline, now I was getting to see what the other part of living in Bastion was like, and it made me think that many of these base rats have a brass neck complaining about anything out here.

I started to put up my new hanging wardrobe that I had brought with me, pictures of my wife and son went up beside my bed and I quickly made myself comfortable and lay on my bed for about 10 minutes just taking everything in, I could see that Spud had a chuff chart and had been crossing off each day as it had passed. He only had about a month left so I am sure he was going to take the piss out of the fact we had six months to go.

I managed to be left alone for a while and took full advantage of this by going to the phone area and phoning my wife. This would indeed reassure her and I would hear my little boy again and find out what they had been up to and explain what my new facility was like. She was happy to hear my voice and it cheered me up to know that everyone was doing well.

After the phone call, I walked back through the sand swept camp to the UKTHF. I was let in by showing my ID card and explaining who I was. This was to become the normal way for entering a location which was classified to all UK personnel.

I had a chat with the guys before having a shower and getting into my bed, after a very long day and a little bit of jetlag I was completely shattered and quickly fast asleep waiting for what was going to be the longest day of the tour, it was going to be packed with lectures from 0730hrs right up until 1700hrs that night.

I fell asleep listening to the many songs I had on my iPod. Then what seemed like only a few hours later when Rob came in and woke me up for breakfast. I looked at my watch and it was only 0545hrs. What the hell was this all about? Then Rob explained that there would be a massive queue for breakfast and it would be better to get in first rather than wait for an hour queuing up, that I agreed with!

It was only 5 November and our tour didn't officially start for another week. This was the bedding in period and where we had to learn all the drills with the detainees before they left for home. So, we needed to be like a sponge and absorb everything that we were being told.

After a quick shower, I headed to the American dining facility only because they had a choice like no other cookhouse in the world. And shortly after my visit, they made a rule that no British forces were allowed to eat in the American cookhouse. A rule which would not be adhered to by many. After breakfast, we decided to take a brew with us; it was going to be a long day.

We sat through 10 presentations on our first day in Bastion. As an instructor in numerous subjects, it does not take the brains of an archbishop to know that soldiers switch off after about 15 minutes if every presentation. So, this was just a tick in the box exercise and we all knew it.

Some instructors spent some time making their given subject interesting and entertaining. While others were just boring and not worth listening to, they lacked the teaching experience back at their own unit and had just been thrust into the spotlight and you could tell they were struggling with it. You just wanted the ground to swallow them up and start again with a different instructor.

I was waiting for the Detainee handling presentation, and I needed to pay particular attention to it as I would be teaching this to everyone who entered theatre in the coming weeks. Most of the lectures were mundane and boring, however there was one that stuck in my head.

And that was from an American Marine Officer, who was from the 3rd Battalion the United States Marine Corp (USMC) he had spent years learning and understanding the history of Afghanistan and how the tribes worked and the culture behind what we know today.

Because he had taken the time to learn it in such fine detail. It meant that he was passionate about it, and when you are passionate about a subject, it flows very well and is enjoyable to listen to.

He explained how it had developed from a war fighting mission to what it was now, and how it was a counter insurgency operation which needed to start with the hearts and minds campaign to order to win the people over, to get influence within what we knew was a complex Taliban movement.

It was not about putting warheads on foreheads!

At 1600hrs and after what seemed to be a day that nearly broke me being ear bashed to death by everyone wanting to pass on their vast knowledge and experience we all returned to our facility, but instead of sitting down for a hot beverage, John the Royal Marine that was attached to us, thought I would rather have a brief of the detention facility and took me on a tour of the place.

Every time he gave me a brief, he ticked his notebook and stated, "That's part of my handover now complete." Which meant he could relax slightly as I was now briefed to carry out that detail.

This is where my job had already begun and the realisation of the enormous task began to kick in, then I was told,

"Trevor, we have three high profile detainees arriving in our facility at 1940hrs this evening. You and I will go and collect them from the flight line and take them for processing."

Well, straight into the deep end, I thought, but I suppose it will get me knowing the job sooner rather than later, I began to pack my osprey armour the way I intended on using it for the remainder of the tour, I changed a few things around and added more plastic cuffs and blindfolds to my kit, along with capture cards and clear plastic bags for forensics and detainee belongings.

Having listened to most of the guys giving me their tips and advice on how they used certain items and carriage of kit, I knew what I wanted to achieve and how I would move from A to B and how I would approach each task.

They had already spent some time at the *TORCHLIGHT* facility being exploited and brought into our way of routine. We had to call it a routine because again using the word conditioning is an illegal phase thanks to our human rights lawyers.

When we had received word via the red phone (secure means), we had all the other detainees on lockdown. The place had all staff and handlers in position, and we had even closed the road in front of the facility off. This was not the normal procedure, but because of the level of detainee that we had coming in, it was justified.

The vehicle beeped outside, and the gates began to open, it reversed back into the compound airlock, and we closed the gates, no one spoke for the next 10 minutes as a way of showing them that we were in control. They got out the vehicle blindfolded and cuffed to the front.

They had dark black hair and a brand-new dish dash and trousers along with flip flops, as soon as we had moved them into our briefing bay, the interpreter came in. We always had two members of staff and one handler always doing this. However, on this occasion, we had three staff and four handlers all on display to show them numbers in mass and to give an overall show of force, we could hear the other detainees shouting and whistling at the new arrivals. This was to put the detainees into a warm feeling by the other Afghans that were already locked up.

I began to give the arrivals brief to the detainees and let them know the detention rules, this was translated by Dave, who had worked at our facility for some time and was a well trusted member of the team.

He and I would become very good friends by the end of this difficult and demanding tour.

As soon as the brief had been given, we gave each of them a hot meal which of course was Halal compliant. I was very surprised when one of the new detainees spoke to me in fluent English. He spoke in a very soft voice as he didn't want to raise attention to the others that he was speaking to the British. I thought he was going to tell me something, but that was never going to happen he was just adjusting to his new surroundings.

Jack came in and asked me to go with him and fill out the admission paperwork. It was straight forward and only taking about 20 minutes. Photographs of all detainees admitted needed to go on their personal files and their detention number which would stay with them until they were either released having found nothing significant to hold them for, or just as they were handed over to the authorities.

It has just sunk in that this is what I am going to be doing for the next six months, and I think that my soul is about to be taken away from me. I am basically looking after these evil individuals and it seems so far that we are bending over backwards to their every whim. I feel sick to my stomach.

Thank God I am working with a great bunch of guys.

That night was a real eye opener with regards to the detainees. Well, I suppose it's time to crash out, especially with a 0440 hours' wakeup call in the morning.

As clockwork, I was woken up again at 0445hrs. After a cup of coffee and a small breakfast, I filled up my camelback with ice cold water and sorted out my feet. Today was the big event of the induction phase into theatre. It was the two-mile walk to the range, and in this heat, it was always going to be tough especially as they make you go at the speed of the slowest guy leading the walk.

We got to camp 507 and waited like everyone else to move off as groups towards the range. I was with my guys and we just had a chat all the way to the range, it was right on the edge of the camp and it was firing into a manmade backdrop, a little like the ones in the UK, however this was twice the size.

As we made our way to the range, I was tabbing beside Rob. It was a slight shock from the word go, as the pace was very fast but soon slowed down after only 200 metres, to a quick walk and then my bladder kicked in and I needed to go to the toilet.

The road we were walking on was like the roads in Canada. It was very straight and seemed to go on forever. We passed through the American base, and it was straight roads and American sidewalk signs. It looked like someone had picked up a city in America and dropped it into the desert.

We reached the range and were immediately put into two ranks. These would later become details, and then we were all asked to show our weapons clear.

This was a slight safety mishap on the training team's behalf, as a qualified weapons instructor it is your responsibility to check all weapons on your range. You do not ask everyone to show weapons clear as there is always one dickhead who makes that vital mistake, and with this being the first thing the team asked us to do. It meant a real exciting day was about to begin.

I was put into the second detail for firing, and it was starting to look like a terrible day, I could see the first lot engaging the targets and the dust cloud that had appeared from nowhere and was now obscuring the vision of the firers. It was becoming impossible to see the targets.

The wind had picked up and now the targets where not visible from 50 metres, not a great start to a tour, but I suppose we could come back and get zeroed at any time, as we were going to be staying in this camp for the remainder of the tour.

The main thing was to get through all these lessons and be ready to take over from the outgoing team. I got on to the firing point and placed my ear defence on and waited for gaps in the fine dust that was blowing in front, I managed to get a grouping on the target and waited for the safety staff to call us all forward. I checked my group and changed my sights slightly and then fired a check group to verify that I was on target, not that bad, I was pleased with my grouping and made my way to the next stand.

Some of the other guys were not that lucky, there were guys who stayed on the range for over two hours trying to zero, and in that heat, I felt for them...honestly.

With the heat on the range picking up to almost an unworkable temperature and with me being a redhead, I quickly moved across to the tented area for some well-earned shade and a bottle of water; it wasn't long before most of the guys and girls on the range had the same idea. There were quite a few tents spaced out equally around the training area.

After 30 minutes, we began a series of lessons which had all been designed to assist us for the next six months, each lesson had been identified during the previous tour as key to make the tour more pro-active and safer for the troops, as well as a way to achieve the battle-group mission.

The medical stand was by far the best medical stand that I had ever seen, he had put everything into it, the way he showed us how to adapt your kit to make a tourniquet was great. He made us all crawl, carry out lifesaving drills, he used a volunteer to demonstrate and then we all had to show him that we were in fact competent; he made it a fantastic lesson.

Then the depressing lesson on legal powers and what we could and could not do in Afghanistan. There were so many loopholes we could use to our advantage, however at the end of each loophole there would be a public interest lawyer waiting to jump on the band wagon and make a few quid. There were now to many greedy lawyers making millions from the British Army, it made us all feel sick.

Another lesson was showing us all how to make an emergency Heli-landing site (HLS). I already knew this and had been teaching it back in the UK, so I just played along with the instructor, as it would be appalling to just walk off or intervene.

The lesson I had been waiting for was coming up next. It was the detention brief and it needed to be spot on, as there were in fact a few of us going to be watching and we were going to be the new in theatre subject matter experts.

I watched with a beady eye to see how he approached the lesson and his tone, he did a great job and made it very interesting. I could see how I could capitalise on it and make the lesson more exciting, especially as I had conducted frontline operations on previous tours and knew what I wanted from the training.

I wanted to give the guy's options from lessons learnt from my experience rather than a detention brief from very inexperienced guys who just count and lock doors for a living. It had scope for massive improvement.

After the detention brief, we waited for around 20 minutes for the bus to turn up, there was no way I was walking back in that heat, I would have burnt quite well and it was only two days into the tour. The bus dropped us off at the telephone area and we made our way back to UKTHF on the way across the square, we could see the wall of memorial. It looked like it was being looked after, I made my way over and spotted a mistake on the wall. It stated Cpl Mark Wright who had been killed in the minefield during the 2006 tour of HERRICK 4. However, it did not have his post nominal of GC. This was rather upsetting especially as it happened over six years previous.

I phoned the GSM of Bastion and explained to him the mistake, and he stated, "Are you sure?"

"Well of course, I am sure. I was standing looking at it." This turned out to be a game of cat and mouse as I complained time and time again about this and when I left it still had not been fixed.

On arrival in UKTHF, I grabbed a brew and started to clean my rifle, the amount of fine sand was unbelievable. It took some time to clean it off. Once cleaned, I put it in the rifle rank in the office and signed it in. The CSM said he wanted to check my rifle. I laughed and stated that it was only last week I had been checking his in Colchester, as I was qualified, and now we are here you want to check mine and you're not qualified, what has changed?

After rifle cleaning, I shadowed some of the guys and tried to pick up some points and tips that would assist me during the tour.

I was brought into the detainee facility and for a split second the hairs on the back of my neck stood up. I was face to face with these evil people, and I was trying to make friends slightly…what was I thinking, well if I go in with a terrible attitude then it would make my job very difficult for the entire tour. However, if I go in and be professional, then it will be seen as such.

I wasn't going to let myself down just because I wanted to kill these guys. They had all been involved in killing British service personnel.

There is a certain way of dealing with detainees and it needs to be within the law. I looked around the open area outside the compounds and I could see there was guards visible to the detainees. These guys could investigate the compound from different angles and see the detainees either standing outside their accommodation or them praying to Allah.

It made you feel a little at ease. There was also a seat that always sat in the middle with two handlers who would assist the detainees with water and food. They would never leave the compound unless being properly briefed and relieved by another handler. The Detainee compound gates would never be opened unless the staff were present to assist and their hands had been cuffed before they were moved.

I could see into the adapted iso containers, and they had blankets and prayer hats each as well as Koran's. They had all been given a Koran by our interpreter because it was seen as an insult for us to touch it, having now had experience with this. I can tell you that this is something that we are allowed to touch, and the hard-line insurgents just complained about the sake of complaining.

It was getting late, and the medics were coming in, so I watched for a bit and could see the Major walking around and giving medication to the detainees. They would all in turn stand at the fence and open their mouths take the medication and then show they had swallowed it. The handlers and a member of the staff would accompany the medics on their rounds. It looked straight forward, all they had to do know is input all this onto the database of each detainee.

This job was all going to be testing at times, more like bending over backwards to please these evil people rather than dictating our rules onto them. I could see how they were already making demands to my boss and how he had already decided to give them beads and string to make jewellery this was to not upset them and that he wouldn't have to listen to their constant moaning.

It upsets me and many of the staff to see that we were becoming compliant to their every whim than detention specialists and the worrying thing was that this was coming from the top brass.

I finished watching the guys and headed to the phone to check in with my wife and son. It seemed she was having a nightmare with him especially as he had four teeth coming through and was screaming his head off day and night, I felt sorry for her but at the same time, I was ecstatic to be where I was. At least I was getting a great night's sleep.

I said my goodbyes and wished her all the best, then went straight to bed with a big grin on my face. Unless you have children, it is hard to explain how wonderful it is to miss the teething side of your child's development.

Another great night's sleep, I was starting to enjoy this tour far too much, no wonder the Infantry hated the base rats. It was rather cushy to be based in Bastion, okay they all worked hard in the chosen field, but it was very safe indeed.

It was 0520hrs and another day on this induction phase before we could finally be settled into routine at our own place of work. It would be outside all day with Ground Sign Awareness (GSA) learning how to spot signs of disturbed ground to see what has been placed there and how many. This was a vital lesson for the troops who would be going out on the ground as it is lifesaving to spot a potential IED.

The next lesson would be searching, either a person or a vehicle, again this was my bread and butter and I was also highly qualified in doing both having completed several courses at the search school in Chatham and been on quite few search teams on Operation Banner in N. Ireland.

The way that the locals would mark devices was something I had never seen before, it reminded me slightly of Iraq, with the putting stones on top of each other and painting them white, recognising the change in atmospherics would be the key factor for those guys, and I didn't envy them doing it especially having to spot a change in a natural environment that they were still getting used to.

How they would find and mark these suspect devices would also be key in how the reaction times and movement to such devices would be carried out, the more information gathered by the guys at the scene would make it easier for the Royal engineers search team coming in to exploit it followed by the Ammunition Technician Officer (ATO).

Again, I was interested in the searching lesson, it was being carried out by one of our own guy's 'George'. He was a big character and had competed for Great Britain in athletics during his years in the army, he had a way of always upsetting people because of his build and way with words, it made others stand off from him.

He had been a sergeant for 10 years, and not because he was bad at work but the opposite. So, he had upset quite a few people I think, and it just went to prove that some of them who were in fact now Warrant Officers and above still held a grudge on him.

He gave a good presentation. He was confident, and he knew his subject matter. To be honest, I was rather impressed with his lesson, but as my CSM stated, "Look at what he has just put on his head." So having looked at him, I could see he just put a baseball cap on, and instead of being remembered for the guy who just produced a fantastic lesson. He would now be remembered for the guy who wore a baseball cap, and that's the army we have now turned into.

I was very interested in the two lessons that used to be my bread and butter and that was the marking of extraction points for Helicopters and the Casualty evacuation (CASEVAC). These I had carried out on numerous occasions in the past and I hated doing them but also prided myself in getting them perfect for sake of my troops I owed it to them.

All lessons had been perfected over the years and I could see how I might have done things better in the past. I should have had my 60mm mortar man putting down illume for Helicopters to come in with my troops securing flanks for protection of the choppers all wearing mockingbirds that actually worked and being turned to infrared to aid the pilots and to inform them of friendly positions.

But the reality is, the mockingbirds do not get changed in these situations and you spend too much time trying to clear an area for the Heli to land that things go a miss.

A commander now has far too many things going on, with sending a contact report, a 9-liner if it's an IED, a shot report, an ATMIST casualty report, an Emergency Close Air Support (ECAS) 10 liner Grids of possible HLS and dealing with the platoon in contact as well as extracting casualties it was a very serious game to play these days. Then you had the possibility of moving into an area that had been chosen by the enemy as our extraction point which they may have booby trapped prior to our patrol.

Most of this stuff was already imbedded with in me. The basics were being covered rather well. It helps to sell a lesson when the guy taking it is not reading from a pamphlet but teaching from experience. Just as he was coming to his end of lesson drills, a dust storm was approaching so we thanked him for his lesson and quickly got on the awaiting coach.

Many of us including me were fatigued from another long day in the sun, so the drive back into Bastion 1 was well received by the team.

After arriving back at the coach stop, I could see that the guys were very quiet. Maybe the sun had taken its toll on the team and the constant briefs had worn us all out.

We got back and discussed the days lessons and began to put together a crash out box. It was rather surprising to see that with all the guys and girls that had been out on tour before us, hadn't even bothered to produce colour photographs of the detainees or a proper board that could be referred to.

It was on our things to do list as well as many other tasks that had been left to the side for others to pick up. There was not enough space to hold all the rifles if we had an increased threat level. It meant that part of the floor in the office had weapons lying on it.

We all put good points forward and agreed that we needed to change a few things to make the tour a lot more pro-active rather than reactive.

We agreed not to change anything until the outgoing team had left theatre, there was already a hell of an atmosphere within the old team. It was being spoken about by the entire team that things had gone very wrong indeed.

What the hell had been going on. If it had anything to do with the way that MCTC had been running well, then I wouldn't be surprised what had been going on out here in theatre, and I swore to myself that I would not let anyone put me or my team in danger. If it meant me standing up against a Senior Officer, then I would.

The operation's room was our hub of operations yet it was being used by both the CSM's as a coffee house. It began to upset the whole team, especially as they had an office over at the other facility. Yet they still chose to have meetings in our television room and even had the cheek to tell us go make ourselves disappear.

After only a few days in theatre, I was already getting annoyed with some of the guys, and seeing the lack of operational experience in many of them, I did try along with Reders to lift the spirits of the team, but by now he was beginning to pick on the handlers which was not good to see, especially as they had volunteered to help us for the next four months and we were making their tour experience a living hell.

I tried to help them as much as possible with regards to getting them the right kit and equipment that they needed, but every time he found out about it, he would give us shit jobs and state we had broken a direct order.

The next day, we were up again at 0540hrs and ready to attack another day. However, I had managed to fit in a bowl of cereal and a hot coffee before I started.

It was going to be a day with mixed emotions. Today we had the vehicle simulator. It was designed to show us that if we kept our seatbelts applied then it would save our lives in that moment of collision. They had put together a mock exercise to see if we could get ourselves out of the vehicle to safety after it had hit an IED and rolled upside down.

This was never my most successful exercise, as I had failed the mock Helicopter one in a swimming pool a few years earlier. I just couldn't sit in that seat as it turned upside down. It meant no sense, and if I could get out before it turned, it was a lot safer.

When we arrived at the start point, we were again put into different groups, but this time there were seven, and this meant seven different stands so another long day ahead.

The biometrics presentation was interesting, and I needed to know how to enrol so to make my job easier. I needed to know how to gather DNA for the exploitation part. This was vital if we wanted to gain a conviction from these insurgents/Terrorists.

A lesson on the Electronic Counter Measures (ECM) would be interesting especially as this was the best and most successful equipment in the world. It had saved me and my guys on so many occasions, I worshiped it.

I was starting to lose the will to live as the instructor was a little monotone to say the least, he lost everyone within 10 minutes of talking. When I looked around, I could see many conversations had begun and not about the subject at hand.

The lesson finished with him asking for all the equipment to be sent to the front and we all got up and left the tent. I wasn't really bothered as we would get our hands on this back at work to practise again.

The next lesson was all about the tactical satellite (TACSAT) another piece of radio equipment to help us get communications from a dead spot where it worked off the satellite rather than a radio wave.

The final lesson of the day was going to be the simulator and I was not looking forward to it. The instructor gave us all a brief on what to do and how to fasten and unfasten the seatbelts. There were pictures of vehicles that had been involved in road traffic accidents and explained to us that if the drivers and passengers had of been wearing seatbelts, then would have survived the crash, basically stating that *YOU MUST WEAR IT.*

I was put into the first group and there was no turning back now, I was trying to be all cool about it, but inside I was slightly worried. I was made Commander of the first vehicle, so no pressure then. I applied my seatbelt so tight it was making me numb, but at least I wouldn't move during the spin of the vehicle. The machine started up and began to turn left and then right and eventually finished up on its side, we unclipped and all climbed out safely, it was easy.

Another scenario took place and this time we had to change seats, and I was sat at the back door. The vehicle went left and then right and began to spin upside down. We ended up in a ditch with the wheels above us. I unclipped myself and stood up unlocked the back door and climbed out.

With only one scenario left, I was feeling confident and began to smile a bit more, then the instructor whispered in my ear than when the vehicle came to a stop, I was to pretend to be unconscious. This should prompt the guys to get me out asap.

This was a test of mental agility. The vehicle turned upside down and I remained quiet. Some of the guys had climbed out and then I could hear the confusion and then command began to kick in, *"Okay we are missing, Sgt Coult, get back in."* He is not moving but has a pulse and is breathing. Okay someone help him to unclip him. I could feel the blood rushing to my head as I was still upside down. They had me out very fast indeed, job done.

With one last scenario tomorrow before we could put an end to the induction and begin our tour, I was looking forward to the small exercise that had been put together to throw everything at us to see how we reacted. On every Commander's mind is do not embarrass yourself!

After the vehicle simulator was over, we got on the coach and relaxed for the rest of the day. I decided to go for a wonder around Bastion and was surprised to see a coffee house that the American contractors had built right out the back of the hospital. It would put Starbucks to shame.

After a great coffee and good company, I headed back to our facility, the Estonian camp looked rather well built, and mostly by a great carpenter, there was a great seating area and canopy made from wood, very visible from the perimeter fence.

When I arrived back at our location, I had to be quiet as Spud was still sleeping having come off night watch duty. I entered the brew room and began to watch TV, then in walked Spud. He had been woken up by the locally employed contractors known as LECs.

This gave me scope to now go in the room. It was an unwritten rule that we didn't disturb the guys who were sleeping.

That night, Jack came into our room and asked what I was up to? I explained that I was writing in my diary for future reference, he then said, "Can I be in your diary," and took his towel away to reveal that he had shaven all his pubes off, he then said, "this will stick in your mind," and then walked out the room.

What the hell just happened, Jack was a typical Royal Marine, no fear and bold as brass. I had worked with Jack back in Colchester in the training wing and had learnt how he did things on impulse and always lifted the morale of the team.

Well, I spent the remaining of the day watching how the team interacted with the detainees and how they had built up their rapport with them. I was just the new guy and I had a lot to learn with regards to building on what they had already achieved. Could I live up to what they had started? Well only time would tell I still felt uneasy with these detainees.

I would do a decent job, but I didn't have high hopes on how I could make this work. I stood back a bit and watched how some of the team pussy footed about them and put them on a pedestal; it pissed me off. I then found my approach and it was strict.

Maybe this is why Non Infanteers should never do this job. It is sickening to see how we bend over backwards to accommodate their every whim.

The next day, I was in my element with Forward Operation Base (FOB) drills, this was going to be testing but cope able especially as I was with the rear echelon guys and many of them had never left a FOB, with a quick brief on arrival at the mock FOB we were quickly broken into multiples of 12 men in each.

The OC of the package asked for Commanders to step forward and all the guys in the MPS edged me to go forward. With reluctance, I did and got picked as the multiple commanders for my team.

A quick brief from the directing staff, of 'It's just a patrol' not a very good brief at all actually. I moved my guys in and broke then into four-man teams, and then showed them the model and how I wanted them to patrol. I explained my scheme of manoeuvre and my intent, we were callsign 10 and we were leaving the FOB last.

Our scenario was supposed to last for two hours. However, with the call signs that had gone before us taking forever to walk 200 metres it had eaten into our time and now, they had to rush us through it, thus not achieving what the package was designed to do. Eventually, we were given the thumbs up to move out onto the exercise area.

I headed to the OC and asked for a UAV or a Predator to be flown over the patrolling area and asked what grid the other call signs where at as well as wanting to see previous patrol traces to see if we had been setting patterns, he just looked at me stunned.

He stated its just to get you out there, mate, I know you've done this a million times but some of your blokes haven't, well he was right to be fair, so I just carried on the motion he wanted.

We patrolled out from the south and entered the mock village, soon we had identified the village elder and could move him to a safe location and conduct a shura, the meeting was going well when the Taliban had gotten up on a roof and shot one of our guys. At this stage, all the locals ran off and I had to send a 9-liner report back to the FOB and state that I needed the QRF to deploy to cover my multiples extraction with the casualty.

Then with the casualty needing to be extracted back to Bastion I asked for a Heli, and we then began to not only treat the casualty but clear an HLS for the Heli to be brought in.

This was a fantastic exercise, and not just because I was EX-Infantry but because it got me back into the way of thinking that I needed to be in, it was all coming flooding back and I was now back in Helmand.

Chapter 14
Knowing Your Enemy

At the end of our final induction training, there was a after action review designed to show us how to improve on our skills and drills while we were here on our tour, a lot of valid points had been risen and they all had the same answer, "If we can get it to you we will." This was like asking a politician his views on a subject. You were never going to get the answer you were waiting for, but you would find out about the deficit.

We walked back to the UKTHF just talking about what our night's plans would be, and what we would do after the Bastion parade, we had to be marched across to the memorial wall and stood in ranks to say goodbye to yet another soldier who had been killed on operations while out on patrol. It seemed we would spend a lot of time on that same square saying our goodbyes to many a soldier during this tour.

After only an hour watching television, we checked ourselves over and made sure we were clean and tidy before going onto the square.

It was a young Mercian soldier who had been killed, the Commanding Officer got onto the podium and began to say a few words about how the guy had been a rising star and had been snatched from his regiment's family. It seemed this was becoming the normal routine in Bastion. Without sounding like a terrible person, this had now become a place to see old friends who worked in different parts of the base and have a cup of coffee after the last post had been played and the order had been given to fall out.

We all turned to the right and fell out and made our way to the cookhouse for evening meal. I walked with Reders and Mick, two of the guys who knew their job inside out. We enjoyed the view from our table and couldn't believe the amount guys who worked in the rear echelon with Gucci leg holsters and top of the range boots, carrying knives and pistols, these guys thought they actually belonged in the Special Forces, it was hilarious to see.

We grabbed a cup of coffee in our issued flasks and made our way back to the facility, it was beginning to dawn on me that when we were working with the Detainees, which were very evil people all we had to do was walk through a gate and into their compound. We slept right next to them in the place of work, not for our own safety, but to be on call day and night in case they needed a medic or a dentist or even a bottle of water. It was very surprising how much rights these insurgents had been given by our government.

We took about 10 minutes to do the walk from the cookhouse back to our workplace, and as soon as we rang the bell, the door opened and all the guys were running around like chickens, we went to the Ops room only to be asked why we hadn't got our kit on. Well, we had just returned from dinner.

There are eight of you going out on the next flight. You will be met by the Special Forces Commander and you will bring back nine captured insurgents. They have carried out a raid and managed to get their objectives... As there are nine of them and only eight of you. Make sure you bring one of their team back as the arresting soldier, please remember to do it or we are in the shit.

So, I decided that I would take that task on. I would grab a detainee and an SF soldier. *Pretty straight job,* I thought, I gathered all my kit together and checked for the essential things.

I wasn't taking any chances having been left vulnerable in the past I made sure I had enough ammunition and then placed a pistol into my Ops vest. I then grabbed my rifle and joined the guys in the vehicle, and we then made our way to the American camp and waited for the Osprey helicopter to come in and lift us.

Jon had come over from the other facility and was looking rather annoyed, he had not been issued his Osprey yet and so borrowed a set from one of the handlers at his facility. It was one of the funniest things I had seen in years and it's not often this type of thing happens so when it does you take full advantage of the moment.

His Osprey had only been fitted with grenade pouches, there was nothing else on the vest and it looked ridiculous. He kept telling us to stop laughing at him, I walked across and said, "All right, Jon, are you expecting trouble?" He told me to piss off, this was met with even more laughter from the team. Once we climbed out the vehicle there was quite a few eyebrows being raised at our unusual posture amongst all these US Marines. We then received the thumbs up from a Marine that our chopper was about to land. It had only been 17 minutes since we had arrived, the guy came running off the back and broke us into two groups before we embarked.

We took off towards the target area not knowing what to expect. I had an idea that it was going to be well away from the area he had been picked up, especially as it was a secure LZ. For me it was amazing, as for a short period during that flight I felt alive again, a fire had ignited inside of me, and it made me feel great.

The feeling of going into an assault. However, this time though I was only running off and collecting a member of a terrorist group, lots of them so it was going to be one hell of a flight back.

We landed and waited for the tail to drop before running off into our designated arcs. We could see the guys all lined up in two chalks. We approached one at a time and began to strap each of the Taliban members to each seat remembering to leave a gap between each one for one of us to sit there. Then I noticed that the SF guys were all disappearing into the night again. I got back off the chopper and grabbed one of them, he started to complain and try and struggle.

I was determined not to mess up and explained that I had been told that he was to come back as the arresting soldier. He had no option but to get back on the chopper. We all strapped up and flew back to the HLS at the back of the Exploitation building *TORCHLIGHT*.

I knew I had done the right thing. If you detain someone, then you must accompany them back to the facility for the mountains of paperwork that follow on from it. Then you must have your prints eliminated from the enquiry as well as sign to say they have not been assaulted or hurt during the initial capture period. The amount of hoops these guys must jump through was ridiculous, and now they needed to be seen by a doctor to state all of this was correct, and he needed to sign the document to acknowledge it.

As we all left the Heli and holding a Detainee by the thumbs, I noticed there was more than one SF soldier who had come back with us, they were annoyed and looking for our boss.

Then more senior SF guy had a very broad Scottish accent, I could tell his hair was dyed jet black as it didn't suit him. However, I was staying well out of his way. His equipment was small precise, and job suited and enough to start a small war.

The Handling team at *Torchlight* had been expecting us, and the cells were open and ready. We took them in one at a time and not one person spoke during this phase of the operation. We sat them all down facing different points of the room and kept on their blindfolds then closed the door and left them to be exploited.

On our way back to the UKTHF, we were quiet; it was as if someone was waiting to say what they had done, but then laughter drowned out everything else as someone said, *"Jonno, what the hell were you thinking?"*

He started swearing at us again as everyone began to have a go at him, he then started to get called Grenade for a while.

When got back into the television room for a rest, we began to clean our weapons from all the sand and dirt that had been blown onto the weapon during our trip out, it was only then that someone said, *"Has anyone seen the Royal Navy Chief Petty Officer (CPO),"* and I hadn't seen him since before we got onto the Heli; it had in fact turned out that when we landed to collect the detainees. I had dragged a guy back on the Heli and there were no seats left so we had to leave him on the ground with the UKSF teams.

This did not go down well with both parties, but it made a hell of a story for the guy dumped on the target area. This type of thing should never ever happen, but we are all vulnerable to making mistakes and to be honest, he was in great hands.

Well, it was only the start of our tour and we had already made a colossal mistake. I am sure it would be a learning curb. We had made a few calls and discovered he was with the team on the ground and would be back with us the next day.

It was the topic of conversation for the next few days, well as we had now all started to de-bomb our magazines from ammunition as a way of helping the springs to relax, I heard "Ouch…aah." Reders had indeed tried to cut corners by taking the spring out with the rounds of ammunition still compressed and it flew up at speed and hit him square on the eye, funny for all of us, but not so much for his new black eye!

His reaction when we all looked across at him was spectacular also, he just looked down covered his face and said, "Ouch." He was in pain and his eye was completely bloodshot. I did try and conceal my laughter but had to let it out, what a day today had been. We finished de-bombing the magazines.

After a long day and learning from a few mistakes, it had to improve and quickly. Again, another day done and ticked off the calendar in Camp Bastion.

Before going to bed, I decided to go in with the old team and have a good look around the detainee compound. It was freaky especially with all these evil insurgents all staring at me and trying to find out my name, some would just smile while others were trying to work me out. It wouldn't be long before I was searching for them every day and getting to know how they worked.

We had files in the office on every one of the detainees. They could be read by us. The whole team had decided that they didn't want to know why they were being detained in case it swayed their views or the way they treated them would change after reading it but wanted to know each and every one of them as I needed to know for peace of mind.

The next day, I got up early, around 0500hrs as I wanted to be ready to watch Spud carry out his duty handover. This was something that I needed to master for when I took over duties of the facility. However, no handover in the world should ever be started without a hot cup of coffee. So, I grabbed mine and began to watch. It all started with a brief of the night's adventures, had anyone been detained and if so, what detention numbers had been given out. How were the detainees feeling and were there any mood swings amongst them, this all needed to be logged.

I then watched the medics arrive and go into the operation's room to sign in and leave their weapons safe and secure, before they made their way around the detainee compounds, each detainee being called forward by their own individual number. This was etched into a plastic cuff and around each of their wrists as way of identification. It was checked and then they were told to open their mouths before being given medication, this followed with a drink of water and then they had to show us inside their mouths and that they had swallowed it.

I then made sure that the doctor's cabin within the compound was unlocked ready for the cleaner to give it a once over before the doctor arrived with his list of names. A member of our team always stayed with the doctor, and we had three interpreters that lived on site with us who worked 24/7 and for good wages I may add.

Dave the interpreter and I would become very good friends, he would help me with learning the language and writing the numbers in Pashtu and I would do my best to improve his accommodation and his living conditions. I could already see that he was not 100% with these detainees. Some of them snarled at him and he wanted to keep his identity hidden, so he wore a shemagh wrapped around his head with a baseball cap on.

He was worried that if they found out who he was then his family would be in danger, and he would be killed. Shortly after the doctor had been and checked all the detainees for marks and illnesses, it was recorded on our database and in the doctor's notes and we gave them 30 minutes to have a brew before we were going to conduct the ritual of a Talashi. Talashi being search in the Pashtun language, we made sure that it was never done at the same time each day and we mixed it up as not to set a pattern.

We started back after a coffee and a chat about who was doing what job, this would take three members of staff and four handlers. This was not only a show of force towards the detainees but also a safety precaution.

We would get them all to move to one side of the compound and get behind a line we had painted on the floor, as we began to search the toiler area and where they slept including their belongings, which included each of their Koran's.

Then one at a time, we searched each detainee. Some of them messed about while others had the look of hate etched across their faces.

I was beginning to put numbers and names to faces, as the day went on, it was imperative that I was able to know each one of them. This would make life for me easier when it came to appointments and medication timings.

After the search which had taken the best part of an hour, everyone was doing their own thing when I made my way into the operation's room.

I started to fill out the logbook of the mornings events when the boss wanted to know who was responsible for cleaning the rifles at night, because his was covered in dust. I explained that it was the individual's job to clean his own rifle, this did not go down well and I found myself having to walk away again and bite my lip, what a tour this was turning out to be.

I had to remember that I logged that six of the detainees wanted to begin Fasting, and this needed to be implemented before the lunch was collected from the cookhouse, the lunches had all be prepared Halal compliant and that all animals had been blessed before being used as food!

So soon after that Reders and I rounded up the detainees that wanted education the rest we left alone to talk in their compounds. This was another activity that we had thought up to help pass the day and make it more constructive for the detainees. However, on this day, they all wanted to do education and the group was far too big to let them all in one compound together, so we decided to split them into two groups for safety reasons.

This was not accepted by the detainees, and they all started to complain about their treatment by us. They wanted to go back to their own compounds and be left alone. Well, it suited me fine.

We escorted them back to their compound one by one in handcuffs, we left the compound and I finished off being shown a few more parts of the handover/takeover, then I had all the facilities ammunition signed across to me.

His handover was nearly complete, and I had begun to take over most of his tasks, this gave him a little bit of downtime before he had to catch his flight. Reders had spent most of the remaining part of the day showing me the database and how all the logs had to be completed. It was rather straight forward and I just needed more time on the job and to run things the way I wanted; fresh eyes always see new ways of doing a job more efficient.

As soon as everyone had left the operation's room, I went across and began to look at the detainee files. I wanted to know why key detainees had been detained. I read very detailed notes on certain objectives that had been on the Special Forces most wanted list and known as the Watch list, this list had been put together by the Americans and contained the most evil men on the planet, it was shared by the UK however it had a slight twist, basically both nations upload the worlds most wanted men onto a database to be used by coalition forces.

But the Americans control the list and give us what they only want to share with the UK, and we upload everyone we enrol and tell them everything. A slightly one sided 70/30 share.

It was a very weird and uneasy feeling coming face to face with these detainees. They would try and befriend me and some of them spoke perfect English. I wanted to know where they had learnt to speak so well, so I began to sit down outside their compound which resembled a cage with razor wire on top to stop them from climbing out. One of the detainees told me he learnt listening to the prison guards back at Guantanamo Bay prison.

He had spent six years there being interrogated by the Americans and was released without charge. He then travelled to Pakistan and began to fight the US soldiers. He had learnt to hate them after being falsely detained, so basically, we were making the Taliban bigger by detaining innocent people. This was a no-win situation that we had found ourselves in here in Afghanistan.

I decided to not take their word for anything and looked more and more into their background. Some of the guys we had locked up had attended the Royal Military Academy at Sandhurst (RMAS) the most famous officer training establishment in the world. We had trained these insurgents in our very own tactics, it made everything come together. Now I knew that during my previous tours why it was so hard to find enemy casualties and enemy KIA. This was because their own casualty extraction was as good as ours, if not better.

I had to watch what I did or said in front of them, they were still working out how to take me as a person, many of them struggled to understand my thick Irish accent, and I was glad in a way.

They began to try and interact with me by smiling and asking my name, if I was going to be there for the next six months, I needed to give them a way of communicating with me, so I told them I was Sgt Trevor. Now they all were calling me, I had to do it, even known I was burning up inside having to be nice to them, I started to understand why we were both in this position fighting for a cause.

I was in theatre to look after the detainee's welfare, whether I liked it or not, it was my job, and I would do it to the best of my ability. I would build on my rapport towards each of them and then hand over to the next guy.

The next day, I had to go to the Reception, Staging and Onward Movement Integration (RSOI). This is where I watched the detention lesson one more time by Reders. He conducted himself very well and I picked up a few tips that would be relevant in my lesson when I began to teach it. I had now watched two lessons by two different guys. The next time I was here, I would be teaching it to 500 soldiers who were arriving in theatre, and it would be from private soldier up to Brigadier, so it needed to be perfect.

I had to make this lesson interesting and make people sit up and listen. My fellow staff do not ever go on a patrol so why would they listen to my patrolling brief. Well, it was up to me to make them, so I set about putting a new lesson together. I knew it would be met by some of the old and bold as *'who's this smart ass'* so it was going to take a bit of time to tweak it. I began sitting in the brew room and running through my presentation to Reders and Tom. They liked it but it wasn't there way of teaching and Tom had never actually taken a lesson so it was a learning curve for him.

I decided to use my previous tours as the start point of my lesson and explaining why searching was important and that understanding the cultural beliefs needed to be understood, why searching women was frowned upon and that a village elder or local religious mullah needed to be present during the search and how it needed to be carried out away from public eye to give respect to the female. These were all lessons I had learnt from previous tours and I wanted to pass this knowledge onto them.

I had many things that would assist them. How to utilise the attachments and get the best out of the interpreters with regards to treating them well in return for great work and understanding. If they see that you respect them and are clearly respecting their culture they work harder and enjoy working for you.

The soldiers would enjoy my teaching methods, and it would give me that feel good feeling seeing them walk away with a smile having learnt something worthwhile.

His lesson finished and we waited for our transport to pick us up, we were right out the back of the American base Camp Leatherneck, and there was no way that we would be able to walk back before evening meal was over. It was a few miles away and near the perimeter fence.

Good old Dan turned up and drove us back to the UKTHF. We arrived back, and I got cleaned up rather quickly. The OC and the CSM were there waiting to talk to the outgoing team as their tour had come to an end.

They had done a fantastic job here in Bastion and the team working in the UKSF outpost called Varsity had also worked extremely hard. They had overcome a lot of in-house problems and many a service complaint had been filled in. The Hierarchy had cut many corners during their tour and lives had been placed in unnecessary danger because the boss had been either ignorant or lacked experience. Either way, heads were certainly going to roll back in the UK.

Tonight, we decided to hold a Bar-B-Q in our detainee overflow area, which was just across the road from our facility. The OC had finished their operational inserts and was calling on each of them to get them to sign it. However, due to the tension within the team and how the old boss had come to loggerheads with most of the team. He had written bad reports for most of them.

This would surely not be the end of it, many of the team were intending on reporting the senior Officers to the Brigade Commander and the Provost Marshal on their return to the UK.

I was just hoping that at the end of my tour I would have a smile on my face, after seeing my operational insert. Only time would tell.

I knew that I would drop a bollock on operations, the problem is, how big and when I would drop it. I looked at my watch and it was already 1937 hours and the curry dinner that had been organised by one of the guys was now in full swing. All the Military Provost Staff from Bastion 3 and Bastion 1 had attended along with the handlers and the medics.

I got to see old faces and have a laugh before they all went on their final journey home. They shared some tips on how to work with certain detainees and where to go for a rest period when things got on top of you, and it was nice to be allowed this 30-minute downtime.

I made sure I got around most of the team before the night was over; we all had a soft drink and I made sure I had seconds as the curry was fantastic. I was offered a cigarette and I started to smoke again for a bit. I knew things were not great but I had a job to do.

One of the guys had made up awards and had certificates made for the troops leaving theatre, there was Matt who had been awarded the best-groomed member of staff, while Rob was awarded the second strongest male in Varsity 'Varsity being a detainee holding facility.'

One of the female medics received the best distraction award, it made us all laugh and had the medic going bright red through embarrassment. The whole night came to an end with a curry that the chefs had made for us especially, and it was fantastic.

That night, I lay on my bed and turned on my laptop for a chat with my wife and son, I told them how things were and what my routine consisted of of but could not explain to them the layout or who and why we had who we had. There was operational secrecy (OPSEC).

The next day started with Spud giving me and Reders an early call at 0605hrs which didn't make sense, why the extra five minutes? Anyway, I had to get my kit together for teaching the RSOI detainee handling package to all the new arrivals in theatre, I had decided to change things slightly on how it was taught, however still hitting all the headlines that needed covered. It was being taught by guys before me who had no operational experience from the frontline in Afghanistan and did not know how the frontline soldier worked. So, I took it on to use my expertise to revise them on their drills.

Bob offered to drop me off at the ranges ready for me to set up the lesson, it was after a good breakfast and 0715hrs he dropped me off. I could see the groups moving in a gaggle around my teaching area. And wondering who I was and what I was doing. Bob had gotten slightly lost on his way to the ranges which meant it had eaten up my fudge factor time and I was going to have to just start the lesson straight away on arrival.

I jumped out the vehicle and took two minutes to set up then I turned to the audience and said:

"Sir, Ma'am, ladies and gentlemen, welcome to search & detain. I am Sgt Coult MC and it's up to me to remind and revise you all on the training that you should have already received back in the UK."

I can see some of your heads beginning to drop already so let me make myself clear. I already know this subject inside out and it's my job to make sure that after this presentation you all will to, if I catch you sleeping regardless of rank, I will have you leopard crawling to that burn pit just over your right shoulder so sit up and pay attention.

It was right there and then everyone had a bit of laughter and I had softened the mood, just as I had intended.

I used my experience to great effect and had everyone coming up to me at the end telling me it was a good lesson, especially the guys from the intelligence cell. Who thanked me for explaining how vitally important it was to use gloves and gather intelligence as well as look after all captured personnel, because they tend to speak a lot more if looked after. And when you hit them, they will not open during exploitation and we then lose that intelligence that they withhold.

I walked away from the lesson feeling good which means I had achieved something. When you see guys and girls watching your every move and taking notes it means they are enjoying what you are doing, and it gives you even more confidence. And I loved the feeling of passing on information that I had learnt from others.

Some of the lesson content was about to make them sit up and pay attention. I explained that every piece of intelligence they get and send up through the chain was written down and acted upon, so send it, the Special Forces task force go out every night to react to that intelligence and bring back objectives because of it, it made them all realise how important they are to the bigger picture.

This can be as hard a six-month tour as you make it, if you get it right from the start then it can have a positive impact across the battle group, much of the exploitation side of operations begins from the minute you decide to detain someone, from that initial interaction it can produce wonders. If you treat them with respect then they can offload some vital information that the human intelligence (HUMINT) has needed for some time, or if you're a complete twat then they will become stubborn towards you, and they are very well trained in not giving away anything that will have their families targeted.

Well tonight we had to say goodbye to five members of staff who have completed their time on operations and we have now fully taken over the detention facilities, every additional task and all 53 detainees in three different locations. All I must do is again keep myself busy, and the fact that I am phoning home every night and seeing how routine there is, it is making my time so far go by very quickly indeed.

I managed to find the time to ring home, and Luba has been getting very little sleep because Sebastian is teething. He also keeps touching my face on the canvas that we had made so time before I deployed, I suppose it is a two-way thing. If I didn't have to be here, then I would not come on this type of tour, baby-sitting the Taliban was not on my things to do list, if I could get away with it, I would easily shoot every one of these evil scumbags.

Today is 40 days from when I go on Rest and Recuperation (R&R) and I am not counting the days at all. My son will be starting to walk now and once that happens, I reckon life as I know it is over for good. I will have to learn to have eyes on the back of my head.

I have only been in theatre for 10 days and its only now that I am beginning to settle into a routine. The guys are working around the clock and putting in the hours with the detainees so they can learn everything they can. I can already see that we are building on Rapport and the detainees are starting to realise that it is our team that is now in charge, so they either respect us or they only get what they are entitled to and do not get the tea-urns for 10 minutes longer or get to talk to us for that brief extra minute.

I've now had the chance to read up on many of the detainees and see why they are being held here in detention. I have a sick feeling running through me now, knowing what some of them are here for, nearly every one of them have killed ISAF soldiers, the ones that have not, well they called the shots to have British soldiers executed. It now kicks in that we are bending over backwards to accommodate their every whim.

Today we had a delivery of board games that we had bought to entertain the detainees, and the CSM now wants us to teach the English as an education lesson, then we have dental check-ups and medical care, and because of the International Committee of the Red Cross and their fantastic recommendations. We now must let all detainees get a 15-minute *Skype* call to their family. Regardless of what is going on in theatre, so if **Operation MINIMISE** is called, everyone must stop using electronics and communications, i.e., phones and internet. Guess what? We are not allowed to cut the *Skype*, in fact nothing and no one is to interfere with their private calls.

And when **Operation MINIMISE** gets called, the detainees start to cheer, as they know what it means, this has started to upset me inside, but I will not acknowledge to them that it upsets me, I have begun to just smile at their behaviour, but it angers me.

Chapter 15
Controlling the Watch-List

We are now at the stage of running scared as a Nation when it comes to Terrorist or Insurgent activity. The human rights lawyers and public interest lawyers have left us vulnerable as a nation, especially after the Baha Musa investigation which disclosed, he was arrested in Iraq while working as a hotel porter, and while he was in British Custody and being detained by British soldiers. He was beaten so badly by our guys that he died with multiple injuries.

Now it has come to light that the soldiers in question had not been trained properly in looking after Detainees, so that's where the Military Provost Staff come in. They would now take over all detention facilities and conduct training with the troops to ensure that this type of incident would never happen again.

However, as we progressed with the detention on Ops it was as if all soldiers had deleted what they had done wrong and where now pointing the finger at the MPS as if they had caused the death of a detainee while in custody. Again, another exercise that sometimes green troops should not be used to look after Prisoners of War (POW) because one of those guys has probably just had a friend killed by him and the red mist hits everyone at certain times.

We are now starting to get Taliban fighters being detained and claiming to be only 14 or 15 years of age. They know that if they state this, then we will have to record it on our logs and documents and that means by our pathetic law we are not allowed to tactical questioned (TQ) it is as if someone from our side is telling them all our techniques and how we do things, or then again because we are British we put everything on the goggle search engine and you can read about how we carry out our drills.

So they have us over a barrel there, and after spending nearly a year learning how to use our biometrics equipment and getting hits every time you take a DNA swab from an Afghan male's mouth or a fingerprint and Iris scan, you feel elated to know that you have just received a positive result and can arrest and detain someone, but to then explain to them after their tour, having lost three of their guys through IEDs that the guy they caught went to court and was released without charge because the Afghan Authorities do not recognise biometrics in their country.

It is classed as white man's magic, will not go down well with their families. The government has a lot to answer for.

The only way to get a conviction in Afghanistan is to have photographic evidence, so now we must take pictures with the insurgents with all their weaponry to gain a conviction or sit them beside two tonnes of opium and cocaine.

It is very draining on morale to watch these guys walk out the gate having been paid for wrongly detaining them because of a corrupt Afghan Government. It was how we were approaching in our hearts and minds campaign to gain the trust of the local villages and spread good word amongst the different tribes, hopefully ending the attacks onto coalition forces. Who were we trying to kid?

It is an insult to the families who have lost dads, mums, sons, and daughters. How do you explain that we had let the killers go as a good will gesture for that specific village and it would spread the word that the British are okay.

Each day that went by, I would get ready and go into the compound, I would have to explain to every single detainee that I was going to search them and their belongings, as well as each bed space. I would then wait for the Interpreter to translate every word into Pashtu so that they all had no excuses when I approached them.

Now once they have been briefed as part of their conditioning, which is a word we are not allowed to use anymore in the military. They all move and stand behind the yellow line which we have painted inside each the compounds on the concrete floor.

I call them forward one at a time ensuring my hands are covered with gloves and start from the head and make my way down each of them. The prayer hat is removed and I begin to go through the hair with my hands then I break the body into four equal parts, top left and right followed by bottom left and right. We even check the sandals. This will happen over 180 times during the tour.

The search is followed by the two cleaners that arrive on queue after each search, we must lock the detainees into their iso container. For the local cleaners to be safe, especially as they treat everyone who works for ISAF as a traitor to Islam and a target.

At the start, I always watched the cleaners and made sure they carried out their job and did not leave signs of being there or messages. To be honest I was a little paranoid and trusted no one, but after seeing that the Taliban keep their Korans in a urinal and shit in the shower, it made me think what kind of animals these people are.

The smell had begun to make me sick to the stomach. They wash their hands and feet but never seem to shower, and I wonder why they have survived for so long without catching a disease.

I have begun to watch detainee **2592**. He seems to be a proper fanatic and reads the Koran for hours each day rocking backwards and forwards, he has the look of a crazed man, his eyes stir right through me as if he wants a chance to kill me if I let him, not a great detainee to have in your facility, even the other staff are very wary of him.

He stops rocking every few minutes and looks at me with a smile, little does he know that I have read his file and know how evil he really is, he has been linked to the deaths of many ISAF soldiers, and a real die-hard Taliban Commander, so dangerous the Special Forces had him as an Objective in their target packs.

The day has been very eye opening with getting a little closer to the detainees, they think they are earning my trust, but having gotten to know them I am slightly worried of how we have moved into a position of giving everything they ask for, when will we stop.

Each day is completely different from the last and a challenge. They know how easy life is in detention and are always complaining about not having enough food, or wanting extra green tea, and snacks at 0300hrs because they are fasting, and guess what!

You guessed it, we ran around Bastion finding extra tea containers for them, they got everything they ask for.

Today brought a new low to their requests, they have complained that the attack alarm in Bastion is upsetting them during prayers. What the hell do they want us to do about it, tell their friends not to attack during prayer times?

Well, I have been here in theatre for two weeks now and the flag has flown at full mast on three separate occasions, soldiers' loose limbs here every single day, if not British then Danish American, Estonian, Canadian, or Australian.

There are many nations here, but these are the ones that are with us in Bastion Camp, and I have worked with them all at some time in the past on the battlefield.

Every few days, we gather at a battle-group on the square in rows of 20 or 30. The words of comrades who have spent hours perfecting their speeches to give a fitting send off to the fallen is spoken softly we all hear about each of the guys and how they lost their lives trying to make Afghanistan a better place to live in. It now begins to fall on deaf ears as many of us now want to leave this place to them to sort out their own problem.

After the first speech, we then hear the Garrison Sergeant Major (GSM) giving his bit about the battle-group now being even more determined to see the job through, followed by the Commanding Officer of the battalion who lost the comrade, then the Platoon commanders and Platoon sergeant followed by his best friend, all stories are the same, he died doing the job he loved. Then we hear the last post being played, it puts a lump in my throat every time I hear it.

All the Officers and Warrant Officers salute, the gun fires shortly after followed by two minutes silence before we hear the revile, the salutes are sharply cut away, then the GSM says, "For your tomorrow, they gave their today." We all stand to attention as the VIP guests make their way off the parade square followed by a *'FAAALLLL OUT.'*

As I make my way back to the detainee facility, I see that there are four soldiers who have collapsed during the parade and are now getting treated by the medical staff.

Having stood on that square in that heat, I now know why these guys passed out. I was nearly joining them. You feel the sweat dripping down your back and into your eyes. The only thing that stops me from passing out is pride and respect for the guys who have lost their lives. It's a test of strength to walk off that square.

It has now reached the stage that every soldier in the British Army knows someone who has been killed in Afghanistan, such a reason is because how small we are now as an army. The cutbacks have been so severe that it has been felt in every unit, and now no one feels job security anymore within the ranks.

On the way back to my place of work, I cannot help but drift off into a time where chaos and confusion were ripe. A time when I was in the middle of death, my friend Luke had been killed. Then my mind jumps to when Paddy was shot in the neck, Cupples was blown in half, Paul being killed in Musa Quala, the list was endless.

Memories are great to have when they are of beautiful, but when they are filled with traumatic sights and danger. They tend to take over your mental state and scar you for life.

The one memory that has now turned into a nightmare is when I received screaming down my radio. I grab the medic Caylie and we both run to the front of the platoon to find our interpreter with no fingers and nose missing from a blast, then we see my radio Operator Justin. He was a double amputee, and I can see that he is dead. However, Caylie goes at him with everything she has, she spends every giving second trying to revive him but he has lost to much blood and the blast has taken a chuck out of his back. No one would have survived that; the scene is so horrific. I will have this on play in my head until the day I die.

It has now reached a critical stage in my life. I am not getting any younger and this job has taken its toll on me. I still do not really know why we are here thousands of miles away from where our families are, it's a WAR, but no one will admit it. The only ones who have seen the end of this are in the body bags that we keep filling, for every soldier that gets killed in action there are another three or four that are wounded.

The news back in the UK is only mentioning the dead, dare they mention the 5000 soldiers now off work with injuries so horrific that they will never be able to work again. We would have a revolt in the National press, and this is being hidden from the news.

The recruiting offices are beginning to fill up back home, they see us fighting and think it's all on television and it looks exciting. What are these young kids thinking?

Well, another day has just started here in the UKTHF. We start again by counting all the detainees and conducting roll call, followed by checking all the fence line and locks, bolts and wire. We are looking for signs of disturbance and wear and tear, it needs to be 100% or these evil bastards will try and escape into Bastion. There are signs that the razor wire has been broken as the sharp bits are being broken off inside their compound.

This will be picked up during the search, but we must make everyone aware that they now have a sharp instrument and could use it as a weapon.

The handlers have all came in are all busy preparing breakfast for the detainees, they enjoy eating the same foods as us, but will not eat pork. Detainee 2604 is now smiling at me telling me he killed a Lance Corporal in the British Army. This upsets me and I go and check his file only to find out that he had been picked up by a Special Forces assault late one night, he had been a member of the Afghan Army and detainee *2604* then used his knowledge taught there and defected to the Taliban.

It was during a routine joint patrol with our Mentoring teams that he turned and fired his weapon on the team resulting in wounding four soldiers and killing the Lance Corporal. This has me questioning my own professionalism as part of me would love to shoot all the detainees at this facility.

Then the other side of me kicks in and I must remain focussed and in good order. I also have a family to support, and it is the only reason I am here to start with. On looking at the wall of remembrance, I see that it is nearly full of names, all who have been killed here fighting this meaningless war.

Every couple of days, I speak with the GSM and ask why Corporal Mark Wright has not had his George Cross post nominal added to the wall, and he states the same reason, "We are looking into it." Pretty pathetic answer if you ask me. Just add the bloody thing before you send my anxiety levels through the roof. It's only been five years since he gave his life and that means you're a complete prick for not having noticed it before.

I am sure it will now be fixed having been moved to the National Arboretum Memorial.

The detainee handlers have begun to complain to me that the Taliban detainees at nighttime keep saying, "Britannia…Britannia." And then showing the sign that they will cut our throats. This is not to be laughed at as we all know they will give half the chance.

This has been taken rather badly bad one of the RAF detainee handlers and in response he has thrown a bottle of water at the floor, which bounced up and hit the fence in front of the detainee, and in response to that, the detainee threw a hot cup of tea over the handler. Now as us British keep the stiff upper lip in all types of incidents, we had the handler removed from our facility as he has now lost face in front of the detainees. He now works at another facility.

This type of reaction from my boss is not appreciated by the rest of the team, we understand what had to happen, but we need to start looking out for each other, not the other way around.

That night, I get a phone call and an order. I am to get three of the High Value detainees and prepare them for a transfer out of British custody. However, they are not going to the Afghan Authorities. It is the first time I have ever been given such a bizarre order, but I am not allowed to question it, as it has come from the Prime Minister.

It seems these three detainees are on the American watch-list and are amongst the most wanted men in America, and part of the STILTSKIN case I have been ordered to collect all documents that they are in or part of. This includes all medical documentation. Every single trace that they were being held by British is to travel with them. They are very happy because they think they are going to Lashnagar.

If they end up in Lashnagar, they will surely be set free to kill more soldiers, so we cannot afford for this to ever happen.

Little do they know that I am flying them to Bagram Airbase where they will be detained and exploited by men who do not pussy foot about, having checked the flight manifest to confirm timings; it seems that this flight does not exist.

The destination is not spoken about and the two detainees now do not exist. Sometimes this is for the good of mankind that these things tasks take place.

Most things we do at a high level is for the interest of National security, everyone is expendable when they are a threat.

The next day arrives, and I am excited about the prospect of being part of such an operation.

I went straight across to the staff iso container and check that my plate carrier and equipment along with weapons are in good order. Sgt Steve comes with me and is looking forward to this operation just as much as me.

Then we hear CSM shouting out commands. He wants to check that all the paperwork is in good order and that we have everything running smoothly, because of the nature of this Detainee delivery, it has been kept in a very small circle of people this has been classed as a need-to-know operation. I then go into the Ops room and begin to check each file with detail, everything must be signed and in place.

Each file is scrutinised by me and then Steve, we double check everything. The CSM has asked to escort detainee *2164*. He was detained by the Special Forces and is the Brigade Commander of the Taliban in Helmand, a very high-level objective. His beard and hair are jet black and he is very well groomed compared to the other two.

Steve has been tasked with escorting detainee *2163*, he was the Commanding officer of upper Gereshk Valley and was a hard knock capture by the Special

Forces also, and he wants to kill the brigade Commander because he has disclosed information on the CO hoping it would give him a lighter sentence.

Then there is me, I have been entrusted with the safe delivery of detainee *2161* who is part of the Taliban MOD high commission, another great capture by the Special Forces. These are on the American run watch-list and are extremely dangerous men, with hundreds of ISAF deaths on their heads.

I have now placed all our lunches on top of each of our backpacks and the files are safely inside each of our bags, weapons are oiled and prepared and my handling kit is ready.

Steve walks over and hands me a 9mm Sig pistol with magazines. I tell him that his paperwork is in his bag. All three detainees have been separated from the others from early hours in the morning to not get the rest of them to cause an argument or even worse, a riot. We have been briefed by the Intelligence team that *2163* and *2161* are to be kept apart at every possible moment, basically the Taliban high commission member has told our Exploitation teams everything to do with the Commanding Officer and now he wants to kill him.

That's the same story in the UK, the MPs always hang our officers out to dry to save their own skin, so it looks like we do things the same way, and corruption comes in many ways and forms.

We place the rigid cuffs on all three detainees. The blindfolds have been applied as well as the body armour and helmet. We cannot afford these guys to be injured they know too much intelligence. I also know that my career is certainly on the line. The bus arrives outside our place of work and we walk them all onto the awaiting bus. A United States Marine Corps Major is sitting on the bus with dark shades on, he says morning and watches all three of the detainees to ensure they are completing this journey.

After a quick check, we drive towards the flight line, there sitting on the runway is a prepared C130 Hercules transporter with its back ramp down and the pilots sitting there waiting for us. No one in Camp Bastion has got a clue that the guys who have been calling all the shots in theatre are now in custody. If only it would all stop, we could all go home, but someone else has been ordered to take over Taliban operations.

On arrival at the aircraft, the flight team get into their position. We walk them off the bus and onto the aircraft, it looks like we are the only ones flying today, but then again, this flight does not exist. I made sure that I placed my detainee on one side of the aircraft and he is not facing the other two. I then strapped him in securely. The other two do the same and as soon as we are in the air, I remove his blindfold and give him food to eat.

I give Steve the thumbs up when he is finished and then replace the blindfold. The same happens to the other two detainees. The flight was carried out in silence, this was all very new to me. I knew our government carried out behind closed door deals. I personally thought this trip was a little too far. We had already exploited these guys, so why would another nation want them, unless this was a joint Special Forces Operation.

Then I remember, regardless of who is on the most wanted list. The American control the WATCH-LIST and we comply with the White House. They can have intelligence sent to the pentagon and be back with them within the hour, however we must wait a few days to get our intelligence back from the UK, and it begs a question. Do they find out our intelligence before we find out?

We will soon be landing in Bagram camp, and its prison is very well known for its hard regime and how they are hard on the detainees, this is probably hell on earth for any terrorist network on insurgents.

Then again, these guys are responsible for the deaths of hundreds of ISAF soldiers.

Well, I'm sure that that the Americans have a great team awaiting their arrival and whatever information these guys have will be exploited/extracted from them.

After one hour and forty minutes we finally land in Bagram, the ramp goes down and I see lines and lines of Blackhawks, in the distance there are two CH27 helicopters coming into land, this place is awash with war planes and US Marines, I cannot help but notice the American fighter jets and so I try and count them, I give up at 67.

After waiting for seven minutes on the aircraft with these three high profile detainees a bus pulls up with yet again more US Marines, three Marines come over and try to take the detainees away from us. However, they belong to us until they have been officially signed for so we refuse to hand them over, so we all get on the bus and begin to move around the airfield. It is bigger than Stansted airport. The road begins to turn into a dusty track as we leave the airport.

Then I see the signs everywhere, *MINEFIELD*. We are driving through a minefield, and it is a scary feeling, but after everything I have been through to date, I just laughed it off, what else could possibly go wrong in my time in Afghanistan.

After driving through what seemed like numerous minefields, 20 minutes later we arrived at the gates of Bagram Prison?

The bus came to a stop and we all got up and left the bus. We were taken to a wooden shed and placed are weapons and ammunition in there. We then systematically were searched by the soldiers from the US Army. I didn't feel like I had properly been searched as I had metal objects still on me, but the sentry post looked very well equipped.

The whole facility looked like a reinforced the perimeter walls were over 6ft thick and every door had keypads and codes. Once inside this vast secure facility, the detainees were taken to three separate rooms and were all strip searched, all belongings where then put into a pipe and sent straight to the incinerator, their papers had now been signed and they belonged to the Americans.

I decided to watch how they carried out their duties with regards to processing them, so I went back towards where I had left my detainee and found him wearing a facemask and his hands are now cuffed behind his back. A US Marine went to ask me a question about the detainee and all I could bring myself to say, was, "Look, mate, he is not my problem anymore, he is yours."

I then got a reply of laughter followed by, "You're right there, sir, he sure is."

Seconds later, all three detainees were put into red boiler suits. We said our goodbyes to the Marines and left the facility. We collected our weapons and got back on the bus. All three of us were a little quiet. Did we just witness that, wow we really are weak in the British Army, why did we bend over backwards for these evil bastards.

Before we headed for the flight-line, we stopped for a few photographs, we meet up with a Staff Sergeant Hubei, USMC, he stood at over 6ft tall and light blonde hair and he hated everything, every second word he spoke was fuck this and fuck that.

On arrival back at the C130 and were told to make our way to the cockpit, the pilots explained that because we were the only people flying back that we could remain in the cockpit and see Bastion from a place that not many get to see. The view was fantastic, and I soon fell asleep in the seat. I only awoke when Steve tried to creep past me to get a better view, we spent a few more minutes there then went back down the stairs to the main holding area.

As we made our way through the aircraft, we could see that everyone else, i.e., the other two guys were fast asleep sprawled across the seats. After a quick drink, I decided to get a kip before we landed to what might be a chaotic day at the UKTHF.

On arrival back at our detention facility, the OC was in a very good mood. He had been told the transfer of detainees had in fact been a smooth transition, and only now he could relax knowing they had gone. The other detainees were still in shock knowing that the so-called big commanders had been removed from the facility.

Just as things were running smoothly in theatre, word had been received that one of the sergeants from the previous tour had made numerous allegations that his fellow peers were incompetent and cut corners on operations and that he was concerned as a member of staff, talk about having big bollocks. It made me laugh for days, as he was a member of the Royal Military Police (RMP) and now he was MPS, not exactly good drills when you are looking to get promoted.

This didn't really phase me, until allegations that a SNCO had made a safety mistake on one of my ranges. That SNCO was in fact me. I remembered the incident in question. And it had in fact been an error in drill and the shot had been fired after instructions had been given.

And only a trained skill-at-arms instructor would be able to identify it. The member of staff who made the complaint was clutching at straws to help build his case and what he lacked at judgement he made up with his charm towards senior staff members, and after making such allegations as a member of staff he would forever be on his toes.

Reders will be returning this weekend so I am sure he will have a few stories to tell everyone from his escapes during his R & R. Hopefully, he will have sorted out his life for once and is finally on the right track. It annoys me to see good guys going through bad times especially when you are stuck in Afghanistan for six months; it plays on your mind every day.

My wife is at home raising our son and I am sure it is difficult, so I make sure I phone home at every chance I get and find out how her day was and what they had been up to. It takes you away from the pressures of work and for that entire phone call you can be anywhere in the world.

It made me laugh when she explained that he was already answering back and then hiding in the kitchen, typical chip off the old block. The parcels were now coming thick and fast from my parents and Luba and were very well received. The one thing I loved but could not ask for it was chocolate, and that was because if they send you chocolate, it melts all over the remainder of the contents in the parcel and is a real pain in the ass to get out.

Inside the Christmas parcel was a Christmas card with my Sebastian's picture on it with him wearing a Santa Claus costume with his hands in the air. It is small things like that, and that can really make the difference to a shirt day at work. I put it on my wall with the other 12 pictures of my family. I have a shrine now to my family and it's great to look at before I go to sleep each night.

I am now looking forward to R&R and its only 22 days before I go home for a well-earned break from these detainees. His first birthday will be very special indeed, and we have arranged for family to pop across and spend it with us, Luba has put a lot of time and effort into making it very special.

I notice that the mood here in our facility has taken a slight dive, my boss Geordie has started to detest the ICRC because of their constant demands and interfering it looks like they are not as transparent as they let on. They are supposed to be squeaky clean but it is obvious to a blind man that they favour the Taliban every time.

They now want us to provide maps to the Taliban and teach them where countries are in the world, what the hell are they thinking, so here is the UK and here is Afghanistan and this is how you get there. No wonder many countries despise them.

Now Tom keeps making trivial mistakes because he has personal issues, and the boss has started to micro-manage everyone. I have been in the Army for 17 years and this is the one thing I didn't even due to my troops back at 1 Royal Irish. This will make me snap and who would blame me.

Just as I am beginning to find some head way, I get told by the clerk that my R&R has been messed up by the RAF? This does not make sense as they have me coming back on the morning of my son's birthday. This is strange as it can be the flights that they change and not my R&R slot, let's see how this unfolds.

After some negotiations I manage to get new kit and equipment for the guys I am working with, Dan gets his new boots and three of the guys receive new Gore-Tex jackets and trousers along with softie jackets. The temperature has dropped dramatically at night and the guys need this stuff. They arrived in theatre from the Royal Navy with very little gear as they were told they would be issued the kit in Camp Bastion, and we all know that this is not the case.

Well today is 4 December and I will be replacing Tom on night duty. Basically, I am the night duty sergeant, it's my job to keep everything running smoothly and check periodically on the detainees and listen into the net for the end state of the SF night movements, if someone is captured then they get in touch with me for that one off unique detention number. I have to record all captures in the logbook.

Well, I listen to the guys, sign the book, and begin my night-watch. I seem to have mastered it and can only become more sufficient with getting my routine faster, having mastered it in one night it becomes very apparent that an idiot would be able to do this job, it's not rocket science. And it makes me appreciate that I earned my HERRICK medal the hard way.

Looking in the mirror would be very hard for me if I had never been on the front line. I see pride when I look in the mirror as I know it was earned through sacrifice and hardship, even now I work with detainees in the rear echelon in camp Bastion, I find it hard to say I earned it. Some of the guys who never leave camp should be blessed that they didn't get to see the terror of the front line to.

There should be separate clasps every tour, especially as our guys are being blown up, wounded, and killed nearly every day, I watch the J-CHAT and incidents occurring every hour without fail whether its IEDs small arms of a find is the topic of most outposts or FOBs.

Everyone now just wants to have a quiet Christmas. However, we know the Taliban have other ideas. They do not celebrate Christmas in Afghanistan and will be very determined to upset our plans. I just hope we can get through it will very little casualties.

Chapter 16
Staying Impartial

Well again, I find myself sitting in the operation's room watching the clock tick by. I have already carried out four checks on the detainees and made sure the compound is 100% secure and they have what they need. And that they do not die on me throughout the night, which would be a disaster and we wouldn't get to see them suffer the rest of their lives in jail, death is an easier way out for these people.

I have noticed that some of the detainees have begun to roll up their socks and make footballs out of them, they are very resourceful, and they keep kicking them into the razor wire then complain that we need to get it for them. This is okay for a few times but constantly throughout the day has become a pain in the ass, so I put a stop to their football by confiscating it.

It caused a bit of a reaction as they all began to spit at me and give me hand signs of a knife cutting my throat. Now this is very alarming especially as I must spend every giving minute with them, but I have already decided that if it's my turn to go I am at least taking some of these bastards with me.

Well as night duty comes every three weeks, it also comes with a downside and that is that I cannot phone home not just because I am on duty, but because **OP MINIMISE** has been called again. It seems that there has been quite a big engagement with enemy forces just south of Sangin DC. Having looked at the J-CHAT, it seems that the Rifles Battalion have been involved in several attacks throughout Helmand and the casualties have been mounting up. 4x CAT A Casualties which is serious. These are on the verge of living or dying, only quick extraction and vital timings mean the difference.

The USMC have also reported to have striking an IED and a British Armoured Husky vehicle has been destroyed also by an IED, 2x Afghan males have been killed and we have detained 3x Insurgents with PKM assault rifles.

This is just a typical day in Helmand, but a far cry from previous tours in this shit hole, and I am glad those type of combat tours are well behind me. It's a young man's game running around getting shot at and most of all, enjoying it.

Well, Reders is back from his R&R now. And he seems to be in good spirits, this could be the turning point for him. He came on this tour to get away from work. He clearly missed his time in his old regiment and needed to get back to soldiering. He seems to rise above all the petty chit chat of the mess and come good at the right times. He is a very intelligent bloke. I could see him making great changes for the better.

Having said that I find myself questioning what it takes to make a great Warrant Officer, as back in 16 Brigade, the guys have a bit about them, and from my previous career, they were all respected having got it the hard way, here in the MPS they lack flair and professionalism in spades.

The last four Warrant Officers to deploy on operations have all have complaints made against them for not knowing their job specification, which is slightly alarming from a military perspective and embarrassing from theirs.

Having come from an Infantry background, I have been taught by my previous platoon sergeant and CSM the way to lead men and how to get the best from them yet still maintain discipline. It's all about respect and giving them the space to make their own decisions. When it goes wrong, you then step in and show them the right way unless it is dangerous then you lead the way.

Well after another long day here at the UKTHF, it is now 0455hours which makes it midnight in the UK, with only two hours to go before I can get to bed it begins to drag in. All the detainees are sleeping. I have decided not to open their iso containers to count them. This is another thing I am supposed to do as part of my duty. However, one guy and two handlers opening a container with 12 evil bastards is a pretty stupid rule to have to stick to, and I think I would rather be charged than killed.

Well, the handover is imminent, and I have everything ready for the handover takeover. The detention book and on-screen logbook is both up to date and now I am fully awake again. I handed everything across to Steve, had a quick wash and climbed into bed. Within only a few minutes, I had fallen asleep thinking about my R&R.

After only a short rest of three hours, I am ready to tackle the day again. Maybe it's excitement or am plain crazy it is yet to be decided, or maybe it's the dozen or so cups of coffee I have drank throughout the night, and the bright ideas that I am having about improving the Ops room.

It seems that every time people pass through here on tour, they have added something to make it easier for the next team that is coming out, so it is our turn to add to the infrastructure.

I have just sorted out the key press and moved it to another wall where it is more secure and away from the door entrance, and the detainee board which has been put together in black and white has changed to colour pictures.

There are a few jobs that I need to get on with at night, but with no laminating sheets I cannot finish my board, so it will have to go on the back burner for now. Nights are great and I seem to get a lot done, this is why the CSM keeps giving me tasks that he wants me to do each night and they only last about 30 minutes each, so with my checks and jobs, it still leaves me with a few hours to kill. I have now discovered that you can use the internet while on nights, it works from the computer that I use to log the detainees in. This means I do not have to go to the internet facility anymore, and another way to keep us completely locked in this facility and only need to leave now for food.

This is also a way of catching up on idle gossip and seeing new pictures of my son and wife that they have uploaded, it's always good to know what is happening in the world, and with two weeks left here before I actually go on leave it is going to be epic. It will be our first Christmas together as a family so I am determined to make it very special.

The atmosphere here at the UKTHF has become depressive because the CSM is constantly at loggerheads with the boss of the facility. It is having a negative effect on the rest of the team and making socialising very awkward indeed.

I have now had the chance to speak to Tom about his failings and he brushes it off with jokes about life and then calls me mate. This is supposed to be a cream of the crop of the MPS…what next?

After the CSM has briefed us that he does not want us drinking or eating in the Ops room, which is right beside where we sleep, he then asks for a cup of coffee to be made for him, and guess where he is? You guessed it, in the Ops room.

I am having to learn a whole new way to deal with issues in the world of rear echelon.

There is more than one war going on in Helmand, the one that's the guys and girls are fighting on the front line and the one inside the wire, with dress regulations and bullshit. Each day the dress list gets bigger, my own CSM has joined in on the game and sideburns are his pet hate, Jesus Christ, I understand dress policy…

This all becomes trivial when **OP MINIMISE** comes on again and the J-CHAT is showing there has been a few double amputees from the battlefield, this brings it home that this is real and why are we being so petty at our place of work.

My eyes remain firmly glued to every message that comes across the J-CHAT. It is very depressing; each message displays that we have had an incident and taken casualties. I go off for a quiet cup of coffee to reflect on the day. I wonder how the guys are in his team and did they get the chance to give payback to the Taliban. It's always bittersweet when you get to take some of these bastards with you.

It's times like this I think back to the great soldiers I had working with me on my previous tours and were injured or killed. I also had unfinished business with these evil men.

I can feel rage building up. I have never been so annoyed in my life; I also know that it is disgusting behaviour from myself towards a CSM. This type of attitude I have developed would never be tolerated back in my old unit. Then again, the Warrant Officers back there have all earned it the hard way and are great guys. They have tactical knowledge in spades and I would never question them.

I can only do what I believe to be morally right, as I was told by Frankie, Spencey and Jon, *"Always have integrity even if it is not what others want to hear."* I have since kept that as part of my trait and it always sets me aside from others.

Well today was different. After breakfast in the main cookhouse, my CSM overheard a Para CSM tell a young tom to get rid of his hero sleeves, and he has brought that great quote back to our place of work, because now he is walking around telling everyone to get rid of the hero sleeves, what next? This type of jargon does not go down well with me especially from a person who has never fired his weapon outside of a range.

I just stared at him thinking, *go on say that to be your pompous prick.* Because of the way the tour has started and carried on. I am very much on guard with everything he says now, today Craig is at loggerheads again with him and is getting frustrated with his micro-management approach towards all the Senior

177

NCOs. It has gotten so bad the Territorial Army OC that we have has now got involved in the ruckus.

'Captain Ideas' was in the army and left after 22 years, and like many of them in the MPS they join the TA and hey presto. They are now back to finish something off as an officer. This guy sounded like the real deal until he brought a plan to the table and every time it fell apart.

It has now reached critical point where we are not enjoying being here each day. The atmosphere is at boiling point, and the detainees can sense that something is not right with our team, this should be a relaxed working environment but it's very stressful, and I need to walk away for a brew outside of our place of work. Having spoken with Steve, Reders and Sgt D, we have all conclude that the CSM needs to be told, and the OC informed of how we all feel working here.

Having had a chat with the OC, he is slightly worried about the situation and has stated he will speak to both parties and have them compromise over issues.

It seems to have done the trick (for now) and the atmosphere has picked up, again it is a breath of fresh air, there is more spring in the handlers step and smiles have begun to materialise at long last, even the detainees are happy.

I have started to spend more time with the detainees and listen into why they joined the Taliban, *2604* just smiles and tells me that we should not be here in his country and that we will be beaten by the Taliban, his English is not great, but he knows enough to communicate with me.

The lift in spirits and morale is not for everyone though, as a detainee handler who started off her tour in Kandahar has now been sent to work with us. It seems that Lisa has been having a relationship with more than one person, and that a young Officer from the Navy has been having an affair with her. This has a negative effect on the team, one she has compromised the team and two, why could it have not affected my working regime.

The Officer has now been flown to Bastion for an internal investigation, when she arrived from Kandahar, Reders and I were sent to collect her.

Doesn't anyone have standards anymore, some of the guys believe what happens on tour stays on tour. Well not this callsign. I believe that what happens on tour will affect you for years to come. And I have a head full of shit to prove it.

These memories are the only thing that cannot be taken away from me, and over the last five or six years my wife has given me good memories, having travelled together to Tunisia, Thailand, Nice, Rome, Malta and many other beautiful locations. My mind is beginning to drown out the old with new fantastic memories.

Our house looks as if the occupants have nothing to do with the military, my memories are all in the spare room and mostly boxed away, my uniforms have been packed away with only one set in the wardrobe for work, and the rest is placed in a box.

During our first overseas holiday, I awoke having a nightmare and was naked in the corridor saying, *"We have to save them."* So many triggers that can send me over the edge now. I find myself struggling to keep in control of my own life. It is my wife and son that stop me from cracking up.

I am looking forward to him turning one this January and taking him to football and doing all the things that my father did with me. I had a fantastic childhood and just hope I can be half as good a dad as my dad was to me.

I was always being pushed to achieve and reach great heights, he took me all over Ireland and N. Ireland and after a few years doing Judo, I was crowned as the All-Ireland Judo Champion with countless wins in my category.

I got bored after a while with Judo and changer sports to take up running, and after a few years in the sport, I was beginning to make a name and was soon known in my age group as a decent runner. I ran in the N. Ireland fell running championship and came first which in turn gave me the captaincy of the team and I competed for my Country in Grasmere where I beat the whole of the Irish team and was ranked 7th in Great Britain. I tried to keep this up during my career in the Military and prided myself with the basic fitness tests. It was only after 'Derek McG' left the military that I came 1st for about eight years without a decent challenger to compete against me.

With such a competitive background, I will ensure that my son has tasted defeat before he starts off on a journey of success. It's only those who have truly understood losing that can make them into a true winner.

I am hoping he does not follow my footsteps into the Military and he gets a great education, this will set him onto a bright path and help with his choices of a career, I secretly hope he becomes a pilot and can then look after his parents (or am I wishful thinking).

Well, it's not long now until Christmas day and I can see that the spirits of the team have risen, many of the guys are receiving gifts through the mail and are making their bedspace and chill out areas very Christmassy with tinsel and decorations. Then at work, we hide it from the detainees, as they do not celebrate it, so things like Christmas hats can be worn everywhere except were we work, as we wouldn't want to offend them.

I am looking forward to Christmas, as I will be spending it with my wife and son. It will be our first Christmas together and I am excited about it.

Today is a typical day here in the UKTHF, Talashi carried out on each of the five compounds, each with the capacity to hold 12 detainees, and we are pushing towards capacity because we have a juvenile taking up a compound by himself.

Task Force 196 have just brought us six more detainees from their nighttime excursions, Reders is taking the RSOI lessons today which frees me up to help with the inductions of the new detainees. Tom has begun to sulk again because he is not allowed to teach RSOI, will the truth be he is more than capable to do it, but he has not got a teaching qualification. This I am sure he will get as soon as he gets back to the UK.

Having said that today he made several mistakes resulting in everyone at some stage of the day having a go at him, then he accused every one-off picking on him. If he was to take this job seriously, he would give none of us an excuse to shout at him, he is still to step up to the plate, and when he is ready, I think I will have retired by then.

Reders is a guy to watch in the future once this mishap has died away. I can see him catapulting forward, and he will remember all those who stepped on him over the last few months. They will be in for a shock. Reders is an intelligent guy and thinks before doing when he isn't drinking obviously.

His annual report was the worst I had seen in a few years, and all because his actions in the mess, rather than his work ethic, which should be wrong to report on, but hey it's the MPS.

He had worked very hard and was not given the credit he had deserved, this was not what I needed to hear from Reders, especially after the head to heads I have been having with the Hierarchy this weather, and I am already on a knife edge.

Looking at this from another point of view, at least he received a Mid-year appraisal (MPAR) whereas my OC had forgotten to write me one. I think this was down to the fact that he was preparing to leave the military and had a few things on his mind and writing reports were not one of them, if promotion was going to be on the cards all I had to do was provide a good operational report and put it to the board.

I already knew I was proactive and had been knocking out the courses required for promotion, but I lacked that side of compassion towards others, I called a spade a spade and the hierarchy didn't like me for it, I had already had my cards marked by the CSM. I knew the Careers officer very well and asked him if he knew anything about the seeding/ranking and he told me that he had seen and heard I was number 5 in the Corp.

This was a surprise, and I knew if I carried out my tour well and added more stuff to my portfolio, it would be a great asset for the board to look at.

The news had put me in a good frame of mind, and I began to have a fresh approach to the tour and new zest for the job, thinking that rewards waited for me at the end.

The rest of the day was rather fast and furious, the Prime minister and Prince Edward had arrived in Bastion, this ruined the whole day as *OP MINIMISE* had been enforced so that no one in theatre could tell anyone back home, and a media blackout was now in full swing to enable the visit to be safe and quiet. Not a single person was able to talk with their families and all flights in and out of Bastion had been cancelled until they had left theatre, the only flights out was resupply and casualties.

Air support was still readily available for the odd Troops in contact (TIC) or for the threat of an aircraft being shot down which was now a high threat, the Taliban had been overheard on the ICOM scanner that it was one of their priorities, and now we had to play it safe when moving around the battlefield, and thanks to everyone knowing this the only flight up would be his so it would be easy to presume that if you hit a chopper you were hitting the PM.

This had a negative effect on all troops in theatre because now there was a three day backlog of flights to the UK, so guys waiting to go on R&R to see their family had now missed out on a few days leave, though guys already on leave had a few extra days, so not everyone was a loser on that front.

I am sure it will all be rectified before I leave on 24 December, tomorrow Gary will be arriving at my stand for day two of his induction package, so I am sure he will be keeping a keen eye on my lesson. I will give him up to date teaching practices on detainees handling and in return, I hope to find out about the promotion board, that's if he knows anything. Most of the time, he is not allowed to tell anyone but our Gary loves to have one up on most of us, and I always try and bribe him with a brew or some food.

I am sure there will be loads of gossip that I can catch up on, especially as one of our bosses is being suspended for making dangerous decisions as the CSM from the HERRICK 14 tour. There was an investigation on going and over 10 members of staff are involved. The allegations involved every member of the team.

Well, another day begins and it's getting closer to Christmas and more importantly my R&R, so the excitement was already beginning to mount.

It's the 20 December and Reders has woken me up at 0730 hours and its bloody cold. The temperature in the room has dropped throughout the night and my face feels the breeze. It certainly is time to deploy the softie jacket.

After getting ready and walking out of the accommodation, I could see that everyone was wearing softie jackets and gloves, where the hell did the warm weather go, it was as if the ice-age had just come back over night. The detainees were shouting that they wanted more blankets and protesting for more green tea. As good boys, we are we were told to go and accommodate their every whim.

More politics, we had to be seen as world leaders on detention especially as we always had the previous mistakes shoved down our throats at every given opportunity. Well, it looked like the winter was well on its way now and I could see with my own eyes how my hands were beginning to crack and they were sore. I started to rub E45 cream into them to help with the easing process and especially as I had to drive the gator to the lessons. It was about 20 minutes' drive to the RSOI location, so I needed my goggles and helmet at the ready also.

After the drive, I couldn't feel my lips or face. I was numb, so I grabbed a brew and the student's location, everyone was huddled around there trying to keep warm, some of them were jumping up and down, you could spot the rear echelon soldiers through the midst of infantry. They wore yellow scarfs and had red jackets below their issued combat jacket, and it stood out amongst everything else, like a big arrow pointing at them with a caption bubble '*ITS MY FIRST TOUR.*'

I started to set my lesson up and Gary came across to shake my hand. He was excited about getting away from camp duties and trivial rubbish, he tells me with a smile that I have been graded number 3 out of all the sergeants, and that puts a smile back on my frozen face, but I am sure it would be knocked off as soon as I get back to the UK.

Well, it's two days before I am officially on my R&R and there is no way this smile is coming off my face now. I start to pack my kit and prepare myself for home. It seems weird as so far, I have not been stressed that much and for the first time on 10 operational tours, the stress is coming from a CSM who never leaves camp; it does bother me how much of pain in the backside he is.

Man, management is lacking on this tour in a big way. I know once I get home from this 5-star accommodation I will be able to relax even more. I am sure my wife will notice the difference in me from previous tours. I think I have gained a few pounds from all the great cookhouse food. Yet when I was back at MCTC and watching the staff return from HERRICK it now seems daft that a few of them complained of having stress related issues from theatre. Now it is laughable having seen this place as a holiday camp.

Word comes in from across at the Intelligence Exploitation Force (IEF) that the clerk needs to talk to me and its urgent, so I make myself look respectable and go across. Apparently, the CSM has been trying to get Tom back in the UK to complete a dog handlers' course, which is what his next career step is going to be back at MCTC.

To enable this to happen, he has changed my flights to get me back in theatre for 3 January, this would mean me travelling back on 2 January and that is my son's birthday. What was he thinking, he didn't even have the bollocks to talk to me first. Well, I was not letting this go without confronting him.

I confronted the CSM and he denied that he knew of it and it must have been a mistake. I explained that they said that CSM had spoken with them and that you told them to change my flights, in fact there is an email on our screen from you to them, he went red and walked off to his room. If he would just join in and take ownership of his mistakes and talk to everyone like he is enjoying being with us. It might help him to relax while here on tour, yet instead he continues to cause friction and a bad working atmosphere across all three high profile detention facilities.

It was time to go on R&R and the bus was waiting outside the THF, we climbed on board and were driven the short distance of about 800 metres to the makeshift terminal at the top of the road. There the biggest queue of soldiers awaited my arrival. It looked like I was not the only one who couldn't wait to get the hell out of here.

The flight was delayed by two hours and so it was another waiting game. Many checks must be carried out before we get on board. Then we have the RAF who like to upset guys who have nearly been killed fighting, by taking away the

200 extra cigarettes they have bought cheaply, as if they were going to hurt anyone. No wonder they were not very liked by the rest of the Army.

The girl with the Movements sign stood on a chair and announced that we would begin to move through the terminal in rank order. Well, it was now I was glad to be a Senior NCO. I could spot the guys who thought they were ally by their hero sleeves and long hair. Some of them wanting to look as if they were Special Forces.

We boarded the flight and waited for about 30 minutes before we began to taxi around the runway, all lights had been turned off and we were then forced back into our seats by the g-force from the take-off. It was a direct climb into the sky to avoid Missile strike and small arms attack, and we were glad it was a precaution as it's not exactly the moment you want something to happen.

Soon we were in the air and Cyprus bound. This was another failure that the MOD had not planned for. How the hell could a guy go straight out of a combat zone and on to R&R without seeking help from traumatic events that he had encountered from the frontline in Helmand. Yet at the end of a six-month tour, they must complete decompression in case they are suffering from a mental health issue. Many soldiers go without being diagnosed with Post Traumatic Stress Disorder (PTSD) because of these failures.

A short stop at RAF Akrotiri while we refuelled and then it was straight to Brize Norton, where I had a driver waiting to collect me. It was quite a drive back to Colchester finding out about how the place at MCTC had been running and who had done what, not to mention which Ex-RMP had been promoted to keep the police side of things within the unit alive and kicking.

It was an interesting conversation and Alan was always one with his ear to the ground, so not much got past him at work.

The next few days were fantastic, getting to see my boy learning how to walk and spending some quality time with my wife. I explained to her how the CSM had tried to screw me over and she wasn't impressed. I was struggling with the transition from front line soldier to rear echelon and this guy was going to be the reason that I exploded. It was only my wife and son that were keeping me from ripping his head off.

After a fantastic 1st birthday at adventure land and a few more quality days with my family. It was time to get ready and head back to Afghanistan. In the back of my mind, I was never away. My night's sleep was always filled with dreams and faces of many of the Detainees, especially the faces of those who had committed serious offences.

Chapter 17
Groundhog Day

After what felt like only a few days being home, it was time to prepare for the return flight. I packed a load of goodies and along with clean fresh smelling uniform and made my way to the front gate of MCTC, where I was met by big Jim. He was a gentle giant who did everything by the book and I had the privilege of handing over the PRI account to him before I deployed in theatre, and he went through every detail of it. It was between us that we fought tooth and nail to get the regimental admin officer (RAO) and the quarter master (QM) to take missing equipment and written off equipment, off the list.

Jim had a few enemies at work because of his diligence. He would never let anyone bend or break rules and this used to upset staff that were trying to take shortcuts. Even when I wanted to do take the odd meal from the detainee cookhouse, it was frowned upon by big Jim. However, we all knew that with big Jim about, things ran a lot more smoothly.

On the way back, he was telling me how his contract was coming to an end, and he had a few ideas that he wanted to pursue. One being deep sea diving that he was a very good at and had been on several overseas expeditions leading them from the front. It was quite a journey back to the RAF base and we had talked the whole time. He dropped me off at the passenger terminal, shook my hand and just drove off into the night.

Once inside, I could see that nearly every seat was taken by troops returning to Bastion. Many of them were sleeping and taking up two or three chairs. I found a space and settled down for the long wait I had before we were boarded.

After sitting in the lounge for almost three hours, they decided to bring out tea and coffee which was welcomed by everyone in the terminal, followed by a lunch bag, and another announcement by the staff. *"The flight has been delayed until 0200hrs, we will provide vouchers for your evening meal."* This was a kick in the teeth. Well, I suppose it's better safe than sorry, and I am glad they are diligent with all these checks.

After a short delay and good food, I was on my way back to Bastion. For the last part of this tour, I was looking forward to getting back with the guys. However, I knew that the CSM would dampen my spirits as soon as he spoke. He had a way with words that could turn a great day into a complete miserable one.

We landed in Bastion safely and then walked from the plane to the Passenger handling facility (PHF), I could see that the guys were busy, as transport was not there yet. I gave the Ops room a quick ring and was told to wait out for the vehicle.

Shortly after it turned up, a detainee handler arrived with a big smile on his face as he was a young lad from the Royal Navy and a slight hot head but a great worker with funny sense of humour and he was pleased to see a fresh face.

He drove me straight to the UKTHF, and explained that he was on nights and it was rather boring it was 0210 hours and after being on the go for over 24 hours, I was completely shattered however, I always try and complete my day's jobs before I go to bed and that meant at least trying to unpack and put things away. This would save me messing about in the morning. I must have lasted about 20 minutes before I began to fall asleep, so I called it a night and crashed on my bunk.

It wasn't long before I fell back into routine and Groundhog Day had started to take effect immediately. I was told that Tom had now made his way back to the UK in good time to attend his dog handlers course, which means he only lasted three months of a six months tour, excuse me for being cynical but who the hell gives up a six-month operational tour in Afghanistan to do a dog handlers course for MCTC. It's not as if he is Dave Heyhoe and Treo DM attending an Arms Explosive Search course.

I have also noticed that *UKAP002604AFCM* has been removed from the facility. I begin to enquire of his whereabouts and find out something disturbing. The news I hear would upset families of soldiers killed in action (KIA) for years to come.

I have discovered that I very high up person in our UK Government has given the thumbs up for a convicted Taliban insurgent who has been biometrically linked to killing a British army officer, and whose DNA and prints were found on the IED, has been flown out of detention and given back to his village as a good will gesture over the Christmas period 2012.

This will cause friction even more within the team, it has really upset me. Only a few years ago, I was sending my men out into combat to kill or capture some of these guys, and now I have seen the other side of the battlefield and wonder what was it all for, what would the soldiers do if they knew that these dirty tricks were taking place right under their noses. This will cause a storm that may not be able to be stopped once started, our guys were here on a suicide mission because sure as God, we were not stopping this bloodbath any time soon.

It seems that as we try and gain the initiative in Afghanistan, it is the front line soldiers that are being used as pawns in a battlefield that we are not willing to fully commit to, having seen that we are capturing high level personnel who are level 1 to 3 and on the Watch list and then exploiting them and letting them go back onto the battlefield is not going to win any prises for being nice back in the UK.

There were several occasions that staff had upset the boss (Geordie) and were given quite a few warnings, but this was all in one ear and out the other. One of the guys was constantly telling jokes and befriending everyone to make up for the countless mistakes and then they tend to fall away unreported.

We have now been told that big Al is coming out to theatre to replace Tom, this is great news as we all know that Al is a grafter and works well. I am sure we can all learn a thing or two from him. He has bags of detainee experience from operations and he is also a fellow Ulsterman, all 6ft 4 of him.

Until he gets here, I am on nightshift and not before time. It's actually a breath of fresh air to have a break, and we all like a break every so often. Not because we are fed up but because we all need a break from the CSM and his constant whinging about trivial stuff when we are trying to do our job.

I am beginning to put together a plan with Steve and Reders on bringing the operation's room up to a decent standard. It's not what you would expect from at least 30 senior Non-commissioned officers who had been through that location before us on HERRICK 15. I am sure together we will get this place turned around in no time.

The next few days dragged in waiting for my flight to return home for some well-earned rest. I was excited at the prospect of seeing how much development had happened in my son. It was exciting times watching how he had changed.

However, I was a little happy I had missed out on the sleepless nights and nappy changing duties, but I would never tell the wife that!

Time had come and I was heading towards the airframe and making my long journey home. I had learned a lot about the Military Provost Staff and how hard the troops worked in theatre. The guys with knowledge of operations and a good background knew how hard these tours could be, especially from an Infantry unit. I had worked 10 times as hard before I came to this job, yet from an MPS perspective they all thought they were badly done by. It made me fill with rage to see them complain about paper on the floor, and an empty cup in the Ops room, which nearly resulted in someone being given extra-duties!!!

When my wife had opened the front door of the house, her expectations were of a guy who was frail having been in the sun all day carrying heavy equipment and looking after his men, she was astonished to find a man who had put weight on and was immaculate. I had even managed to grow my fingernails.

She couldn't understand why, so I explained that I had a great bed and mattress, I have sky television, play-station, a phone on tap, internet, a brew room, a gym, pizza-hut, coffee shops, shops, we had everything and it didn't feel like a tour at all, fresh rations and sometimes good company!

This was when she started to sit back and relax, my previous tours had well and truly come to an end and now it was a retirement job and money in the bank for old rope!

After a great rest, I was dropped off at MCTC main gates and had to listen to the guys telling me how hard they had had it when on operations. I swallowed pride and explained I knew what they meant as its very long hours. I could see the shake of the head in agreement which spoke volumes.

No sooner have I returned from leave I find out that my son Sebastian has started walking and causing my wife to pull her hair (not literally). He is constantly moving around, and he is only 1. I think we are going to have our hands full... Well, Luba is anyway as I am stuck out in sunny Helmand.

Working nights are good for a few things. It helps me to sort out my personal administration and keep my diary up to date. I have been doing a lot of thinking and talking to a few people at the Intelligence exploitation force (IEF) and have started looking into a possibility of a career change. I have applied for work with other government agencies and now begins the waiting game to see what if any correspondence I get back from it.

I have begun to plan what we need to do when I get back from this terrible operational tour. I think I have done enough time out in Afghanistan and will not be coming back. I had endured some horrendous tours of Afghanistan, but this has been the most relaxed.

I have thought about who the real enemy is and I am struggling to come up with the right conclusion, is it the Insurgents who are killing us or is it the UK Government who are letting these guys off the hook through secret handshakes and ghost flights that leave theatre with no flight manifests and destinations that never took place.

Well finally Big Al has now turned up and the energy has lifted around both the Camp Bastion detainee facilities and competition has begun to see who gets him working in their Ops room, whoever gets him will find the workload a lot easier as he is a workhorse.

Let's see who wins the battle of the minds. As far as we are concerned, he has been sent out to replace Tom which means he belongs with us, but after a bit of juggling with the Orbat I am sure he will end up in Bastion 3 and one of their guys will end up in our THF.

It's now 12 January and I am still on nightshift. My personal administration is complete and now CSM has asked could he borrow one of my watches as his has finally packed in. I have agreed to lend him one. After all, I am professional and try to keep harmony in the workplace. It's just a pity that the workplace is also the rest place, eating place and sleeping place, so it is hard to stay away from him.

Well, there has been a few jobs left for me to get on with, which is great as it will help the night pass more quickly. It also gives me time to put my diary in order and plan for my future. A lot of guys on tour spend many nights thinking about how to improve so they can either progress through the ranks or change career completely.

I am getting annoyed with outside influences messing everything up. These are our lives that are being put on the line.

Today the US Marines were caught urinating on four dead Taliban, and it has caused a right diplomatic problem and our detainees have found out through Skype calls to their family. The Americans have disrespected the Muslims and we are being told to be extra diligent, now American outposts being attacked more frequently because of their Marines actions and we now must watch the

Skype calls with more caution in case this they are given orders to attack our staff.

Al is on the in-theatre induction course and we are getting Mac to replace him. Mac is a good guy and I already know how he works having worked alongside him in the training wing so I am sure it will be a breath of fresh air to get him in here. And to top it all off, we have Bob back from Varsity. He has made it to here to prepare for his R&R flight, which is tomorrow, but I am sure he will upset the CSM before he goes, as the CSM does not like his laid-back approach to life. However, Bob is a fountain of knowledge and CSM gets annoyed by it as Bob has a habit of shouting, ***"Trev get the kettle on,"*** and standing outside for a we cuppa.

Bob shook my hand and enquired how things had been going down here at the THF. I really didn't know where to start with how things had been. We both grabbed a brew and went into my accommodation for a chat. I was joined shortly by Reders who let off a little steam about the boss. It was hard to comprehend how bad things had reached and how we were all still holding it together, God knows!

This tour had begun to make me realise that there was no job in theatre for an MPS Warrant Officer. They were getting in the way and trying to get involved in day to day running of the detainees when it was not needed rather than get into the files and help to close them down and send them back to the UK. They would sit and complain about the most trivial of stuff, sideburns and colour of t-shirt and lunch timings. All the stuff that didn't matter when you should be relaxing when not with the detainees rather than brushing the sand with a hard brush.

Well today proved that the civilian engineers make a big mistake when designing this million-pound facility to hold detainees, and that is the lack of drainage around it. It poured down throughout the night and it was worse than any rain I have ever witnessed in the UK which in turn had the Taliban soaked to their skin. The roof began leaking and the seal around the windows was broken and now letting rain drip onto where they all slept.

No sooner had we reported it, we were sent into somehow fix it. We tried our best with mops and towels and clean bedding, but as soon as the OC found out… You would have thought it was the Queen. He would not let us rest until the Taliban were happy. This made the detainees very happy and now they requested new Korans, shirts and food. Which we had to run around Camp Bastion and collect, anything and everything to keep the enemy smiling.

My tolerance level has just exploded with the bending over backwards to accommodate these requests and the fact that the CSM had sent us all over the camp to fulfil all these demands has really upset the team. When you have seen what we do to these murderers, it gave me a sense of worthlessness.

The OC then decided to send the staff to the shops and buy beads and games to keep the detainees entertained. He has the understanding that if they are occupied making stuff, then the staff will get less threats and abuse. I suppose it may work, only time will tell.

I have now been sent to the hospital in Bastion to post a sentry. We have an injured detainee in bed getting treatment after he was hurt during an attack by our Special Forces during the night, and he had tried to put up a battle but received some hot metal that will take some time to heal.

As I walked into the ward, I couldn't help but notice a young Afghan boy who was smiling at me. He looked extremely fragile and had metal staples across his tiny head and through his chest. His body was covered in cuts and bruises along with his left foot which had been amputated and his left eye was closed. I took a deep breath and started to fill with emotion. He had lost his whole family in a suicide attack by these lunatic Taliban scum. I posted the sentry and walked away.

This was one of a few things that moved me while on the tour, and I still do not understand why the CSM has not even spoken with the team and asked us how we are or how we are doing in this messed up environment. It would be nice to know he was looking out for his guys but I am getting used to it.

That night, I had broken sleep, seeing that young Afghan boy with nothing to look forward to in life, and the battlefield casualties that are mounting up daily is beginning to make me feel sick. I have seen both side of the spectrum now and the end state of the capture is quite shocking.

Why have fighting troops and Ops rooms when Downing Street is pulling the strings and deciding who is important and worth living and who is expendable.

Some of these reports should never be for humans to read. Yes, I have a duty of care to my fellow soldiers and some things are put out in such a way it seems reckless to put them into a public forum but labelling everything as confidential and secret just to cover one's backside is disgusting.

Dirty wars and black Ops are just punchlines that should say, *"We can do what we like."*

Now I have to go and teach six groups of troops that have just entered theatre, this includes the provost Marshal (PM) and a Colonel who wrote part of the Joint Doctrine Publication (JDP) for captured persons. Basically, the bible for detaining people.

I was confident of my abilities and needed to deliver a great performance with her listening my every sentence with ears on stalks in case I taught the wrong information. This would be damaging to me. My unit and the battlegroup, so it needed spot on. The more I thought about it, the more I got nervous, so I decided to just run with what I had already been teaching.

The guys didn't help much as they were telling me to get it right, and don't mess up. It was just the old army banter and them trying to make me get even more worried than I already was. I thought what's the worst that can happen.

I began by introducing myself and explained that had experience from the frontline and it helped me tweak the drills that they would need to know out on the ground. They seemed to enjoy my hype and excitement of teaching.

I explained that searching was vital and how command wire can be worn as a belt and how to look for it. I then went on to highlight that after all these years and overseas operations they still had not come up with a reasonable way on conducting the search. This had the Colonel sitting up and giving me a look of disgust, however I knew I was right.

If the search was carried out from head to foot and systematically, it could be done any way you wanted. I did stress however to do it as if you were searching you own son or daughter, and that meant respect the person you are searching and do it with judgement, cautiousness and be respectful of peoples belongings, no matter what they have in their pockets it may be important to them.

From my point of view, I was hitting all the main heading and giving a shock approach to the troops, and when it came to the detaining of suspects, I made sure they all knew that from the point of capture until handed over to our team; it would set the tone of how these Afghans would cooperate. If you treat them badly, then we lose the Intelligence that we otherwise could have gained from them.

And if you are nice to them, *NO MATTER WHAT* they have done, it helps with exploiting the information that we would get from them. The intelligence gathered by all green troops is vital and it helps build that bigger picture, not to mention keeping *TF 196* with a job to do at nighttime.

193

At the end of my lesson, I got a few people clapping and the Forces Provost Marshall (FPM) and the Colonel came across and thanked me for a very well thought out and planned lesson. It gave me a sense of purpose to know that I was teaching the right stuff and doing it well.

Well, another day completed with lessons. I am sort of glad the guys cover duties when we are teaching, as a day in the sun for a guy with ginger hair tends to give you a headache, and I am truly exhausted with repeating the same lesson over and over again.

When I got back to the rest room, Craig had made me a coffee and spirits had improved. He has just received a parcel from home to go with his other collection of 30 parcels he has in his room, he he… Well, when the boss is happy, we are happy!

Just when everything is running smoothly, the handlers come in and explain again that they have nowhere to sit and carry out their job when the weather turns for the worst, and I agree with them, in fact we all do. However, every time we bring this subject up with our boss, 'The CSM' tends to ignore it and states that they should wear Gore-Tex and keep warm, not really a solution just an excuse to pass the buck. We and I mean the workers are now looking at a solution to keep the handlers warm, it may take a while, but I am sure we can resolve this issue.

The heater in their tent has broken and we are now waiting on the civilian contractors to come across and fix it. They say it could be a week or two which is not great news, but then out of nowhere, the detainees begin to complain about their heater not working properly, and 'The CSM' gets straight on the phone and shouts and within 30 minutes we have three engineers here to get the problem sorted. It puts a bad taste in my mouth of our staff at our facility; it is always nice to know where our loyalties are!

Tensions are now at an all-time high. It seems the stress working with captured Taliban and Al-Qaeda is creating problems and lowering the morale. I have never witnessed this type of behaviour and self-induced stress before. The infantry does have bullshit be we know it is for a reason and to keep us occupied during some testing times, but this is appalling atmosphere is horrendous.

The CSM enters the Ops room and finds me on duty filling in the register of the mornings events and Craig is going through the database. When he politely asks us to check the area around the facility for rubbish and cigarette butts as the Brigadier is flying in from the UK to check the detention facilities, this seems like a reasonable request and I stated, *"Sir as soon as I have finished here, I will get onto it."* Then Craig says he will walk around now, and I agree to follow him. Everything is running well.

I followed Craig's footsteps and found a few bits and pieces, but nothing to write home about, just as I sit down and answer the phone, then the CSM appears at the door and shouts, *"What is this is my hand."* I was on the phone, he then shouted louder, I turned and said, *"Sir, I am on the phone, give me a minute."*

"No, I will not," shouted the CSM.

At this stage, I apologised to the officer at the other end and told her I would phone her back in five minutes. I then stood up and said, *"It's rubbish, isn't it? And you have finally broken me. The fact that you have walked past four bins to bring this shit to my attention proves that you are a waste of space with no operational experience and a complete twat, now piss off and put it in the bin before I knock your head off."*

He just stood there stunned and started shouting, I then lunged forward at him only to be grabbed by the other guys, I was truly broken, this was meant to be a tour were life and death decisions being made every. The fact that he had thrown this rubbish on the Ops room floor to make a point sent me to boiling point.

I left the facility and went for a coffee, as far away from him as was possible, I sat there wondering where my future lay. It surely wasn't with this unit. I felt sorry for some of the great guys and girls that were also disillusioned with the job. What would my next chapter be, and how was I going to recover from this outburst, mud sticks in a small corp. I was done worrying how to climb the promotion ladder, it was always going to be who you knew and not what you knew.

With a very high profile visit about to take place, the CSM now decided to take his R&R. What a great guy. I am sure we can get through the visit without any showstoppers. The OC has now come up with a plan for the detainee/insurgents he wants us to grade them for stage 1 and stage 2...exactly the way they are graded at MCTC!! Another brainchild and now we are being told to introduce sports and re-integration, what the hell is going on, these have killed British soldiers and we are giving them sport!

This news sent shockwaves across the troops in the other facilities. We knew this job was being made extremely hard by our CSM and OC...rumour began to circulate that they were chasing some sort of recognition for their implementations! How they had missed the whole picture, these evil bastards had killed our men and women and our boss was after an MBE for services to detainees!

We have now all be briefed that no one is allowed to speak to the Brigadier unless he approaches us to have a chat.

This is normal in every unit. I am sure he has enough to be dealing with without hearing are trivial rubbish. We spend the next day and a half checking that everything is up to date and in good order. The place is scrubbed spotless as per inspection criteria and we are soon ready for his arrival and his entourage that will surely follow him like lost sheep.

Just as the CSM is trying to leave theatre and enjoy his R&R, we discover that there is a slight problem with the aircraft and the guys all return to our location for a brew and sandwich while they wait on any news coming in about the flight. The guys are a little upset but that's understandable considering the build-up of emotions and wanting to see loved ones. Things here need to improve slightly and I am sure the break from the boss is just the ticket for morale.

Chapter 18
Feeling Betrayed

Having exhausted all avenues in making sense of this mess, it seems to me that we are at the beck and call of the captured insurgents. I am under the impression that the human rights act has now taken a turn for the worse and I think we have lost the battle to public interest lawyers; it is now about the individual making money rather than doing the right thing and what is in the best interest of the people.

I went and had a look in one of the Iso containers and the evidence we have gathered in it still amazes me. Even when they are brought in with Semtex explosives, weapons, four mobile phones and detonators. We note it all down and the Biometrics that confirms that the insurgent has handled it and his prints are everywhere...we still fail to get a conviction in the Afghan court.

Another day has come to an end here at the UKTHF and we sit around chatting about the jobs that need to be carried out before the provost Marshal arrives. It seems we have been left to carry the can if things go wrong. Then what came next sent rage running through my veins. A list had been left for us to carry out tasks prior to the visit and it consisted of the following.

1. Haircut registers for all detainees.
2. Register for purposeful activity for all detainees.
3. Register for detainees who need clothes exchanged.
4. Games register for detainees.
5. Phone register for detainees.
6. Skype registers for detainees.
7. Register for footwear shoes/flip flops.
8. Register for detainees' food requests.
9. Register for detainees who want education.

Now forgive me for being blunt, but why the hell are we bending over backwards for these people, they want to kill us and now they are demanding…yes demanding that they are all allowed into the one compound to have prayers!

Surely this would be a massive security risk for all of us, with so many of them in the one place and only eight of us at the very most to move them all, especially as we must move each one in handcuffs and this is very time consuming.

It must be a joke, let's just wait and see what happens, then word comes in from Craig. He has refused the detainees to be placed in one compound, this is great news for all of us. Craig has many years of experience in this forum, and it comes in very useful when put under extreme pressure for the top brass.

I fear that one day a detainee will try and attack one of us and then the rest of the detainees will join in. I just hope we manage to gain control of the situation as weapons are not allowed to be used within the facility!

I've decided to go into the operation's room where we keep all the sensitive information and have a look at the detainee files. I am always in sheer amazement at how much intelligence our guys are able to gather on high value targets, especially when it seems that we have many informants working for us, the intelligence is so precise.

"Objective Alpha has moved into building 1 and is meeting with Objective Bravo they are discussing an ambush onto Coalition troops in the green zone; they spoke about a device that has now been assembled and is in place. Objective Alpha has handed over 2 x long barrelled weapons to Objective Bravo and has given him a new mobile phone."

They moved out of the building and walked south towards the well. When this took place a dozen men moved around the area and it seemed they were looking out while talking on the phones. Objective Alpha brought two more weapons up from the well and gave them across before walking away from Objective Bravo.

Objective Bravo placed all the equipment into his car and headed east towards Sangin.

Now to me and to everyone I know, that is enough evidence to state that this guy is part of the insurgency and he is about to kill ISAF soldiers in an ambush, well you would be wrong as we now have to wait to be engaged before making a move, the days of Card 429 are well and truly over and Commanders have to beg on a daily basis to have more use of force rules of engagement given to them.

With all this in mind it is back to reality as I have just heard someone shouting, "Don't forget to iron your combats." I just sit here with my head in my hands wondering what we have actually become…what have I become, if there is one thing, I have left in this broken body it is integrity and I will not jeopardise that for no man.

I get up and just comply with the rest of the team. I begin to make sure I don't let the team down, we all are trying to get each day to roll along without incident, working in such a volatile and dangerous place we all have to watch each other's back and if one of us is off our game then it puts the whole team into jeopardy. As the tour rolls on, I can see cracks starting to appear in the friendship we all had for each other. Some of us are not caring about the others, Tom has fallen in love with someone he has just met online and before he has even met her in person, he has spent a lot of money on her for Christmas.

This has all of us scratching our heads, is this guy really in control of his faculties? So, we begin to watch how Tom has developed a relationship out of thin air, which keeps us all entertained for the foreseeable weeks to come, beneath all that front he is the most down to earth guy in the corp. He has been known to lend his car out for weeks at a time and would do anything for his friends, it is just a pity that many of the CSMs take advantage of such generosity.

We have just received a phone call from the guys who left the facility yesterday to go on leave and it seems they are stuck in Dubai as the plane has a fault. This happens a lot with the RAF and much of the time it is just part of the process that comes along with being in the Military. We just hope it never happens to us when we go.

I went to sleep that night wondering how we were actually going to get rid of these detainees. The juveniles have been brought into detention because of evidence that has linked them to placing explosives into the ground that have killed ISAF soldiers. Yet it is illegal to tactical question them. We can't even ask them a question. This has gotten very embarrassing for everyone concerned. We know they are guilty we can prove it with Biometrics but the Afghans who asked for our help will not take Biometrics into account when convicting their own population.

Another day has started here at the secretive holding centre. I grabbed a coffee and began to catch up on the detainee files that I have not read yet. Just as

I progress down the screen I nearly chocked on my coffee. It seems that detainee **2757** was responsible for the death of Captain Lisa Head. I remember her death being very significant as she was a member of the Explosive and Ordinance Department (EOD) her role was to make the area clear of improvised explosives, so that the ground troops could patrol safely.

She had cleared quite a few devices that day and they had set one up to specifically catch her out, it resulted in a massive drop in morale throughout the battlegroup, however this guy has now been released. I was confused by this and asked the other guys about **2757** and they all told me he had been released over the Christmas period. They tell me with anger in their voice, as a juvenile it would be seen as a good will gesture to the village that **2757** was from.

On hearing this news, I was devastated and now at an all-time low, why would someone in our government make such a ludicrous decision? How would the family and friends of Captain Head react to the news, it would all be kept quiet from them in case the media would find out, this was going to cause a storm. But as always when things begin to drift out into the public domain the Government quickly react by sticking a D-NOTICE onto it.

The Official secrets act (OSA) which is in place to keep our Country safe from threats and for National Security has been hijacked by the Politician's for some time now. They have twisted everything we do into underhand individual gains for themselves. Secrets we can live with, however dirty deals and corruption were now an everyday occurrence they fell into the OSA, and we must follow orders yet still trying to uphold the Army's values and standards policy which begins with Integrity, it is basically laughable.

How could anyone live with a clear conscious knowing what was being covered up, it now feels like we are all expendable if we uncover the truths of the minister's secrets.

Only time will tell if this will ever be told to the parents of soldiers who fought for their country and died for their country and then were betrayed by their country, so that politicians could remain in power.

The mood amongst the team is worrying. We all know what has taken place and one of our own soldiers has been betrayed. It becomes common knowledge within the team that our prime minister and his cabinet are either corrupt or Naïve, either way it's just pure ignorance, to not know what is going on is woeful.

When the Prime minister came out to visit us in Sangin DC back in 2008, he made it very clear on his priorities and how he would implement change amongst the military we would be looked after as long as he was in Number 10. Fast forward and he is finished with his military toy for a while and had destroyed the cohesion throughout the services, we all fear for our jobs on return to the UK.

Well, it's back to routine in the detainee compound with carrying out searches of each building, and then searching every detainee. It should be getting quicker as we are used to it, however if we do the searches to quickly then there is always a possibility of missing something like a piece of wire and once, we relax, then it could end up in our throats, there is no place for complacency. And we are all professional to realise that.

Just as we are halfway through the searches, we are starting to see a pattern emerge, the detainees have made little pouches from their own clothes and that is what they are keeping the Quran in. It seems okay to me however they are destroying the clothes we have given them, and they are breaking bits of the fence which means they now have razor sharp blades on their person, this is a big worry to us, and the searches take a bit longer than usual.

Well after a few hours carrying out checks we are done; the detainees seem to be in good spirits and have begun to play football using rolled up socks. I know it's not allowed but I turn a blind eye for about 15 minutes and this way they think they have gotten away with it.

Then the gate rings and it is the Legal Advisor (Legad) he arrives once a month and explains to each detainee why they are being held by UK Forces and asks every one of them if they understand.

So, I get help from two of the handlers to escort them one by one to a port-a-cabin where he is waiting with Dave the Interpreter, the first one is simple. "We are holding you on behalf of the Afghan Authorities and when they are ready you will be transferred to them." Some smile and give a nod while others say they are enjoying the clothes and food.

Then I get ready to collect detainee **2592**. He is a Taliban Commander and has been at this holding facility for nearly four months. He has jet black hair and very well groomed. He speaks English very well when he wants to. He is told something completely different from the other detainees, "You are being held by UK Forces because of your involvement in the insurgency." He is such an important capture to the coalition that to release him would cause more deaths and help the Taliban gain the initiative.

He then starts to talk in Pashtu to the interpreter and states that he was sitting in his compound having a cup of tea when men came from the sky and brought him here. I nearly laughed but held it together during the interview. We knew he was talking about our SAS troops who had brought him in.

I took him back to his compound and released his handcuffs. He just stood and smiled at me with look of disgust etched across his face. I knew he wanted to kill me, so it just made us all weary of him, not that we were becoming complacent.

As I was coming back from putting **2592** in his compound, I could see the detainees in compound 3 were trying to hide what they were doing. They had tied their towels onto the fence so we could not see inside. I shouted to the sentry if he could see and he replied, "No." I then got the other handlers to come with me and I asked them to take it down immediately, they just laughed and smiled, I asked one final time and they ignore me.

I got the keys and opened the gate to their compound and on moving towards the towel they all began shouting. I began to untie the towel when detainee **2842** grabbed me with force. I threw my hands in a chopping motion upwards to force him off me and in doing so I had thrown his hands across the razor wire. He lost a pint of blood within seconds. I wrapped him up and took him to see the Legal advisor known as the Legad. He was shocked at the state of the detainee I had brought him. I explained and then got the medics to bandage him up.

I then spent the rest of the afternoon writing a statement and asking the other handlers if they would write one also, then a statement from the guy on sentry. All of these were typical these days of stopping the leach lawyers and detainees from prosecuting us.

Every day spent with the detainees is like walking on egg shells as one mistake can very soon snowball into your career ending, and we have all quickly learned a valuable lesson that when it involves detainees, then your Hierarchy turn their backs on you until you personally can prove you were in the right which is impossible to do when your colleagues are told to back off and you end up riding the wave of allegations by yourself.

Well, it's getting very close to the visit and I still have a million and one things to do. The Interpreters need one some work carried out on their roster and the pay needs to be reviewed before they all go on strike.

Dave, Kamal, and John who are our best interpreters would like to try and find a way to resolve the changeover at the other facility known as TORCHLIGHT. This is a name that has been given to it by people that have never been in there. It is supposed to represent torchlight being put in the face for interrogation purposes. However, with today's PC Brigade, we are not allowed to use the word interrogation so we changed the word to Exploitation to get around the red tape.

I am having difficulty in getting the interpreters to agree with the new contract that has been sent done from brigade HQ. They want all the Interprets to be on a basic salary not exceeding $1000 a month. However, what they do not realise is that our interpreters are working 24/7 and earn their pay. The interpreters that work out on the ground get paid a lot more because of the dangers and that I agree on.

What is not mentioned is that our interpreters were out on the ground and got injured and so now work with us and because of their injury they do not take a pay cut... Our government really did not look after the guys who are on immediate death threats for helping ISAF, it least the Americans took their interpreters back to the USA for a better life, we could learn a lot from the Americans on hospitality.

Well, it seems another storm is brewing back at the facility as the boss has decided to try and enforce the same regime, we use with serving soldiers at MCTC here with the detainees...is it just me that thinks what are these clowns trying to achieve? And moreover, they have explained that they have asked for a sports pitch for the detainees! And they say crime doesn't pay.

Many of the guys are now disillusioned with what we are here to do, we know the law and how it works, but this is rubbing salts into the wounds of our already tired and exhausted frontline troops. Now I know why this place is classed as secret. We do not want our troops to know how well we treat these evil bastards.

We have an old man who was being held in compound 3 because he was passing weapons to and from the Taliban. During a call to his family on Skype, he began to laugh and told them all to get arrested by the British because the food and clothes he gets given are fantastic. He said he has never been treated so well, this made all of us shake our heads. Now you could argue that this is coming from the top brass, but being here and seeing how things are changing it is coming from Captain Ideas and his sidekick.

Things are beginning to change atmospherically inside the detainee compound, a new detainee knows **2592** and they have been caught talking. It seems **2592** is not happy about the new detainee being held here. This has been noticed by all the team and we have been told remove him at early hours and avoid confrontation with the other detainees. They must not know where he has been moved to.

So, at 5am, I get up and slip into his compound quietly with the other handlers and we extract him. We drive him away in a blacked-out vehicle to *TORCHLIGHT* where he will undergo more exploitation sessions and hopefully, they will gain some vital intelligence from him. With **2592** being such a high-level Taliban commander, it could be the intelligence that we need to either gain a conviction on him or at least lead us to others so **TF-196** can swoop in and grab them.

As we take **2894** away from the others, the look on his face tells a story of fear. He thinks we are going to kill him as many of the Taliban believe that we kill them once we capture them. He fears what might happen. He then begins to speak English and asks us what is happening. I explain that he is going for a chat and some tea. After that, he just smiles at the both of us.

After I drop him off, I make my way back to get ready for lessons. Today we have 800 new arrivals in theatre, and they all need reminding of the procedures that we do with captured persons.

More importantly why we detain, mainly three reasons but two are always being used and they are threat to mission accomplishment and Force protection. The troops arriving always know this however once they sit down and get asked their minds always go blank. I suppose being put on the spot is not always great way to learn.

I jump on the Gator, which is a small vehicle that looks like a golf cart and we are off. As I drive through the American camp of Leatherneck, I can't help but notice how this camp is so big it has two cookhouses a superstore, pizza-hut, bus stops for people going to work, a gymnasium and many more surprises around each corner. As I arrive at my teaching destination, I can still see many guys and girls zeroing their personal weapons on the range before they start with lessons.

We have got some great instructors here, from medical to cultural awareness and from legal advisors to myself captured persons and evidence, my lesson was always split into two parts and it flowed rather well, from the point of capture and then handing across to the RMP where they teach how to preserve evidence and how to gather it correctly. All in all, it's a great lesson which pays dividends in the long run.

When I returned to my place of work, I am told that Kamal who is one of our interpreters has had his flight cancelled and will miss one of his days leave with his family. This could have an adverse effect on the interpreters if not solved and quickly. After a few phones call across the brigade, we manage to get him on the following days flights into Kabul and give him an extra days leave.

Just as I am about to relax with a hot coffee, I get asked to carry out a big talashi (search) of compounds 3 and 4. During routine checks, the handlers have noticed that small pieces of razor wire, which includes tiny blades have been broken off in several places. This is very serious as these could be used to slice us open and it's well documented that they want to cut us open, especially as they keep giving the hand gesture of cutting one of our throats. This will take all hands-on deck to make sure not an inch is missed and with the threat of being cut by a detainee will have all of us on edge and watching every movement.

We keep pushing the boundaries every day, what are we trying to achieve with all these implementations. I am now being sent to buy a set of hair clippers and nail clippers and nail files so the detainees can do their own hair and groom themselves. If I could get away with it, I would knock them both out. These are the type of people that need self-gratification all the time, look what we did without being told if I have said it before I will say it again, chasing MBEs will get you nowhere.

Just when I arrive back with the goods, the team are looking at me as if they are about to break. They realise we have lost the battle here with the, and let's not forget these are captured insurgents.

The only thing left for me to do now is to see who needs a new coat and who needs a new prayer mat. This may sound like it's my idea, let me tell you this has nothing to do with me and has come for the OC. This type of treatment to captured insurgents would only ever come from people who have never witnessed sacrifice or bloodshed on the battlefield, because if they had a tiny glimpse, they would not be doing this.

When I think about how we are treating the enemy, it annoys me to a degree. Yes, we should treat them well and show them we are different and hope that they pass all this back through their own ranks and hopefully…yes hopefully, they may want to negotiate with our top brass in finding a solution to this mess, but when you look at their way of life in Afghanistan, they treat women like second class citizens and use boys for pleasure so they will never be able to integrate with western values and how our own society works.

It seems that the higher up the Taliban chain you go, the more it's accepted to use young boys as sex objects; this is normal in their society as a whole.

The detainees at our facility seem to be in a very good mood these past few days and it probably has something to do with the fact they are very much in charge of this jail.

I am sure that someone somewhere is breaking the law with regards to this detention facility. I agree that most of these evil bastards need locking up and the key thrown away, but surely, we have some form of legislation or document somewhere. This facility is known as THF which means temporary holding facility and we all know that 28 days is the maximum we can hold detainees here before we (by law) must pass them onto the Afghan Authorities, but if the Afghan Authorities are not ready for them, then we have no choice but to keep hold of them.

What we are then forced to do is ask for a Parliamentary extension for that detainee. I know it all seems rather straight forward and it shouldn't cause a drama, but when you keep asking for an extension on the same detainees it all adds up, so we have some detainees here for seven or eight months without a conviction yet we know they are guilty through biometrics hits on our equipment that the troops on the ground have used, yet we know that is not good enough for a conviction here in Afghanistan.

So, all we are effectively doing is watching the clock tick by until our tour is finished and handing the same detainees across to the new team that arrives in six months' time. Then as soon as this operation has end and we all go back home for tea and medals, the public interest lawyers who have been watching with a close eye on how we have conducted operations will be across to say, "*Which ones were held by British troops.*" The queue will form, and every single insurgent would receive compensation from the UK taxpayer. Every soldier that gets injured in Afghanistan will receive 10% of what the enemy get and many of the soldiers will never be able to work again.

It seems this token gesture we are providing needs to be done so that the front-line soldiers think we are winning a pointless operation, nothing has been put in place after the firefight has been won. Yet back in the UK, the news tells of a different spin altogether, the news states we are doing a fantastic job, yet we are freeing the enemy to fight on a different day at a different location, does this sound familiar? Then I remember the Good Friday agreement and would not be at all surprised to find out in years to come that our government has given them all pardons!

Another day has arrived here at the United Kingdom Temporary Holding Facility and it's Valentine's Day everywhere else but here, then the post is brought across and my wife has sent me a beautiful card; it doesn't suit the surrounding here and its very much appreciated in amongst this chaos. I did send one home but with limited stock in the shop here and nearly 5000 men trying to buy one, I assume she didn't like it.

Then I decide to retire to my bedspace and realise that the Taliban sleep less than 10 metres from me and it's here that I take five minutes to myself and ponder how my wife and son are getting on back at home in Colchester. My boy is growing so fast that it is sad to miss out in such a special moment. These moments that servicemen and women give up defending and fight for our country should never be forgotten, the military families always look out for each other, and they should as we all know that the government forgets our sacrifice very quickly…unless it's the voting season then they stand in our corner.

When I wake up from my bed, I see that Craig has had quite a few parcels from his wife. His smile is from ear to ear and he doesn't spend time in showing us his treats. It cheers us all up because we all know that a happy boss makes a happy team and rest of the afternoon could not possibly go wrong!

Then just as we are all in a great mood the phone rings and it's the Brigade Provost Officer with her usual charm. She has been informed that we have been ordered to release a detainee at the front gate. This does not go down very well with the team as we know all about this particular person, his is a juvenile and regardless of what his crimes have been, we are not allowed to ask him questions, which is another failure in our justice system and a disgrace to the men and women this detainee has killed.

He is a renowned Taliban bomb maker and was detainees with many munitions which is a great find, he had detonators, timers and Semtex as well as a substantial amount of cash. Now in many countries, this would be instant jail but not in good old Afghanistan; we are beginning to be known as the detainee hotel and it is for good reason.

I go into the office and decide to read up on this young Afghani before preparing him for release, and it shows loads of evidence to why he was detained, his prints are linked to improvised explosive devices than have killed or maimed servicemen, yet the Afghan courts will not accept this as evidence. His **Annex G** is very precise with intelligence gained from the ground.

I begin to read the file of ***UKAP002592AFCM*** and like many times, it sends shivers down my spine as to what kind of man he is. This guy should have been shot on sight in my opinion like many others. He has now become a burden on the UK taxpayer and keeping this man alive will surely cost us with deaths in the long run.

The only problem is that all the evidence we hold on to him has come from a third party which will not hold in court so realistically we do not have any concrete evidence to even have him in custody, which will come back and bite us when the conflict is over.

Every time we bring this matter up at our Orders group, we are told the same old party line 'Parliament are currently looking into this.'

When you have heard this more than a dozen times, it just rolls off your back and you think nothing off it. They might as well be saying we are doing what we want to at this precise minute and time and once we have a plan in place, we will let you all know the outcome.

With so much going on and having to keep quiet about my job outside of the detention facility, it all starts to mount up. How can anyone possibly believe we are above the law. Surely, we are breaking many laws that we are expected to uphold. When we break a rule or have a lapse in judgement our career is hanging by a thread, yet here we seem to be judge and jury.

Our Commanders love the power that has been bestowed upon them, out here in theatre they are like gods and they make sure everyone knows it. Their demands remind me of the days of Hitler or Stalin as they take advantage of the soldiers, they command with the woeful decisions that have been made. We are now being ordered to have yet another airlock so that the inside gate can only open so far before it locks.

This may sound like a great idea, but to us that use it more than 20 times a day it is impractical and dangerous, this means that only one person can either enter or leave the detainee compound at a time, so if they were to break free and charge the gate, then one of us is going to either be seriously hurt or killed.

We have exhausted ourselves trying to explain this with both the OC and the CSM but it's very clear they have already made their decision and it's not the common-sense approach. The CSM is overheard saying that the OC is trying to leave a legacy behind at the UKTHF, which means he will be solely responsible for any injuries that come from his actions.

The Royal Navy personnel that we have attached to use are working like Trojans, they seem to be on a roster that has them working for six months flat, now I know I have an infantry background and have had some ferocious tours. But even during the darkest days, I still managed to be on a rotation that gave my guys six hours sleep a night and, on some days, we rested pretty much all day.

However, our boss has been aggressive towards the handlers and most of them came to us for advice on how to tackle it, the SNCOs sat down and we came up with a better rotation which meant they had more down time to do administration and rest. This was frowned upon, and he wanted them on five hours on and five hours off for six months; this was in my eyes unacceptable, and the guys and girls could not be responsible for their actions in a highly volatile environment if they are fatigued.

I start to try and give the troops some morale and on top of the wall outside the Ops room I have wet the sand and begin to work on making it look like a village. I have made walls and compounds out of mud and it starts to set shape, the guys all love coming across and having a cup of tea of coffee and looking what has changed. Each day, I add buildings and eventually, I will hand this across to someone else who will look after it.

It sounds like I have lost the plot but in fact I am trying to improve moral, which is already at an all-time low. Anything I can do to change the atmosphere around here I am sure will be greatly received.

The Interpreters are beginning to get restless again and complaining about their wages Ishmael has stated he is owed money from his last assignment in the region of $1300 which is a hefty amount of cash for an Afghan male. I have looked through all documents and it seems he was sent to work with us before he managed to get paid. This is something I need to rectify before the other Interpreters lose faith and trust in me.

The tour was coming to an end and I was counting the days until I could relax without the boss telling me to carry out a pointless task, as a Sergeant and having earned my stripes from the relevant courses I felt dejected and worthless as an MPS member, I could not let this go on!

Chapter 19
Exploitation

I had been back from operations for a few weeks and I was struggling to make sense of what was actually happening in Afghanistan. I had been indoctrinated to believe that our mission was to help the Afghan people and that we were actually making a difference, but our own government was carrying out deceitful tactics that put Taliban fighters back out onto the battlefield after they had been captured.

This was horrendous and very disturbing, yet at the same time was being accepted by those at the top of government. We had known for some time now that the Afghan government was corrupt and that high value targets were being released in Lashkargah, but we were completely powerless to intervene.

I would try to use my connections to bring this up in conversation so the information could be known. However, under the OFFICIAL SECRETS ACT, all serving personnel are bound under OATH to remain quiet about such dealings. The OSA was a cover title to not only keep things secret but to cover up failures and dirty tricks by our government and we were complicit in letting it happen, the deaths of our own service personnel was happening, and we were aiding and abetting our enemies!

The more I thought about this, the angrier inside I would become. I tried to continue in my role in teaching the detainees at MCTC and also all the staff with their Military Annual Training Test (MATTS). There were very few people in the Corp that had the qualifications to teach the lessons so the pressure of keeping operationally effective without a training officer of qualified training Warrant Officer was testing.

I continued to write the training programs along with the other guys, Steve, Kris, Sherpa and Dave each of the guys brought their experience to the table and it worked, we were a great team and I had respect for each of the guys. Then we had a new instructor join the team called Karen and she was a breath of fresh air and brought a different perspective to the training team.

I noticed a ramp up in the duties and the teaching side of things, due to the operational commitment to Herrick we had now to supply Detainee Specialists to training teams across the UK and to Canada, and supply three teams for Afghanistan, Operational Training Advisory Group (OPTAG) and the in Theatre training team (RSOI) and now we needed a team to carry out Post OP Stress Management (POSM) plus it took 15 members of staff to run the two companies, Education, and both gates, with two shifts per day it was using up 30 members of staff at a time and the staff were now becoming fatigued and stressed.

I had also been told that my name had been put forward as the first ever member of the Military Provost Corp to go to Sandhurst as a Detainee handler specialist. I told my wife and she was happy and after a few days with the family I decided to accept the offer and began to ensure that all my qualifications were in date. I booked myself onto the various courses that I had no real interest in like the 'Drill Course', I had no interest in marching people around, but it was a course requirement, I continued to put together a battle-box/teaching aids box.

My uniform had to be made to measure from our tailors and a set of Blues had to be ordered for such occasions at the Royal Military Academy.

I wasn't given any time to prepare for the course and I had to attend an induction course in Sandhurst. I came off duty and drove to the Academy. I was tired after such a long drive but I completed the fitness tests and requirements and then returned to Colchester and sorted out my uniform for the following days' work. Then back onto a set of night duties which was a rest compared to the training each day.

The day finally arrived and a started my Sandhurst selection Cadre, the guys and girls were all quite good at taking lessons and each candidate brought their own unique experience to the table. I got to know some fantastic guys and I still class them as friends today. Each day was nerve racking and we all headed to the wall to see who was taking the lesson as it's the most self-induced stress I had faced off the battlefield ever. After the first few days, we started to get into a routine and our fitness was at a good level.

We all had to carrying out different lessons and make the lessons exciting and have a reality that mirrored real life on a battlefield. I enjoyed my lessons, but I was extremely nervous every time my name was called. I got confused when I was picked to give a field-craft lesson on reaction to effective enemy fire.

I was screaming at the guys to put down accurate fire and giving fire control orders. The guys worked hard and theirs faces went red and by the end of the lesson I could hear them all saying, "Fuck that" and "Holy shit". I made it as realistic as I possibly could.

Then out of the blue, the Officer from the Signals regiment said, "If you could do that again would you change anything and why?" I said I was happy with the effort put in by everyone and I believe it went well. I would have loved it to be darker so we could use tracer rounds to give it a more realistic scenario.

I was stunned and confused when he said, "Well, I thought you were far too aggressive and that's not what we like to see when you're teaching young officers. You can't scream at people like that and expect them to do what you want!" It was at this point I looked at the other Senior NCOs and they were all looking at the floor as they seemed a bit embarrassed by what had just been said.

He asked me if I can any comeback! "Sir I do, I'm afraid that on this occasion you are wrong!" I could see the look on everyone's face as if to say, "Here ends your time at Sandhurst Trev." But I needed to show integrity and due diligence and I wasn't afraid to give my own experiences.

He said, "Explain." So, I explained that if there's any time whatsoever that you need to shout and scream it's when there are bullets bouncing in and around you and you are taking casualties. I had witnessed it first-hand it was in my experience how you got heavy fire onto the enemy position.

It seemed I had hit a nerve, but I did have some great feedback from the other potential instructors, and they all agreed with my approach to the lesson. I had passed my appointment and now I was free for a few days while everyone had their chance to take a lesson, the first week went well and I was pleased with my progress. I noticed a few of the candidates had been sent back to their unit for coming up short on basics tests. A few guys had been injured and couldn't continue. This was sad as a guy I got to know called Mark had been exceptional but had picked up an injury.

I had made it to week 2 of the Potential instructor's course and was looking forward my lessons in First aid and Skill-At-Arms, though to be honest I was not looking forward to the drill lesson and marching, I always preferred field-craft and weapons.

I could start to see the professional soldiers and separate them from the others who had lacked operational experience, you can spot soldiers who lack knowledge of the battlefield. They have usually spent most of their career in depots teaching recruits and have moved onto Sandhurst as their natural step but can't teach about their operational experience for the lack of it.

My lesson on the SA80-A2 was pretty straight forward and consisted of the nine key point check list, very basic for any instructor to teach if you break it down into sections and demonstrate it as if you are teaching children. When your lesson is going well, the instructor tends to move you on and then asks to begin end of lesson drills as he is confident that you are competent in the subject matter.

I was starting to find my feet here and get to know the layout of the place, the routes for running and the way instructors have to conduct themselves, I had met a guy who had been awarded the second highest gallantry medal in the UK. His name was Mark and he had been exceptionally brave to be awarded the Conspicuous Gallantry Cross, second only to the Victoria Cross, an outstanding soldier from the Mercian Regiment.

Those who had gallantry medals never spoke about the events surrounding it, most medals are given out due to life and death situations and having had to of come face to face with enemy combatants. Most memories of this nature involve traumatic events and the memories of such events are kept under lock and key in our heads. To revisit these events can very easily trigger off mental health issues and it's when this happens our lives begin to unfold piece by piece.

It was now week 3 of the Cadre and I was enjoying getting to know the guys. I made a friend in a guy called Roy. He was a seasoned soldier and very capable of any task set before him. His lessons were of a very good quality and he made it easier for a few of us. At the end of each day, a few of us would stay behind to ensure we had our lessons prepped for the following day. I was now in a routine and enjoying my surroundings.

It was becoming very obvious who needed guidance and that extra help from the instructors, we noticed two potential candidates who started to befriend the course instructors in the hope that they would find out who was taking the up and coming lessons, not a great way to get through a course, but I guess its everyone for themselves in a selfish sort of way.

I had now started week 4 and was feeling very confident. We had been broken into teams and about to start the assault course, competing against each other for nothing more than pride and to show each other what we were capable of. Each team could be awarded penalties for not finishing tasks that had been set up along the route. After each task, we received a debrief and then we started the clock and moved to the next one.

We finally reached the assault course and the 12ft wall, I got me back up against the wall and helped a few of the team over. It was my turn to get over. I was thrown up buy a guy who was built like an animal. I came off the wall and landed very awkwardly. I felt a tear in my right knee. It shook me and I felt instant pain. I got up to move towards the low wire and began to crawl through. It was agony dragging my right knee and leg, at the end of it I got up and tried to jog with the team. I now had tears streaming down my face as I tried to continue. I shook my head and stopped. I apologised to the team, but I couldn't continue.

A member of the Directing staff approached me, and could see the pain I was in, they told me to report to the medical centre then once finished to report to them with an update. I limped like an idiot to the medical reception and the nurse and doctor looked at my swollen knee and told me that I had torn ligaments. I was told that my course was now over and that I was being sent back to my unit on medical grounds, I was absolutely gutted.

I was given light duties and told to remain at home for the next two weeks. During this time, I received an operation on my right knee and I had my cartridge removed through keyhole surgery. It was a time when I had no idea what my career direction was going to be. I was disillusioned with my job and didn't have an aspiration to move through the ranks due to Ex Royal Military Police having all the key roles.

I was supposed to be sick at home yet constantly being messaged about detainee handing kits and to help put training aids together to help the other staff. I then received a phone call from the Training Warrant Officer asking me if I could go to Poole and teach the Special Boat Service (SBS) a lesson on detainee handling as they were about to deploy to Afghan. I explained that I wasn't well and couldn't drive.

A few hours later, I got a call from the Warrant Officer begging me to go and he would drive me. I wasn't happy and was told I could wear tracksuit. I still had crutches and my knee was very delicate. The trip sitting in the car made my knee swell and we pulled over so I could stretch it. Once we reached Poole, we both booked in and had our pictures taken for temporary passes. We then made our way around to the hanger and entered the side door to find a complete Squadron of SBS troops sitting listening to another lesson.

I heard the end of the lesson and then walked in to see my surroundings. I was stunned when the Squadron Commander came over and said, "Hi, Speedy, it's been a while mate." It was an Officer I had known for a few years who used to Command A-Company 1 Royal Irish.

I said, "It's great to see you, Matt." He asked me if I had a power point presentation, and I said my lesson was in my head so I wouldn't be using any of their equipment.

Matt then called his troops to sit back down and it was at this point my escort Warrant Officer looked at me stunned, I said, "Right, troops, thanks for having me today, I'm not here to teach the basics on how to put a pair of goggles onto someone's face, that's just insulting to guys of your calibre. Instead, I've tailored this presentation to give you the answers to your questions. We all know why we are in Afghanistan and the reasons why you detain, Threat to Mission accomplishment, force protection and the other reason is to assist the Afghan authority. As UKSF personnel you need to know vital information on the ground and you need it yesterday, for future Ops I'm not telling you to break any law, but I will advise you to manipulate the timeline in order to have maximum time with the High Value Targets that you capture, you can actually assist us in the Exploitation facilities by not sending the arrest reports until you are about to land with your detainees, this means the clock starts to tick when you send it, we will then get our four hours from that moment. If you come across men that you believe to be under 16, do NOT ask them their age, wait until you've questioned them to get the information and then if they say they are younger than 16, by law you cannot ask them any more questions!"

I told them to use the law to their advantage. I then showed them a few techniques and asked if they had any questions! Matt stood up and said to his guys that now was the time to get their worries off their chest and that he loved my no-nonsense approach and that it was the best lesson he had ever received on this subject. My Training Warrant Officer was annoyed that I had left out the basic stuff that we would normally teach other units. I didn't care. He didn't even know the lesson structure or could he teach a lesson.

My job was done and the OC of the squadron deploying was going to give my Commanding Officer a ring to say he was impressed at my lesson.

I was still recovering from my operation but now back doing work, I was called in to the Deputy Commandants Office where I began to receive an education from him. He gave me a story about his rugby career and how he had been injured, but instead of quitting, he told me that he carried on. He said to me that he 'Maned the fuck up.' I said I understand what you are saying and ill return to full duties…this was when he said, "Oh, I'm not telling you what to do, I'm just telling you that I MANED THE FUCK UP."

I understand sir, I know what you're getting at…

I was now in a confused state of mind. I had issues with the direction we were going and still couldn't get me head around our conduct with our enemies. The internal climate within our own unit and the underhand dealings being conducted by our Officers. We had a Company Sergeant Major at home under investigation, me had a Captain trying to manipulate the staff, we have a Naval Senior Non-Commissioned Officer under investigation and 10 Senior members of staff all writing statements, not to mention my training officer had signed off and was leaving the army. The Regimental Sergeant Major had signed off and I had no one to go to for advice!

For the next few days, I kept having staff members ask me if I was going back to Sandhurst, I had lost my zest for adventure within the military. I was sent to work in Garcia platoon which was the induction platoon and all the new admissions to MCTC had to come through me. I was to teach them the ropes and to assess them in mental health and to find out about their crimes and the path they were to take next. I had another member of staff working with me who I thought was a good guy. He had many years of experience and I enjoyed working alongside him. After I had recovered and could walk around properly without the aid of a walking stick, I was sent back to the training wing to teach Herrick Specific drills and MATTS.

I was back to teaching the Staff, the Detainees and OPTAG lessons on detention.

Chapter 20
The Breakdown

I really enjoyed teaching lessons to the detainees from A-Company, they were the service personnel who had not broken any laws but had broken standing orders back at their own units, many guys had been absent without leave (AWOL) usually they had taken a few extra days leave and had now been sentenced to 28 days jail for doing so, this also had a double punishment as they would lose a month's pay on top of jail. We also had a few guys who had been involved in a fight and been awarded 28 days depending on how serious the fight was, and then we had the odd fraudulent invoice being claimed for by guys trying to beat the system.

All the staff in the training wing knew that I had training aids for everything, I had left no stone unturned when it came to Herrick specific lessons and wanted the troops to go back to their unit knowing their jobs inside out.

I was now throwing myself at work. I would get in at 0700hrs and prepare my classroom for the first lessons at 0900hrs, checking my register and marking off who I was teaching. I had started to not care if I had other staff in because I didn't need anyone and stopped relying on others. With the report writing and the training roster and the training program, I was busy constantly and it kept me focussed on other things that to worry about my own demons.

I would receive emails every day from several staff members asking me if I would 'be a mate' and give them a paper pass at their weapon handling test or their map reading and first aid, it just added to the already pressures that were building up. My training officer would come in from time to time and say hello then leave, I asked him if he would spare some time to sit in and listen to one of my lessons so he could say I was teaching the right subject matter, but he never did. It was the time of year when our mid-year appraisals had to be done to help steer us towards our confidential reports... I kept asking him and because he was leaving the military, he never bothered to write my report!

With all this going on and my own mental health wavering, I was supposed to carry out Traumatic Risk Incident Management (TRiM) to all the staff going and returning from operations, quite alarming that I was the Unit TRiM Coordinator and was looking after the staff but there was no one qualified to look after the TRiM Coordinator.

My home, work life balance was non-existent, and it was pushing Luba and myself apart, I was on edge most of the time and the noise of Apache helicopters constantly flying above my home was becoming frustrating.

Then I woke up one morning and walked into work. The walk wasn't even long but it was enjoyable and only across the football pitch to the gates of MCTC. Today I was teaching the Orders process to the detainees, a straightforward lesson that had a pneumonic known as REEPI, receive, extract, estimate, prepare, and issue. Each of these headings was broken down further and I had everything prepared.

I collected the troops from A-Company along with Karen, we then separated so I could take the lesson and Karen continued with her work in the office. I called the nominal roll and then told them all to grab a quick brew and cigarette before we begun the lesson. I was feeling anxious for some reason and now panic was beginning to settle in. I went outside for fresh air and the detainees took this as that I wanted them all back inside. They walked past me calling me staff and saying hello and took their seats in the classroom.

I took a few deep breaths and went back into the classroom, everyone now looking at me for today's lesson. I couldn't find the button to turn the screen on, though I had turned it on and off hundreds of times in the past. I felt stressed and now my heart was beating out of my chest, I then didn't know what the lesson I teaching was was, I looked down at my sheet and it said 'The Orders Process'. I then didn't know what that was and I struggled to remember it. I felt the hairs on my neck stand up and I began to panic and struggle for air.

I told all the detainees to go back outside for a coffee and cigarette for 10 minutes and I walked into the staff changing room and sat on the floor and cried my eyes out. I had no idea what was happening and how to fix what this was. My mind was lost and I was falling apart. I can't even remember which member of staff came into see me but I was a mess. I got myself together and left the detainees and walked over to see my RSM. I knocked on his door and walked in, he could see that I was upset and told me to sit down. I looked at him and I just broke down, he said he knew I was on the verge of breaking but didn't want to intervene, he phoned the Medical Officer and organised for me to have an appointment.

It was the last time I ever got into military uniform and ever taught a lesson. I had no idea what lay ahead or what I was to do next. My head was all over the pace and I had no idea what to do, when you're in that frame of mind you need direction and help, my unit chose to see an individual who only spoke about his disabled child and how he was struggling. I ended up giving him advice and I was left to fester away. I was put under the Mental health team in Merville Barracks and started to receive treatment from a fantastic therapist called Leslie.

My had to find a start point for her to be able to treat me. We spoke about my previous tours of Afghanistan and my working relationships in the training wing, she was already seeing numerous members of staff who had all had a rough time and needed help. I received medication from the Doctor which was a tablet called Propranolol which was a tablet designed to reduce my anxiety, but it also slowed my heart rate down. It didn't stop me feeling like shit of stop the thoughts of death and my guilt of losing my friends on the battlefield.

I had to go through a complete month on this tablet before my therapist spoke to my medical officer and between them, they decided to male me have a higher dose. This left me like a zombie and my wife was feeling the pressure to carry out every single task in our family, she was now becoming the mum and the dad and my career. It was such a tough time for her and learning to adapt to this new way of life was strain on all of us.

After the second month on this intense therapy, doing EMDR and learning coping mechanisms I was then put onto a new medication called dronabinol which was stupid. It wasn't until my wife read about the side effects that we discovered that they had given me a tablet that caused psychosis and actually made my mental health worse so we asked for a new medication and where given Venlafaxine which was certainly a lot better and helped to keep me calm and relaxed.

I was not being filled with medication that was actually an anti-depressant, it seemed no one in the medical world knew how to treat PTSD. The only avenue they knew was to throw anti-depressants and an illness which had nothing to do with depression. I wasn't depressed, I was having thoughts and reminders of my people that I cared about who had died, and that my bosses in work had not treated me fairly with regards to reporting. I was being left in the training wing intentionally due to my experience and qualifications.

My son was only three years old and needed his dad but unfortunately, I was a mess, I was not a good dad and needed help to fix the mess in my head, I would go for a drive and just cry by myself. I felt like a burden to my wife and to my son. Then one day while I was out in my car, I lost all thoughts and felt calm, I had made my mind up and I was going to rid myself of this awful pain I was carrying and for the first time in a long time, I was relaxed; the weight seemed to just disappear. I had found the wall that I thought was solid and I drove my car into it at speed hoping to kill myself.

I'm not sure what went wrong but it didn't work and instead of ending my life, I was just sat there in the front of my car crying my eyes out knowing that my wife was going to go crazy at the state of the car.

Luba didn't even shout at me. She knew what was going on in my life and was very supportive. I now needed to get help and get it very fast indeed if I was to continue to be a dad and a husband.

I was now assigned a Personal Recovery Officer (PRO). He was called Stuart and a guy I got on well with. He enrolled me into the Help for Heroes recovery centre, and I was given a room. I was told that when I needed a break from home, I always had a room on standby in the facility known as Chavasse VC House. It was in here that I got to know lots of veterans who were all suffering in their own way from injuries sustained while serving their country.

I decided to put in a service complaint about my career and how for the second year in a row my boss had failed to write a report on my and he had also failed to give me a mid-year appraisal. This meant that I hadn't gone to board twice in a row and has effectively been career fouled by my unit. This along with the extra duties and the constant travelling away to different locations to teach others was adding to my stress levels; it was making me become angry and I was already starting to speak out and tell those in higher authority that they had caused my mental health to deteriorate.

I decided to ask my peers if they would write statements about how they had seen me change and to put on paper what they had witnessed. After two weeks, I was able to put eight statements from different members of staff to my own and make copies to go forward to the tribunal. At first, I had to speak to the Brigadier about my allegations but unfortunately, he had moved on and instead I was left to speak to the Colonel. This conversation never took place and I received a letter from him telling me that he had investigated the case and found that the Deputy Commandant had nothing to answer for.

I was surprised at this when you consider that I had eight statements. My personal statement and medical references along with my therapist statement, so I investigated this and discovered that the Colonel and the Deputy Commandant were in fact good friends. It was at this point that I started to make calls and get legal advice. After a few days and talking to several solicitors, I knew I had a case against the military and I hired a law firm. My solicitor requested all my information and started to put together a case.

My treatment and my case against Military Corrective Training Centre (MCTC) started to move along nicely. I asked my PRO if it was possible for a house move out of the Garrison as waking up every morning to the noise of ranges and Apache helicopters flying over my home was not helping me with my recovery one bit. It took around two weeks and he had a place for my family to move to, we organised the movers and began to pack up the house, our new home was within the married quarters of 23 Royal Engineers known as the 'Airborne Sappers'. No one knew who we were, and it was nice to be out in the Country and new Rendlesham Forest, a place I could go for a walk to and relax.

We decided to look at the nursery within the military community and after a quick introduction we put our son into it and got to know a few of the families but didn't stray too far from our own doorstep. A few of the engineers befriended me and when word spread that I was a Patron for an Engineer charity and that I had a Military Cross and was suffering from PTSD; it wasn't long before one of the Engineers began to fire fireworks from his back garden and start to aggravate my mental health. I was extremely lucky to have a friend who was the Royal Engineer Chief General, **General Mark Mans** who was also a Patron for the Engineer charity.

After I exchanged correspondence with him, he visited the Regiment, and everyone was in full ceremonial uniform for his visit. Then the next day, the RSM kept driving past my house but for some reason didn't knock on my door. The petty behaviour from the Engineer stopped immediately.

We remained here for seven months while I was undergoing treatment at DCMH in Merville Barracks, Colchester. Every week, a taxi would arrive at my home in the morning and take me to my therapy and then bring me home. The therapy always opened old wounds in my mind, but I had to keep doing it. It was the only way that I thought would help fix my broken mind. It was during a very intense therapy session that I had broken down in front of Leslie and said I couldn't see a way out that she told me that it wasn't about curing my PTSD but more about learning coping mechanisms and ways to manage it.

This made more sense to me. I needed to find a way to get through each day and get back to being a husband and a dad, and my focus was to just be a better person rather than an angry man. On the way home from therapy, I didn't speak to the driver, I was thinking about ways in how I could move forward. When I got home, there was a letter from The Ministry of Defence waiting for me, my first thoughts were that my claim was being investigated or the MOD had accepted liability.

How wrong was I, the letter was the biggest kick in the teeth I had ever received. I was in the middle of treatment for my PTSD. I was struggling with life and now the *Secretary of State* had sent me a letter to explain that I was no longer a member of the Armed forces and that my family had six weeks to vacate our military property or we would be placed into sheltered accommodation. I really had nothing left in my tank to say or do, I felt worthless at this stage, I went for a walk to the forest and just sat there for about 30 minutes thinking of what to do. I had tears streaming down my face and I was completely lost' I had failed my family and I contemplated suicide!

This was not how I should be behaving. I had a beautiful wife and son and I had to find a way out of this. We started to apply for houses from the local authority, we registered with Suffolk Council and after three weeks of being told no, we finally applied for a house, and we were the only ones who bid.

I received an email confirming we had been successful then followed up the next day with 'We had noticed you have no connection to the local area, so your bid has been refused'. This applied more pressure onto me, and my wife and we just had no other option than to privately rent, we found a nice three-bedroom home not too far from our married quarter but it came a huge cost to us, they wanted over £850 per month. This is a huge amount when you've just lost your job and home and dealing with trauma.

My wife began to work while I was the stay-at-home dad during my treatment. She would work long hours to earn enough to cover the rest of the bills and her boot camp business took off rather well, my treatment continued until I had been out the military six months. I was then passed over to my GP and the NHS. After several appointments and telling my story to every Tom Dick and Harry, I began to lose hope in ever receiving the proper treatment.

The only way I could cope with my own mental health was to keep busy and find a focus on something that I loved. This way, I wouldn't have time to think about me own issues if I was thinking about other things. This worked and I felt alive in doing something worthwhile.

I had witnessed first-hand at the many failures in dealing with mental health and it became my focus. It became everything to me, and I started to use my Gallantry Medal to get my voice in the media. It opened many avenues and I started to be able to speak out on behalf of the thousands of other veterans who had faced the same type of behaviour from our own MOD. I put together a social media page which over time had grown to 45,000 followers and the messages coming in from veterans and their partners began to overwhelm me. I had SSAFA caseworkers join my page as admins and who were working very hard to help these families.

My network of journalists just expanded over a period of three months. I was helping a great Journalist called Sean Rayment in highlighting the many issues that veterans faced, suicide within the veteran's community was rising each year and the figures were shocking. With the help of almost all the newspaper defence journalists, I started a campaign to hold the Ministry of Defence to account by embarrassing them on the front pages of tabloids. This didn't go down well with some Members of Parliament and I was soon blocked on social media by the Defence minister Mr Tobias Ellwood who refused to acknowledge any of the issues that was being reported on, he insisted that the MOD were working hard and had injected a further £5 million pounds into mental health, not a single penny of that money would ever reach therapists to carry out sessions and it was almost always swallowed up by the big charities.

I started to dig deep and find out what the big charities had in their banks and where all these donations were going. The increase in suicide and homeless veterans and mental health referrals were at an all-time high but so was the investment by our government and public donations had increased. So where was all this money intended for our veterans, someone somewhere was certainly making a living on the back of so much misery.

I put together a list of the top five military charities and what they had disclosed on the charity commission website. I hadn't made the figures up. But after writing it all down and putting it onto my page on social media, it was shared over 12,000 times with eight thousand comments, soon it was after it was on *SKY NEWS that the military charity sector was sitting on £3,000,000,000.*

Finally, I had managed to get the public to sit up and take notice of this disgraceful practice. The big charities started to release statements of why they needed to have a 10yr plan of investments and why they had so much money hoarded but it didn't wash with the veteran's community. I was now getting asked to do more veterans articles on mental health and was soon after putting into a category in the military **#PATHFINDER magazine** and one of the most influential people in the military community.

With so many people wanting me to do #Podcasts for them and journalists asking me to give them quotes, I was very much in demand. I refused to do dozens of podcasts as the presenters always came from a biased background and who I knew would sing the praises of the charities I had in fact found out to be hoarding donations. I decided to have my memoirs published and tell my story about my operational deployment in Afghanistan; it helped me to put to bed some of the demons I had from Helmand, it would be called '*First into Sangin*' and the name itself caused a lot of controversy with many units putting claim to have been there before my platoon. It got the military community talking and backstabbing each other. I noticed almost straight away that I was not being harassed and trolled by other veterans which was absolutely horrendous.

It wasn't long after that my tweets on Twitter started to be taken up by Members of Parliament and my voice began to get noticed. I had Anne Marie-Trevelyan, And Johnny Mercer starts to engage with me. I had several Celebrities now helping me to spread the message that our Veterans needed to be looked after, and no sooner had I engaged with the Chief of Defence people, Lt General Richard Nugee CV CVO OBE, that he had invited me to the first of several meetings at the MOD.

During my first visit to the MoD, I explained my own personal journey and the letter I had received which led to a drop in my mental health. I gave evidence of the letter that had been sent to all those who were trying to recover and the General was concerned that this letter was causing extra stress to those going through recovering. He had his secretary take notes and a plan was drawn up to give all those service personnel leaving the Armed forces through medical discharge an extra year in their service quarters to enable them to prepare financially for civilian life.

I was over the moon to have had a slight impact on just one area when a plethora of issues were causing such an impact to injured veterans. It seemed money was being thrown at these issues by the government, but it was never reaching the troops that needed the most help.

I got word out to my friends in the media that General Nugee CV CVO OBE was working extremely hard behind the scenes to improve the veteran's community. Then I tried another angle as Prince Harry made a speech insisting, he would dedicate the rest of his life to our veterans. This would in fact benefit the direction I wanted to go in and I soon reached out to the Royal Foundation and asked Harry to help. His office returned correspondence to me very quickly and he was on board. The headline in the tabloids was '*The Royals must do more*.' It prompted the Royal foundation to call me up and I was soon told by one of Prince Harry's team to back off and not to get Harry involved in veteran's issues. It confused me as I thought that he was dedicated to helping our veterans.

I needed to rethink my strategy and fast!

I was asked to help in the campaigns in the media '*Save our Soldiers*' and I had just finished off helping the *BBC* with their '*OUR WAR*' series. The first series that was directed by John Douglass had won a *BAFTA* for its frontline documentary of our fight against the Taliban, and it seemed most journalists wanted to be part of this newfound heroic type of journalism.

I don't remember John or his team at the BBC inviting any veterans to the glitzy star studied night, but I soon realised that 'We Veterans' are a bestselling commodity when it comes to television and ratings. I kept this all in the back of my mind and when the BBC asked me to take part in a second series, I had a plan of my own.

Chapter 21
Campaigning for Justice

I had now become a small voice of reason for veterans. I wasn't everyone's cup of tea but I didn't set out to be everyone's voice. I set out to fix some of the issues that those who had mental health issues faced and the difficulty that we are a community had in claiming compensation for an injury that couldn't be seen. It was almost impossible to receive anything from Veterans UK. They were very well known for stringing veterans on for up to eight years as they waited for settlement.

In many cases, it resulted in self-harm, marriage break-ups and domestic violence, drugs and drinking to self-medicate and eventually suicide for many. With the numbers reaching close to 100 veteran suicides each year in the UK, it made sense for the government to keep veterans dangling on in the hope of an out of court settlement. These settlements never came, and it meant the MOD saved millions of pounds by not paying out for injuries.

I was determined to have this addressed but it came at a price, my own mental health was not good and the constant messages from other veterans and charities that wanted to help was at times overwhelming. I would get calls from veterans every week who were about to take their lives and I spent hours on the phone giving them different options and eventually talking them into getting help from PTSD Resolution. They would always send me thanks in private and it made me keep going. They gave me the strength I was missing.

My mental health was an ongoing battle at the time, and I would seek comfort from my GP, but she was learning about PTSD from me and did her best. I was still crying by myself and going for walks, but it never really left me.

I would travel to London to speak with numerous people who could help influence funding for veterans, I was asked by John Rees Evans to help out in his new political Party 'Democrats & Veterans Party' and he made me the

Deputy leader. This catapulted me into the media even further and I was now being inundated with veteran's issues. I enjoyed the chance to give veterans a real voice and started to be more and more in the tabloids.

It came with other veterans attacking me personally and trying to derail our progress, we met with Steven Woolfe MEP, and he was interested in what we wanted to do and the direction we were going in. I was asked to attend and speak at a rally in Manchester and I took this opportunity to not only do it but call in on Charlie Lawson who was a Belfast actor and who helped to run a veteran's breakfast club in Macclesfield.

It wasn't long after this that membership to our party started to really take off and I was asked to attend a party meeting in Belfast which was in the pace I had grown up. I knew the place and the people and enjoyed seeing the old faces even if it was only for a few hours before heading back to England.

There was now lots of messages being sent to me about veterans and that we needed to push in the direction of veteran's homelessness which was now estimated to be around 7500 living rough and the veterans suicide rate which was increasing to around 80 plus. Both these areas really upset me as in the back of my mind, I could be either one of them.

Then just as things had started to take off and I was being thrown into the media limelight, we had an issue within the Party and the member's forum that I wasn't willing to support.

Stephen Yaxley Lennon, more commonly known as Tommy Robinson had been arrested outside a court for trying to film men who were appearing there for grooming young girls. How this had anything to do with our Party is beyond me, however the party members began calling on me to make a statement and display my disgust in Tommy being arrested. I had no intention of giving a statement on someone I didn't know. A topic I didn't know or an arrest that I didn't know the facts about. I didn't support Tommy he wasn't a friend and he only supported veterans when it suited his agenda.

After several days of tit for tat messages from the Party board members and all the infighting within the Party, I just posted a statement explaining that I had no intention of bending or losing my moral compass on this matter and I decided to step down and leave the Party that clearly have moved from being a centrist party to now displaying signs of far right views. My leaving made it into the media in Belfast and I was supported by many party members who all chose to leave the Party as they had felt I was pressured into supporting something I wasn't willing to do.

I took a few days away from all the hype and then threw myself back into veteran's issues once again.

My first novel was doing well on Amazon, and it had reached the top five best sellers list and had now received over *150 Five-star reviews*, it also had a few Paratroopers who had given in 1 star and had stated it was a book of lies. My claim to be the '*First into Sangin*' had well and truly upset their egos and would put to be future war stories of landing into enemy territory and fighting these men hand to hand combat.

I wasn't even good at writing but I wanted to get all this crap out of my head in the hope it would help me move on in life, with so many people wanting to interview me and hear my story of combat first hand it helped to remove the thoughts from my head and each time it became easier to explain. I did a fantastic interview for an Irish history magazine called '*A journey into Hell and back*'. The interview took up three of the magazines' pages and it was beautifully written, I received tonnes of positive correspondence from it.

I was soon invited to a charity fundraiser in the House of Lords, a beautifully handwritten invitation from General the Lord Ramsbotham which I gladly accepted. It also gave me a chance to mingle and see what I could do. I wanted to utilise these group of people and push for more funding for mental health.

I now had a great selection of people around me and we all wanted to help improve the lives of our wounded veterans. It was difficult to break the current situation and the government were blind to what the charities had in fact been doing and getting away with. Hundreds of millions of pounds from grants, donations and funding had not been going to help our veterans, instead it was being invested overseas and in long term investments.

Members of Parliament and members of the House of Lords were all part of the charities that were in fact hoarding millions of pounds donated by the public and it would never reach the front page of all major newspaper!

The charity journey can be one which is unrewarding.

My relentless pursuit to highlight charity failures and raise funds for charities then began to take a real nasty turn. I had over the previous two years set up and raised over £30,000 which had been split down and sent to veterans, charities and families that couldn't get help. I was commanded by many people for trying to fix areas and fill gaps but unbeknown to me there was a part of the veteran's community that disliked anyone trying to muscle in on their territory. I was soon being spoke about on social media as a thief and a fraud and a person who was living off these donations.

I was reported to the charity commission by individuals within the veteran's community and it wasn't long before I was reported to Suffolk Police fraud investigations team. I was still going through therapy with whoever was willing to help, and I was taking medication at the time. When the phone rang, and I was asked to attend a voluntary interview at their HQ I was absolutely stunned.

I asked if I could have time to put together as much information as I could, so I could prove I hadn't done anything illegal, and they agreed. I quickly sent out message to the charities that I had donated to and to the individuals I had helped. They were all as stunned as me and one lady whose husband I knew had went ballistic; she couldn't believe the amount of abuse I was constantly receiving.

A few days later, I turned up and the police station with everyone I had. I was cautioned and agreed to have the duty solicitor in with me. I was asked several questions about monies I had raised, and I referred to my notebook for the answers. I gave email addresses and contact numbers for the numerous charities I have donated to and contact numbers for the CEOs of the charities. Unfortunately for the police, all these charities were from different parts of the UK, and it meant they had to liaise with multiple forces across the UK to get the information that they needed.

This hit me like a hammer, and I vowed never to raise funds for veterans ever again. It wasn't worth the hassle. The added stress and most of all my mental health had taken a battering. The investigation took me into deep depression and I stopped helping veterans. It took almost one year for the Suffolk fraud investigation team to bring the investigation to an end. After the stress and my PTSD becoming to the forefront, they called me to say that I hadn't be found guilty of any fraud and that it was now closed...

I burst into tears and asked if they could send it to me in writing by email. It was at this exact point I knew that our so called veterans community was filled with toxic individuals who were happy to sell t-shirts hate, flags and memorabilia to make money but would never actually champion those in charge as it meant them losing out in lining their own pockets.

I had helped to find employment for 17 veterans, bought a second hand car, an electric wheelchair, a bicycle, a spinning bike, and helped to house 13 veterans in the two years that I was fund raising, several families had their groceries covered by donations I had made and I was helping to cover the cost of rent and mortgages so families wouldn't default. I loved being able to help in any way that I could but now I had been severely wounded by false allegations and for the sake of my health and my families I wasn't willing to continue.

I took a step back from veteran's issues, and I then had far too much time to think. I started to remember the shocking things I had witnessed, and the trauma started to manifest itself in my head.

It wasn't long before I started having the restless nights once again. I would wake up soaking with sweat and it wasn't long before my wife asked me to sleep in the spare room. She needed rest to be able to function in work and I wasn't exactly helping with my tossing and turning throughout the night.

My doctor soon prescribed me with medication to help me sleep, this meant I now had medication for being awake, medication for anxiety, medication for PTSD and now medication for sleeping. I was quickly becoming a zombie and absolutely no use to anyone. However, I continued to receive emails from veterans asking for help. I received a private message from an old colleague, Sam Benson who asked me if I would be kind enough to post a message on my Facebook page asking from veterans to help look for a friend who had went missing in Belfast and who was suffering from mental health issues, as a result of his time in the military.

This was something I was very concerned about, and I wanted to play my part, I knew the veteran and had worked with him on an operation in Afghanistan… In fact, I remember asking him to drop his bombs on an enemy position that was causing my platoon issues and when I tried to point out the area we had a Rock Propelled Grenade (RPG) come straight past our heads. He looked at me and said, "You can fuck right off, Speedy."

It wasn't long after I posted on my page asking for help to find him that a member of my old unit (1 Royal Irish) and a serving Warrant Officer responded with the most horrific of responses, he had taken this opportunity to not offer help but instead used my platform of 45,000 followers to launch a personal attack at the missing veteran. I decided to not respond but instead I blocked him from my page, and I left his message on there for everyone to read.

I was soon inundated with messages of outrage that a serving Warrant Officer would post such a vile message about a veteran who was suicidal, and I started to receive messages from journalists who were also outraged, the message he posted was so horrific that it ended up on the front pages of the tabloids and a Royal Military Police investigation was soon underway into the conduct of a serving soldier. I was stunned when members of the unit privately sent me pictures from their camp where the Commanding Officer of 1 Royal Irish had placed my picture in their guardroom with a note saying 'This man is banned from Camp'.

This was just petty as I had not been back to my unit in nine years, and I never had any intention to return other that the 10 year anniversary of my radio operator being killed. It was then in the media that I had been banned by my own unit, this was great information which was used by never ending trolls.

It was at this defining moment that I decided to completely detach myself from the unit I had served in, my Military Cross had brought me attack after attack from members of my unit. I remember standing outside the Warrant Officers and Sergeants Mess when a Colour Sergeant whose dad had been RSM said to me that he should off been awarded a Military Cross as his actions were as rewarding as mine. It was at that moment I realised that the envy of my reward ran deep in many of my peers!

I would continue to try and push for better welfare and mental health support for the veteran's community although I distanced myself from the veterans groups and never ever let my guard down again.

I received an email from The NHS and their mental health department, they asked me if I was willing to come to London and give a presentation on veteran's mental health. I was able to see the forecast of events and the other speakers and wasn't really impressed with their line-up. I always struggle to understand why so many veterans put themselves out there as mental health advocates but stayed away from trying to challenge or changes policies that had a massive effect on veterans and their families.

It was as if veterans who were in the public eye only wanted the rewards of fame and fortune but wouldn't dare question the system in case it effected their sponsorship deals and their book sales. I found many of them to be pretentious. (Just smile and say well done you.)

Chapter 22
The Day That Nearly Killed Me

I had now spent the past five years since my medical discharge campaigning for better mental health for veterans, I had written dozens of letters to Members of Parliament and to the House of Lords. Many of my response's came from Secretaries on behalf of their office, I was getting my foot in the door at the MOD and one of my tweets on social media had hit a nerve with the Veterans Minister Mr Johnny Mercer who had responded by inviting me and a team to his office to give advice on how to fix the issues within the veterans community.

I responded straight away with, thank you Mr Mercer MP, can you give me a date and I'll be there. I then contacted several leading experts in the field of mental health, veteran's homelessness, widows and employment. I got them all to meet at the awesome Union Jack Club in London and we discussed the order of presentation and then made our way to the MOD building. I did not go in as it would have been a distraction from the whole point of the meeting. I presented the right people with the right knowledge to give the right information.

I had also informed my friends in the media that it was taking place and they arrived to interview our team just before we set off for the meeting. I was always good at organising these events and getting the right people to the right place.

After the meeting, Mr Mercer MP had lots of information to go on, but he also knew other areas that needed immediate support so left it with him, I'm sure everyone was giving him their plans, and everyone was an instant expert on mental health.

I was still receiving information from my solicitor and being updated on my claim against the MOD, it had been going on for five years and it still had no end in sight. The MOD had refused to believe I had been injured during my 2008 deployment to Afghanistan which was unbelievable considering there was a picture of me in the hospital bed in Camp Bastion and an email from the welfare officer Mrs Moorcroft to my mother explaining I had been involved in an incident but was now stable.

My ongoing mental health issues and my mood swings were becoming worse on the lead-up to September, September was the month I dreaded because it brought back the memories of all my colleagues who had died fighting alongside me. It was their anniversary and I always tried to hide my pain, but it was obvious to my wife and my close friends how much it affected me.

Then came 4 September and it hit me like a brick. I headed out and had some beers as I never touched spirits and when I returned home, my wife gave me the most devastating news. She wanted us to separate and it sent shockwaves into my heart and my head. I had finally broken her, and it was horrendous. I promised to get help, but she had heard this a thousand times before.

For such a tough soldier who gave out the impression of a fearless warrior, I was now crying and begging to get help. I promised things would be different and I had to change. I stayed at home for as long as I could but my wife had already removed her wedding ring and shut me completely out of her life. I felt like a stranger in my home and I would break down and cry every single day. Then it all came to a head when she was doing fitness on a zoom call with her friend. My son was screaming playing online with his friend when I shouted at him to be quiet. My wife came out of the fitness room and shouted at me which I couldn't understand why. I was in the right, but I got upset and told her that this argument was her fault, I pushed the chair and she started crying.

It was at the defining moment I said okay. I took my house key off and handed it to her. I explained that when it comes to the point where she didn't feel safe in her own home then it was time for me to go. I had never hit my wife. I had never even pushed her or would I dare hit a woman. I was loyal and I adored her, but it wasn't working.

I grabbed some of my things and I left my home, I sat in my van and I cried. I cried constantly about the woman I truly loved had given up on me. I got into my van, and I drove away to the forest, I had every intention of taking my life at this point and I took lots of tablets and went to sleep…

I woke up the next day with a dry mouth and a heavy heart. I made the call to a veteran's mental health charity called PTSD Resolution.

I was driving around in my van not knowing what to do, I wanted a cuddle and to hold my wife, but I knew things had reached the no going back point. I had never felt so lost or unwanted before. This was certainly the worst trauma I had ever faced, and I had no one to turn to or to tell me that everything was going to be okay.

I would sit and think about how things had deteriorated to such a degree that a once well thought of soldier had fallen so hard, and there seemed no way out of this mess. I had completely closed myself off from all former colleagues and friends and I was happier and felt safer being alone. I knew that if I did take my life, it wouldn't be much of a big deal and I would be added to the statistics and nothing would change. The Ministry of Defence would continue to be in denial that PTSD is a problem and that I probably inherited it from the Northern Ireland troubles.

I had been living in my van for a few days now when I received a phone call from Michelle Turner from SSAFA. She was friend and knew I was going through an extremely tough time. She was part of the SSAFA Southend Team. We had a chat and I explained what was going on and I broke down crying again, Michelle stepped in with her volunteer head on and immediately took control of my situation.

After what seemed like a few minutes, she phoned back and said that SSAFA had booked me into the Holiday Inn, Felixstowe. It was the toughest time of my life and in was now only a few days away from Christmas. I was struggling to understand everything that was unfolding in front of me, I had to keep focused because I loved my son with all my heart, and he was all I had left.

I got settled into my room in the Hotel and my wife brought my son to stay with me for a few days at my request, I just wanted to cuddle him and show him I was okay, however inside I was a complete mess but I kept smiling at him saying everything was going to be okay. We spent those days walking along the beach and playing arcades and relaxing, it was fantastic, but it wasn't the same without my wife. It felt wrong to be trying to have fun when things were really at their worse.

I had now started to receive therapy from PTSD Resolution and my therapists was an ex-army medic called Debs. She was absolutely fantastic and made me feel relaxed and welcome, it took until our second session before I broke down and explained what was in my head. She was very thoughtful and helped guide me through each session and gave me coping mechanisms to use when back at my hotel.

I was in an emotional mess dealing with not only trauma but my PTSD and medication and now my marriage break up. The MOD were denying any liability to the complete mess that my life was in, and their legal team had strung me and my family along for five years so far and it didn't feel like it was ending anytime soon.

I received phone calls from several military charities who were all reaching out to me, Veterans in Action boss Billy got in touch to offer support and helped me, then Danny Greeno from the Veterans Charity gave me a ring offering help which I thanked him for but didn't need help at that time. Then my friend Jim Davidson called me up offering support along with Helping Homeless Veterans.

I was really surprised to receive a call out of the blue from Lawrence Fox. A great British actor and free speech advocate, he was extremely kind and listened to me offload. It was absolutely crazy, my friends in the media tried to hold the MOD account by publishing an article about how the MOD had let me down, then Ant Middleton contacted me and offered support which was fantastic. Though to top it all off, I received messages of support from the awesome Bear Grylls who explained that I was a warrior and that no matter how tough times get we must always focus on the next step and not the mountain before us.

With so much support coming at me, I had to continue to move forward. I had a son that needed me and I needed him. It was extremely hard to smile when there was so much going wrong in my life. Every time I felt depressed, it seemed I had something positive happen. Charlie Lawson from Coronation Street called me up and lifted my spirits, then Matthew Marsden called from the USA and I began to move forward slowly.

My therapist continued to move me forward slowly and I was beginning to find ways to deal with my PTSD but I was always going to have this vulnerability lurking just below the surface and I needed to keep in control. I had a son that I would now dedicate my life to. I found it difficult to see my ex-wife now as it made me cry and become emotional. I still very much loved her, and it was difficult to see her without me. We started to have conversations about our son, and I promised to continue supporting my son and paying their rent until we had properly divorced then I would take up child support.

I would phone and text my solicitor to see if we were gaining ground towards a court date and he explained that we had a zoom call with the MOD legal team and the Judge very soon. I asked my ask ex-wife to join me and she agreed to help me with the information that might be needed due to my memory being shot to bits and the state I was in.

It wasn't long before the dreaded court day and due to the pandemic it was now all done by Zoom. The judge introduced himself and both legal teams said hello and then the tone was set when the judge asked the MOD defence team if they had come to an agreement that Mr Coult had been hospitalised in Role 3 Camp Bastion in 2008... They said they no!

The judge sniggered and said, even though I'm sitting with a picture of Mr Coult in a hospital bed in Camp Bastion and that I have a copy of an email sent to Mr Coults parents from the welfare officer Miss Amada Moorcroft from Camp Bastion telling his parents that he had been involved in an incident but was stable?

The MOD said, "That's correct, your honour." It was at this point my whole legal team just shook their heads in disbelief and the Judge said, "So that's how it's going to go then."

The case lasted a further 45 minutes and then the judge gave the MOD six weeks to go away and to search high and low for information in the relevant logbooks and destinations to prove that I had been admitted to the field hospital.

It seemed the MOD would never ever admit when they were wrong or take responsibility for their mistakes.

I'm now living in a flat in Suffolk and I continue to work with the media through my most trusted journalist and friend Sean Rayment. I am very outspoken with regards to the treatment of veteran's mental health and I'm now about to enter my sixth year in a case against the Ministry of Defence.

I believe that until we as a veteran's community can come together in a campaign that challenges the current policies for mental health, suicide within the veteran's community will continue to rise.

Each year, we are losing between 80 and 100 veterans in the UK to suicide, our continued ignored of this is helping to sweep it under the carpet. We are losing a battalion of men each year to mental health as they are medically discharged and join the long list of veterans which is over 10,000 who await compensation for their injuries.

It's not what your country won't do for you, but what you've done for your country.

Ingram Content Group UK Ltd.
Milton Keynes UK
UKHW021939220623
423894UK00004B/13